Two worlds of international relations

In the twentieth century the social science of international relations has gone from strength to strength. At first, policy-makers showed little interest in academic international relations, but in the last thirty years they have both encouraged and to a degree intervened in this burgeoning field. For their part, academics have been drawn more and more into commentary on governments' actions, to the point where, for some, the policy debate represents the main focus of their research.

The aims of this book are to discover how significant academic work in international relations has become for practitioners involved in policy formulation and implementation, and to examine the impact of the policy community on academic work and academic values. On the academic side, theoretical, historical and political economy perspectives are presented. On the practitioner side, there are contributions from diplomats, lawyers and parliamentarians. The principal question at issue is whether, if there is a natural partnership between the modern academic and foreign policy makers, there needs to be preserved a respectful distance between the two worlds.

Two Worlds of International Relations will be of interest to all members of the international relations research and teaching community, to historians and political scientists, and to the increasingly large number of academics who have contact with practitioners.

Christopher Hill is Montague Burton Professor of International Relations at the London School of Economics and Political Science. **Pamela Beshoff** holds a doctorate from the Department of International Relations at the London School of Economics and Political Science and is a freelance commentator on international affairs.

Books published under the joint imprint of LSE/Routledge are works of high academic merit approved by the Publications Committee of the London School of Economics and Political Science. These publications are drawn from a wide range of academic studies in the social sciences, for which the LSE has an international reputation.

Two worlds of international relations

Academics, practitioners and the trade in ideas

Edited by Christopher Hill and Pamela Beshoff

1895–1995   An LSE Centenary Publication

London and New York

First published 1994
by Routledge
11 New Fetter Lane, London EC4P 4EE

Transferred to Digital Printing 2004

Simultaneously published in the USA and Canada
by Routledge
29 West 35th Street, New York, NY 10001

© 1994 This volume Christopher Hill and Pamela Beshoff;
individual chapters: the contributors

Typeset in Times by
Ponting–Green Publishing Services, Chesham, Bucks

British Library Cataloguing in Publication Data
A catalogue record for this book is available from the
British Library.

*Library of Congress Cataloging in Publication Data has been
applied for*

ISBN 0–415–06970–X (hbk)   ISBN 0–415–11323–7 (pbk)

To the memory of John Vincent

Contents

Part IV Practical dilemmas and the two worlds

Part V Conclusion

Contributors

F.D. Berman, CMG, QC, is the Legal Adviser in the Foreign and Commonwealth Office. He is a qualified barrister, who has served in Berlin, Bonn and New York since joining the Foreign Office in 1965.

Peter J. Beck is Professor of International History at Kingston University. His book on *The Falkland Islands as an International Problem* appeared in 1988, while his most recent book was *British Documents in Foreign Affairs. Reports and Papers from the Foreign Office Confidential Prints: The League of Nations 1918–1941*. vols 1–6, University Publications of America, Maryland, USA, 1992.

Pamela Beshoff is a former Jamaican diplomat who was awarded a doctorate for a thesis on the foreign policy of the Manley government in Jamaica, 1972–80. She now writes and broadcasts on Caribbean affairs, as well as teaching and lecturing on short courses in International Relations at the LSE and elsewhere.

Sir James Cable is a writer on international relations and naval affairs, who retired from the Diplomatic Service in 1980 as Ambassador to Finland, having previously been Head of the Planning Staff from 1971–75. He has published a number of scholarly books, including *Gunboat Diplomacy 1919–1979: the Political Applications of Limited Naval Force*, 2nd edn, London Macmillan 1981, and (under the name of Grant Hugo) *Appearance and Reality in International Relations*, London, Chatto and Windus, 1970.

Tam Dalyell has been the Member of Parliament for Linlithgow since 1962. He has a well-deserved reputation as one of the last of the great independent back-benchers. His integrity and knowledge of foreign policy are respected on both sides of the House. Perhaps the best-known of his various publications is *Misrule: How Mrs. Thatcher has Misled Parliament from the Sinking of the Belgrano to the Wright Affair*, London, Hamilton, 1987.

Christopher Hill is Montague Burton Professor of International Relations at the London School of Economics. Among his publications in the areas of foreign policy theory, British foreign policy and European foreign policy cooperation, is *Cabinet Decisions on Foreign Policy: the British Experience October 1938–June 1941*, Cambridge, Cambridge University Press, 1991.

Michael Hodges is Senior Lecturer in International Relations at the LSE, where he teaches International Political Economy and European Integration. His most recent publication (with Louis Turner) was *Global Shakeout: World Market Competition – the Challenges for Business and Government*, London, Century Business, 1992.

Zara Steiner is Director of Studies in Modern History at Cambridge University and a Fellow of New Hall. She has always been interested in the area of foreign policy-making, a subject which she addressed in her classic book, *The Foreign Office and British Foreign Policy, 1898–1914*. More recently, she edited the reference book *The Times Survey of Foreign Ministries of the World*.

Roger Tooze is Professor of International Relations at the Trent University of Nottingham. He is well accustomed to the task of making the study of international relations relevant to people of a practical disposition, and he is also widely known for his theoretical work on International Political Economy.

John Vincent was Montague Burton Professor of International Relations at the LSE from 1989 until his untimely death in 1990. He was an authority on the theory of international politics, his later work concentrating on human rights and international relations.

William Wallace is the Walter F. Hallstein Fellow at St Antony's College, Oxford. From 1978–90 he was Director of Studies at the Royal Institute of International Affairs in London. He has held visiting fellowships at the Stiftung Wissenschaft und Politik, Munich, and the Institut Français des Relations Internationales in Paris; he was British *rapporteur* for the UK–Japan 2000 Group from 1984–88, and a member of the British–Soviet Round Table from 1979–89.

Preface

This book germinated in the London School of Economics, for almost a century the principal place in Britain for theorists of society to exchange views with those responsible for public policy. For those working in the School it is always an exhilarating challenge trying to satisfy the requirements of pure reason without flying so high as to be invisible to those immersed in the bustle of everyday life. In the subject of International Relations in particular, the temptations of idealism, intellectual fashion and abstruse methodology have pulled in one direction, and those of realism, policy advice and 'common sense' in another. The result, given the suspiciousness of diplomats towards social science, was for many years that International Relations seemed to have little to say, directly or indirectly, to the policy-makers who were its subject-matter. The latter certainly did not go out of their way to listen, and were far more likely to recruit into their number young people trained in History or Classics than those who had studied International Relations.

This stand-off has been slowly changing, as the academic subject has matured and as practitioners have realised their need of assistance in handling a complex and dangerous international system. The American model of close, interpenetrated relations between the universities and government, is coming much closer to realisation in Britain and many other states. But as it does so, the dangers of the US system, so brilliantly outlined by Hans Morgenthau in his criticisms of Lyndon Johnson during the Vietnam War, are approaching with it. Morgenthau pointed out that 'the intellectual lives in a world that is both separate from and potentially intertwined with that of the politician. The two worlds are separate because they are oriented towards different ultimate values. . .truth threatens power, and power threatens truth'.[1] Morgenthau went on to say that intellectuals could choose to serve, confront or ignore government – all three being necessary roles – but to do anything worthwhile they needed to retain their 'immunity from outside pressures . . . manifested in job security through tenure'. Equally, they should monitor their own involvement in the

academic-political complex in which the interests of the government are inextricably intertwined with the interests of large groups of academics. These ties are both formal and informal, and the latter are the more dangerous to intellectual freedom, as they consist in the intellectuals' unconscious adaptation to imperceptible social and political pressures.[2]

In order to look at how the relationship between the 'two worlds' has actually worked over the last twenty years, and to examine the dilemmas for each side which the trends towards collaboration entail, the Department of International Relations at LSE convened in 1987–88 a seminar series in which researchers and practitioners could present both reflections and experiences to an audience of staff and Ph.D. students. This was the origin of the current book, and the editors are grateful to all those who took part in the original discussions for their ideas and criticisms. This includes particularly Martin Ceadel, David Gore-Booth, Hidemi Suganami, Richard Portes, John Tusa and Michael Yahuda, who gave valuable papers to the seminar which are not included here.

The structure of the book which subsequently took shape is straightforward. After an Introduction which outlines the issues at stake (and also takes a particular view on how they should be resolved) it consists of three parts. In the first part there are chapters by full-time academics, one a theorist, one largely an empiricist, and one with a foot in both camps. The second part presents the perspectives of three practitioners, one diplomat (retired), one politician and one lawyer-diplomat. The third and last part contains three case-studies in which the interaction of scholars and policy-makers can be traced – institutionally, in relation to think-tanks, historically, in relation to the dispute over the Falkland Islands, and economically in the context of advice about new trends in cross-national capital flows. The book ends with the editors' attempt to address the problem of the appropriate distance between the two worlds.

In putting together this book the editors have become, severally and jointly, indebted to a number of people. First and foremost they are grateful to the other contributors, whose patience and good humour have withstood all the ups and downs of collective action. Michael Donelan at LSE helped out with the original seminar and has always provided stimulating conversation on its themes. Michel Girard and other members of the European Consortium for Political Research's workshop on 'foreign policy professionals and political science' allowed Christopher Hill to present his ideas to them at the University of Essex in March 1991; their reactions were invaluable. Fred Halliday, Peter Hennessy, Roger Morgan and Geoffrey Stern gave their time generously to help with queries and comments. Elaine Childs at LSE has provided first-class administrative and word-processing support in preparing the manuscript for publication. Gordon Smith at Routledge has been a sympathetic editor. We are grateful to them all.

Two important acknowledgments remain. The first is to David Armstrong and Erik Goldstein, the editors of the journal *Diplomacy and Statecraft*, for granting permission for us to base Sir James Cable's chapter on his article of the same title in volume 3, number 3 of the journal (November 1992). Chapter 6 contains some new material and it has been edited in accordance with the needs of the book, but it is substantially based on the aforementioned article and we are most grateful for permission to use it.

The second acknowledgement is to Mrs Angela Vincent for kindly giving us permission to include Chapter 2, which is based on the seminar paper given in November 1987 at LSE by her husband John. As all those in the academic world (and many practitioners) know, John Vincent had become one of Britain's leading thinkers about International Relations when he died suddenly at a cruelly young age in November 1990. At the time of his death John was just beginning his chapter for this book, which the editors have completed from their extensive notes of his very well-organised seminar presentation. We have taken care to be faithful to our understanding of John's own work and intentions, and have included points made in reply to questioners, particularly Michael Banks, Michael Donelan, Hazel Smith and Geoffrey Stern. John Vincent continues to be sadly missed by his many friends and to leave a gaping hole in the profession. This book is dedicated to his memory, and most of the proceeds from it will go to the Research Studentship set up in his name at the LSE.

NOTES

1 Hans J. Morgenthau, *Truth and Power: Essays of a Decade, 1960–70*, London, Pall Mall Press, 1970, p. 14.
2 Ibid., especially pp. 16 and 25.

Part I
Introduction

1 Academic International Relations

The siren song of policy relevance

Christopher Hill

The relationship between academics and policy practitioners has become steadily more significant over the course of this century, as the pace of social and scientific change has accelerated and the activities of governments have diversified. Policy-makers have needed to draw on outside sources of knowledge and judgement, while scholars have often been eager to make their own contribution to policy debates on the best ways forward. Yet in moving closer together both sides have suffered damage as well as benefited from new opportunities. The best-known examples are the exaggerated status given to the 'science' of geopolitics by the Nazis, and the prostitution of some Soviet science, notably psychiatry, under Stalinism.

In this story the social science of International Relations (IR) appears as a sub-theme. It can be treated as a detailed case-study of issues which are relevant across the board to anyone concerned with the nature and uses of knowledge. But International Relations also has its peculiarities, mostly deriving from three phenomena: the secretive and security-biased nature of its subject-matter; the controversial, even incendiary, quality of many of the debates which occur across national frontiers; and the temptation by many governments or parts of governments to involve themselves in the generation of ideas and analysis which is usually such a crucial part of the process of political change.

The point at which policy and research come together, notably in international relations, is therefore a sensitive area,[1] particularly for the academic, who tends to need more practical help from practitioners than he or she has to offer in return. But the conjunction also produces at least one sizeable advantage in the longer term. It tends to focus both sides' attention on the fundamental issue of *purpose*. Where it is all too easy for politicians to become preoccupied with day-to-day, superficial, matters, social science scholarship may take refuge in the arcane, the technical or the antiquarian. Each approach can be shaken into considering its ultimate worth and direction by challenges from the other. This was the case from the late 1930s on for academic students of international relations, as the rise of Hitler compelled the gradual abandonment of the legalistic idealism which had dominated the subject's first few decades. Conversely, over the last thirty years academic writing on regional integration has provided the conceptual framework for much thinking and debate about future directions for the European Communities.[2]

Such collisions between the two worlds have become increasingly common since 1945, as the size of the university sector has increased in most developed countries and as the dire consequences of foreign policy mistakes for ordinary citizens have become starkly apparent. Yet there has been little self-analysis by the participants in this uneasy dialogue. In International Relations only Tanter and Ullman have produced a major publication on the relationship between policy-making and academic life, and that was a very diverse collection of essays some twenty years ago.[3] Since that time there have been many developments in which the interaction between the two worlds of policy and of ideas has been evident – such as the rise of international terrorism, a greater concern with human rights, and the passing of terms such as 'interdependence' or 'underdevelopment' from works of theory into common political usage. The time is therefore ripe to take a close and analytical look at the two worlds and the extent of their mutual impact.

There are five major questions which arise from the relationship between policy-making and scholarship, and the contributors to this book have been asked to take one or more of them as their starting-point:

- How far do academics and policy-makers define problems in the same way? Can the theoretical debate about competing 'paradigms'[4] illuminate policy choices?
- Do decision-makers increasingly rely on outside sources of expertise, whether technical, historical or regional?
- Is theory, as Friedrich von Hayek once suggested, the ultimate source of power because new ideas promote change?
- Do International Relations academics take too many cues from politicians? What are the proprieties which should govern the agenda and conduct of research?
- How can academic findings be conveyed to the world of action? Is the indirect route (i.e. via scholarly publication) enough, or should knowledge be mobilised through the use of the media, conferences and political contacts?

These questions are specific to the theme and apply to practitioners as much as scholars. But behind them lie three critical dilemmas of International Relations as a social science, which will be the subject of this chapter, written as is it from an academic viewpoint. They can also be presented as questions:

First is the issue of how far the subject of International Relations should be preoccupied by the contemporary world, and in particular by the current news agenda. This may be termed *the history question*.

The second issue is the place of normative concerns in our subject, which deals primarily with politics and therefore finds it particularly difficult to be 'value-free'. This may be termed *the ideology question*.

The third dilemma revolves around the issue of academic independence, how to identify threats to it and how far to go in its defence. This is *the professional question*.

International Relations specialists naturally face other important questions, such as the relationship between theory and empiricism, the problem of sources and the very standing of the kind of knowledge we lay claim to. But methodological and epistemological concerns are both narrower or wider than the interests of the informed practitioner or ordinary citizen, and are subsidiary to the main theme of this book. Yet while work can be produced which is of compelling interest despite not tackling fundamental philosophical issues, any writing in International Relations which does not consider, at least implicitly, the big dilemmas of 'history', 'ideology' and 'professionalism' will be at best superficial and at worst dishonest.

THE HISTORY QUESTION

Right from its beginnings the academic subject of International Relations has been driven by the issues of high politics of the day. Indeed it was born out of the new determination in 1919 at the Paris Peace Conference to build a better world order in which the crudities of power politics would be constrained by law and collective security. The first chair in the subject, at Aberystwyth in Wales, was named after Woodrow Wilson, and the major figures of the first wave in Britain, such as Philip Noel Baker, Hersh Lauterpacht and Alfred Zimmern were very much dedicated to providing the intellectual underpinnings for the new international system. They were doing, in fact, applied social science.[5] Equally, in the United States one of the most prominent writers on international relations in the 1930s was Charles Beard, who articulated the dominant preference of the day for isolationism over both power politics and collective security. Writers in London were usually in contact with the Royal Institute of International Affairs, which under Toynbee quickly became the centre of an intellectual network, but the huge size of the United States and a rather less comparative approach to the subject meant that the Council of Foreign Relations took far longer to establish systematic contact with the academic world.[6]

In broad-brush terms, the subject has continued as it began. After the Second World War the return to the balance of power between the major powers was reflected in the universities in the dominance of realism.[7] This in turn gradually gave way to a revived liberalism as the Cold War started to thaw, and the consequences of economic interdependence became manifest. In both phases those who could interpret the state of the world to the citizenry also became gurus in their profession: E.H. Carr with appeasement, Raymond Aron with containment, Paul Kennedy on the supposed decline of American power. Interestingly those most successful at doing so were usually those of an inter-disciplinary cast of mind, able and willing to range back and forth across the social sciences.

Now it is almost *de rigueur* for anyone teaching or researching international relations to have expertise on some aspect of contemporary affairs. By definition this usually means an empirical knowledge, and there are both rewards and sanctions for so doing. Endless opportunities exist for commentary on radio and television (even away from metropolie, on local stations), while managerial notions of productivity and 'usefulness' are spreading throughout higher education and imposing subtle pressures on researchers not to follow interests whose harvest might only be gleaned indirectly or in the longer term, for every institution now needs its staff to earn regular outside plaudits if it is to prosper in a competitive market-place.[8]

Such demands do not prevent equal and opposite disparagements of contributions to public debate – and even of the subject as a whole – as 'higher journalism'. During the Gulf War of 1991 the media showed insatiable demand for expert commentary, in which, by the nature of things, and 'against the best academic instincts a simple framework of cause and effect [was] established, quite contrary to the principles of research and analysis'.[9] In other words, academics who wished to contribute to the public debate had little choice but to make what were for them abnormally bold judgements, while neither their more reticent peers nor an often sceptical public showed much understanding of their dilemma. It is impossible to avoid becoming involved during some great drama if one's knowledge and values are engaged (money is hardly the draw), but the consequences are usually unsatisfying.[10] The quality press sometimes provides opportunities for reflective analysis, but if one wishes to contribute to radio or television it is very much on the medium's own terms.

In many who stay well away from current affairs (sometimes because they have not been asked to join in) the pendulum effect can be observed. That is, anxious lest International Relations seem the kind of thing that any half-decent political columnist can run up after a visit to Washington and Moscow, they tend to lard their work with scholarly references, establishing seriousness more through philosophy, history and law than through any distinctive approach of International Relations. Equally, legitimisation and mystique may be achieved through tedious professional introspection, elevating methodological issues to an unjustified prominence.[11]

The consequence of the pendulum effect is that the academic profession is itself internally divided between those who regard themselves as real scholars partly because they do not get involved in contemporary affairs, and those who are scornful of the 'ivory tower' syndrome establishing itself in the social sciences. A small number of writers straddles the two positions, usually in some discomfort. Hedley Bull was perhaps the most successful at gaining respect on both sides. Professional journals reflect the divide clearly. *The World Today* (UK), *Foreign Affairs* (US), *Politique Etrangère*(FR) and *Aussenpolitik* (FRG) to take examples from four different countries, are largely policy-directed journals. *The Review of International Studies, Millennium, World Politics* and *International Organisation* are largely academic in their content and readership (the fact that two are British and two American reflects the dominance of the Anglo-Saxon countries in the theoretical aspects of IR, if not in the policy debates). Although some journals, like *International Affairs* (London) or the *International Journal* (Toronto) work heroically back and forth across the divide, they tend to end up respected by all but followed by none.

It can be argued, with justice, that even the theorists follow an agenda derived from the movement of events – and indeed that there is an inevitability about doing so in the '*longue durée*'. Integration theory flourished while the European Economic Community enjoyed its honeymoon period, yet dropped dramatically below the academic horizon once the impact of Gaullism began to be felt in the later 1960s. The American study of International Relations in particular, partially dependent as it is on grants from the big research foundations, tends to suffer from preoccupying intellectual fashions, which in turn derive from the latest (seemingly cataclysmic) shift in world affairs (i.e. principally from what the US government does). Thus the rise of OPEC spawned a whole school of writers on interdependence, while the end of the Cold War has brought a sense of desperation to the hundreds of experts on strategic studies, who now rightly fear that they could be out of a job. The point is not that scholarship should not respond to major changes in the world; it is rather that the opportunity costs of so doing are not always appreciated in terms of the atrophying of important but suddenly unfashionable areas where the lack of expertise may indeed be keenly felt once the wheel eventually turns again in their favour. In sinology, for example, the USA suddenly discovered after the opening to Peking in 1971 that it needed all the experts it had neglected to bring on during the years in which Communist China was being shunned as a pariah.

Furthermore, it is in practice all too easy to move from a concern with understanding the changing nature (say) of the international system, or the forces which are shaping it, to the far narrower agenda of what the government of one's home country, or the leaders of the bloc to which one's country belongs, is attempting to achieve. This means that academics become, almost without noticing it, reactive to the initiatives of others, rather than pursuing their own professional concerns, which would otherwise intersect with policy issues only occasionally. Creativity is thus attenuated, while the longer time-frame so essential to balanced judgement is squeezed out by the pre-occupations of the day. Even when motivations derive from a critical approach to official policy, and a determination to right injustices, they still tend to be reactive to and therefore defined by what power-holders are doing and saying rather than by the concerns which naturally bubble up from deep knowledge of a subject. Thus academic work which looks at the decline of empires once the decline of key states has become evident is somewhat less original and useful than writing of the same kind which occurs when those states are at the height of their power. It is difficult indeed to free oneself from the pressures and conventional wisdoms of one's own time. But that is precisely what is supposed to characterise a good academic; the ability to pursue an independent line of thought. And if academics are not well enough chained to the mast to resist the siren song of policy relevance, who else is there?

A *de haut en bas* approach to the opinion-forming world of *The Economist* and *The International Herald Tribune* naturally has its own deformations. It is all too easy to pay mere lip-service to a concern with historical breadth. In practice few range easily back and forth in the terrain of post-Westphalian international relations and the vast majority of International Relations scholarship deals with events of the last fifty (or arguably the last twenty) years. Whether we like it or not (and I do not) there is good reason for the historians to say that International Relations is a subject essentially concerned with the period for which the archives are not yet open, and that our task is to write (as Peter Hennessy says) 'the first draft of history'.[12] If our preoccupation is indeed contemporary, then we have little alternative but to accept that we are either social engineers, seeking to influence events and therefore on a par with practitioners, or simply the advance-guard of the historical profession, the shock troops thrown forward beyond the trenches of the Thirty Years Rule. We have the first shot at defining the shape of the past, and then the (real) historians come along to profit from our mistakes and hard-won gains.

This is an uncomfortable picture for the IR professional to accept. It means that the subject has no real identity of its own, and is falling between the stools of political action and scholarly detachment. No wonder so much emphasis is placed by so many on what can (and must) be done with theory! Even those impressive attempts to combine extensive historical knowledge with the defining theoretical interests of IR tend to fall foul of what might be called the snare of the irresistible example (or examplitis). The work of Arnold Toynbee and Martin Wight is difficult both to refute and to believe, as it rests on a bed of rich but necessarily selective illustration. Undermining (or accepting) some of the examples proves little either way. Who, indeed, is to say whether Wight is right in his interpretations of Scottish balance of power policy before 1603, or of Franco–Savoyard relations in the 1690s (to take two of the innumerable mini-cases to be found in Wight's *Power Politics*)? And does it matter? There is something fundamentally a-historical (and very ironical given the training and outlook of the writers in question), about selecting snippets from the past to illustrate an essentially timeless theory of international politics.[13] Perhaps, instead of decking out abstract generalisations in historical garments, we should take a leaf from the historical sociologists and their recent approaches to international relations by providing interpretations of *patterns of change* in the international system and the behaviour of its actors. This does not have to be grand and sociological, à la Hall or Mann. It can still focus sharply on the political relations between states, as in the Cambridge tradition of F.H. Hinsley and Ian Clark, or by preference on the rather wider notion of relations between separate communities, which allows us to break open the black box of the state. Adam Watson's splendid recent book does justice to both history and analysis along just these lines.[14]

What lies behind the addiction with things contemporary, and the corresponding attempt to provide balance with historical scholarship?

The answers are various and understandable: the excitement of politics, a moral commitment, a desire for influence, external pressures on the academic agenda. Evidently nothing can or should prevent that part of social science which calls itself International Relations from engaging in research on contemporary issues. The question is, rather, whether a concern for the present should become a preoccupation, and what the costs might be of working to much the same time-scale and terms of reference as those of practitioners and journalists.

The contention here is twofold: firstly that IR specialists allow themselves to be so hypnotised by the contemporary political agenda that they end up either doing the work of other professions (in some cases notably better than the natives) or becoming mere ancillaries to them. Principally this means that we become historians (of the contemporary scene), journalists (providing depth and some authority), part-time decision-makers (mostly in the USA) and *de facto* pressure groups (whether for radical or establishment causes).

The second contention is that this degree of engagement with the present leads to a sacrifice of perspective – historical, theoretical and normative – and that this is ground difficult to recover once lost. Paradoxically, given IR's tendency to encroach upon other fields, this then encourages outsiders to step in to do our job, often with headline-grabbing and (to IR) frustrating results, as with Paul Kennedy's best-seller of 1987.[15] If we are not to be forced back into the redoubt of pure theory as our only comparative advantage we must try continually to locate our work on the present in a longer time-frame which is itself being continually redefined with the aid of theory. IR is hardly unique in needing to maintain a degree of detachment in order to ensure academic credentials; but it is alone in taking a holistic approach to the political evolution of the world and its component parts. This indispensable quality will be sold short if we spend all our time jostling with journalists and decision-makers to influence this month's foreign policy agenda.

To avoid tilting at windmills it must be acknowledged that a preoccupation with the contemporary world can mean several different things, most of which do not 'consist of today's answers to yesterday's faxes', to adapt T. B. Millar's view of most foreign policy practice.[16] Table 1 presents four dichotomies as a way of organising the analysis. The right-hand column represents the areas where academics rightly have a great deal to say about the contemporary world – they are 'concerned'; but it will be appreciated that slippage into the activities on the left-hand side (where lie the snares and delusions of 'immersion'!) is all too easy and often imperceptible at the time. Examples can be found, however, of writers keeping sure-footedly to an academic path while also making a significant contribution to our understanding of the context in which policy is played out. Such people tend to be either liberal realists or tough-minded radicals, the two schools most willing to concede some possibility of reformism and voluntarism in their outlooks on international relations. Arnold Wolfers and E.H. Carr are the classic examples.[17]

Table 1 Approaches to the contemporary: four dichotomies

	Immersion	*Concern*
(1)	Policy	'Real world' general relevance
(2)	Absolutely current	Post 1945
(3)	Specific proposals for action	Analysis of structures and processes
(4)	The actual	The possible: (a) speculation
		(b) prescription

The irreducible starting-point is that academic IR is half in love with policy and its milieu, and it is therefore immensely vulnerable (especially given the humdrum and poorly paid nature of much university life, contrary to the stereotypes purveyed by refugees from departments of English Literature) to the vibrant image of politics and policy. Hence the careers of Henry Kissinger and Zbigniew Brzezinski. But International Relations will concede the accusation of superficiality if the profession as a whole, pressing to the window to watch the cavalcade go by, then neglects its own distinctive business.

THE IDEOLOGY QUESTION

Most people entering the area of international relations are motivated by some explicit normative concern, however general, whether it is the traditional concern for peace, a desire to see the gap narrow between North and South, or even a determination to protect one's own country's interests by (say) understanding the functioning of the international organisations in which it has to work. This is natural and only causes problems if the motivating values are either disguised (perhaps innocently, as part of a positivist methodology) or exaggerated to the point that they come to dominate the analysis. The connection with the history problem is that a specific normative concern usually leads also to an interest in contemporary analysis, whereas equally strongly held but more general and private concerns tend to lead the scholar into a longer time-frame. Martin Wight, for example, was originally motivated by pacifism, and F.S. Northedge by radical socialism, even if their published work was primarily realist. It would have been impossible to cope with these contradictions if they had written mostly about current policy dilemmas, and so Northedge ranged over the last 'hundred years of international relations' and Wight the whole Westphalian system.[18]

In the restrictive climate of the Cold War, when the idealism of the 1930s seemed to have been completely discredited, it was not surprising that these two distinguished writers should have compartmentalised some of their values. Certainly their views changed as they grew older, but it would be wrong to say of either that they ever completely discarded the values of their youth.[19] More openness would, at best, have risked ridicule and marginalisation. Hedley Bull shrewdly noted the dualism, and observed that 'I have often felt uneasy about the extent to which Wight's view of International Relations derived from his religious beliefs'.[20] Moreover their professional commitment to analytical detachment – ironically echoing the behaviouralism which they both disparaged – gave them a priceless integrity and independence of judgement.

Of course austere scholarly detachment from the world is in itself a normative position with policy implications – and one which can be robustly defended. In brief it means that academics think they do more good by the Candidean pursuit of cultivating their own gardens and leaving the democratic process (for this is a liberal view) to take care of the rest. The alternative could not only threaten academic independence and priorities but foster the kind of elitism embodied by the 'enarques' in France and the 'great and the good' world of Royal Commissions in pre-Thatcherite Britain.

Whichever strategy the International Relations academic adopts, there can be little doubt that what happens in the subject does matter in the wider world. Like it or not, we are 'intellectuals in politics' and 'the study of international relations is not an innocent profession'.[21] Cable considers that abstractions, when not trivial, can be seriously misused, while Peace Research runs the risk of encouraging appeasement.[22] Conversely, Groom has argued that there was 'a spell of unspoken harmony between academics and practitioners' on the power-politics approach, which needed free-thinkers like John Burton to break it and make possible new ways of thinking.[23] Even leaving such contentions on one side, it will be evident that the spirit of an age, the political culture of a society and the preoccupations of a generation are all likely to be profoundly influenced by the output of those who write, think and observe for a living. This is so in cultures where intellectuals are respected, such as that of France (where the Sartre–De Beauvoir lead takes some responsibility for the slowness with which French opinion abjured Stalinism) but also where their status is on a par with that of parish priests, as in Britain. Gunnar Myrdal said, referring to academics, that 'our kind of power . . . is most of the time only feebly related to the politics of the day', but his message was that 'our kind of power' is at least as significant, because diffused and enduring, providing the sources of the ideas out of which social change comes'.[24] 'Power' may overstate the matter; it is always difficult to trace direct links between political outcomes or agendas and currents of intellectual life,[25] while the nature of academic work tends to promote self-cancelling disputes. But whether academics challenge or reinforce the conventional wisdoms of a society they are certainly crucial intermediaries in determining how the mass of people understand the world beyond their own experiences, and beyond the platitudes of politicians. In relation to the Third World, for example, Myrdal's area of concern, they can be both accused of propagating liberal illusions about development aid in the 1960s and congratulated for highlighting environmental concerns in the 1970s.

Policy-makers have no doubt as to the truth of this point. They contribute to making International Relations a political as well as an academic battleground. Sensitive, as we have seen, to both the research and the teaching products of the universities, British governments are no longer slow to sponsor lectureships, promote research centres, send staff on secondment and encourage work on themes of interest to themselves. Even when they remain unmoved by the glitter of power, impoverished universities can hardly turn away from the prospect of hard cash. They are reduced to ever-louder whistling in the dark on the theme of their own essential incorruptibility. Outside Britain things are managed differently, with International Relations usually being at once a smaller and a more intimate world, where the relevant intellectuals and policy-makers are as likely as not to know each other personally and to be less concerned by institutional sensitivities. The exceptions to this rule are the big battalions of the USA, the Soviet Union (as was) and Germany. All of these three states have made no bones about seeing international relations as an important arena to influence. For example Soviet experts in the Institute of World Economy and International Relations (IMEMO) operated as an indispensable auxiliary think-tank for the Party and the Foreign Ministry. In Germany the Stiftung fur Wissenschaft und Politik at Ebenhausen operates like an academic institution, except for the fact that it is funded by the Federal Chancellery and Defence Ministry and works to themes of policy-relevance.[26] In the United States the Congress has explicitly funded the Woodrow Wilson International Center for Scholars and the United States Institute of Peace so as to make major inputs into scholarly debates on international relations.[27]

Accepting this close interest and working with it might be thought to be a form of self-protection, but the opposite can be true. Too much second-guessing in order not to seem naive in front of those who know the 'inside story' can, as we have seen, lead to a loss of academic identity. In fact innocence can be a strength. As with a primitive painter, direct observation, without sophisticated filters coming between us and the subject, can sometimes be devastatingly effective. This is what Hedley Bull did to the behaviouralists who dominated the American study of international relations in the 1960s,[28] and who attracted huge research grants because their 'scientific' approach posed no kind of ideological threat to US foreign policy, rather promising to be able to make it more effective.[29]

Furthermore, there arrive certain conjunctures in history when policy-makers have to cast around feverishly for the *ideas* which are in principle the academic's stock in trade. The early 1990s are one such point, where foreign policy-makers the world over are uncertain as to how the post-Cold War, post-Soviet Union world is developing. Academics cannot forge new realities for them, but what they can do is to interpret trends in a long time-frame and to float concepts which may help to make sense of a mass of confusing detail. They may even, at the margin, be able to influence events through self-fulfilling prophecies.

It is an article of professional practice for social scientists to articulate the major premises of their work. It is certainly essential if the difficulties of the ideological question in international relations are to be met. Normative commitments are inevitable, and there are three possible ways of expressing them. The first path means becoming drawn deep into real-world policy debates, of which the logic is the construction of an applied social science. The basic presuppositions of research tend to be left unstated and unexamined, and International Relations then becomes semi-vocational, like Law, Accountancy and a fair amount of Economics. There is nothing inherently wrong with such activities; the problem arrives when they come to dominate a subject. The lack of an epistemological basis beyond that involved in trying to service the policy debate diminishes its critical capacity, in the widest sense of being able to subject the fundamental assumptions of those one is studying to the tests of history, theory and philosophy. Moreover, enthusiastic immersion in today's problems of the GATT, Somalia or the European Community simply leaves academics perpetually one step behind policy-makers (who control both information and operations), dealing with yesterday's agenda without even realising it. The fact that by the time of publication these examples will almost certainly seem dated, suffices to make the point. There is little point in being practical decision-analysts if the decisions under the microscope turn out to be as elusive as the traditional angels on pins.

The second path that IR academics follow in relation to their normative positions is that of smuggling values into scholarship and decking them out with technical analysis. As often as not this will be done unconsciously. Even though, epistemologically speaking, it is impossible to avoid starting from a particular set of underlying assumptions and preferences,[30] a great deal of empirical work – that is, precisely the kind of research most likely to be noticed by practitioners – is presented in the form of neutral description. Much of strategic studies, for example, has been taken up with specialised discussions of deterrence theory on the one hand and weapon technology on the other, both seemingly devoid of ideological leanings of any kind. Indeed, the knowledge they represent is ultimately comprehensible whether you are the *mujahidin* in Afghanistan or French generals in charge of the *force de frappe*. Yet it can also be convincingly argued that the whole subject of strategic studies embodies a particular view of international relations – largely but not wholly realist – which tends to obscure the peoples and the local conditions behind the blanket concept of the balance of power.[31] Similarly, European Studies have been predominantly pursued by those for whom the goal of an integrated Europe is so important as to be taken for granted. To be sure, they do not go to excessive pains to conceal this value, but nor is it usually made so plain that one can see the links between the conclusions drawn and the premises employed, and compare them with other possible sets of arguments. Until quite recently, differences of belief about the utility of European integration have largely resulted in the sceptics opting out of the whole subject and the enthusiasts using it as a promotional vehicle.

The third path might be thought to be more honest, namely that of directly prescribing general desiderata. This is what idealism has done since the beginnings of the subject of International Relations, and its shortcomings are well known. If ideals are mistaken for facts, disaster can follow; if empirical investigation is neglected, caution and subtlety tend to go with it; if too much social engineering is attempted disappointment is inevitable. But its advantages have become correspondingly neglected in our own times: it is a channel for the normative concerns which run through us all; it requires the discussion of fundamental principles over and above obfuscating detail; it relates directly to the great traditions of philosophy on which all political activity ultimately – if not always knowingly – draws. In recent years idealism has taken on new and more rigorous life in the form of 'critical theory', of which Mark Hoffman has said, paraphrasing Marx at two removes: 'The point of IR theory is not simply to alter the way we look at the world, but to alter the world.'[32]

If we analyse critically the nature of the existing order, and of alternative scenarios (rather than, as in classical idealism, positing a desirable schema on a priori grounds and then working to implement it, à la Ligue des Nations) then we may be in a position to unblock the conceptual and actual impasses which litter the world of international relations. We may be able to stimulate effective debate on the 'significant choices' in respect to the 'direction and quality of life' at the international level.[33]

None the less we are not all philosophers or clerics, even in their new critically self-aware guise, nor should we be. A great deal of the work of International Relations continues to require empirical spade-work which will be impeded (and made inaccessible to practitioners and citizens) if it is constantly looking over its philosophical shoulder. The real 'ideological question' or dilemma is to manage the balancing-act which arises out of giving vent to strong and natural normative inspirations without also becoming side-tracked either by the policy-issues of the moment (where academics have little comparative advantage) or by explicit prescription-writing for the future (research-as-piety). There is a need in many areas of the subject to open up the discussion of underlying values without subordinating our drive for knowledge and understanding to those same values or to the practical decisions in which they become manifest. The vital importance of achieving such a balance will be made clearer by our third and last question.

THE PROFESSIONAL QUESTION

Academics are always concerned about threats to their independence. Perhaps in so doing they betray a lack of self-confidence about their own ability to keep their eye on the ball, but it remains true that there are plenty of genuine reasons for concern. Governments and pressure-groups in mature democracies may well accept that academic freedom is in everyone's long-term interest, but those conditions rarely apply and where they do actions do not always live up to principles, as when Margaret Thatcher's government abolished tenure for university teachers as part of a wider campaign against what it saw as state feather-bedding.

Moreover, the more we strain for policy relevance, even if only to justify our existence in the eyes of society at large, the more difficult it becomes to maintain intellectual integrity. This is as true for opponents of government policy as it is for those advising decision-makers. The greater the involvement in the policy agenda, the greater the vulnerability to the demands of loyalty, ideological soundness, timing, tactics and the rest – in short, the more politics takes over. We end up writing sophisticated tracts on how to 'help determine possible policy orientations by the Community and the member states' towards Eastern Europe, rather than standing back so as to be able to put the changes of 1989–93 in the longer perspective of an evolving European sub-system of international relations.[34]

The central problem is that of agenda-setting. If all social sciences are by definition to some extent 'applied', then there is a world of difference between taking cues from the world of practice and taking them from practitioners. The longer interest, whether of the profession, of society or of humankind is more likely to be served by cool, detached reflection (sometimes running well ahead of politicians, sometimes pulling them back by the coat-tails) than by getting so close to events that we accept limiting terms of debate – short-term, practical and government-driven. This is just as true of International Relations as of its sister-subjects. Looking back at the historical record we can see that there has been an unfortunate tendency for the subject to follow decision-makers' (particularly American) leads rather than to set or anticipate them. For every project in the 1970s on unconventional defence, exploring the possibilities of a world without NATO and the Warsaw Pact, there were ten which suddenly saw the possibilities of writing about energy, human rights or the Strategic Defense Initiative once OPEC, Jimmy Carter and Ronald Reagan, respectively, had made them a respectable enterprise. And it is difficult not to get drawn into taking sides on such important political debates, an engagement which serves neither academic nor political causes. In general the powerfully committed do not make the best academics, while in politics, to paraphrase Yeats, an intellectual passion is the worst. The combination of rigidity and the intellectual's capacity for rationalisation quickly turns politics into the art of the impossible.

Even without becoming *parti pris* in the conventional sense, academics still risk giving up their precious assets of perspective and a reputation for independence if they become too involved in joint ventures with decision-makers. Research has already become yet another lever in the game of bureaucratic politics which characterises modern policy-making systems. In the mid-1980s, for example, the British Department of Trade and Industry (DTI) unusually commissioned a project from the Royal Institute of International Affairs and in so doing drew the Institute into its own internal disputes between free-traders and protectionists. Inevitably the Foreign and Commonwealth Office, Chatham House's usual link with Whitehall, was also affected by the embroglio over whether a commissioned research report should be published.[35] More recently the Ministry of Defence, possibly less than enchanted with the International Institute of Strategic Studies in London, decided to fund a new Centre for Defence Studies a mere half a mile away at King's College. Similarly the European Commission, while happy to agree to appropriate safeguards of academic freedom, is naturally keen to use its 'Jean Monnet Chairs' (whereby short-term university appointments are funded so as to encourage the universities themselves eventually to make the positions permanent) to promote a Community-wide perspective on economic, legal and political affairs. It would hardly wish to see the ideas of the Bruges Group benefiting from its patronage.[36]

In the United States, Henry Nau of George Washington University, whose book *The Myth of American Decline* went some way towards countering the huge impact of Paul Kennedy's ideas, had served in government under both Democratic and Republican administrations.[37] While hardly anyone's poodle, Nau expressed clearly the cross-pressures on someone in his position when he admitted (Preface, p. ix) that 'academic colleagues may feel that my ideas have lost some of their objectivity, while former government colleagues may feel that my experience lacks a sufficient sense of loyalty'. He went on (p. x): 'I expect some readers to criticise this study as an attempt to rationalise the early policies of the Reagan Administration in which I was significantly involved'. The least that can be said of this honest admission is that if Nau had been critical or pessimistic about American foreign economic policy he would have not had the chance to express his views as a privileged insider.

Powerful governments do not, of course, restrict themselves to manning the drawbridge which controls the flow of insiders. They are also used to massaging academic output. As the influential decision analyst Rex Brown said when disputing that politicians tend to calculate human lives in dollar terms, 'if they really needed to put a figure in front of the public, they would get the Academy of Sciences to produce it and then knock it down'.[38]

In short, joint ventures with officialdom pose the dangers for academics of making them reactive to outside agendas rather than holding on to their own more slow-moving concerns, and of dulling potential criticisms through familiarity. Academics should provide a pool of ideas and information on which society can draw in various ways, but it is far too limiting if they seek to act as a kind of adjunct planning staff to the foreign policy executive within government.[39] Occasionally, individuals might be able to serve both sets of masters effectively, as did Hedley Bull in the early 1960s when his path-breaking analysis of arms control drew on his temporary service inside the British Foreign Office, or Francis Fukuyama (ex-State Department) in the 1990s with his captivating theory of the 'end of history'.[40] But this is unusual. Most academics will not get such opportunities. They do, none the less, face continual challenges to their intellectual independence from the perceived pressure to be relevant, and from the very nature of their subject. In other words, the 'professional problem' derives at least as much from ourselves as from outsiders. One should not underestimate the cynicism of those who might want to undermine academic freedom, but at least half the problem is temptation.

CONCLUSIONS

At bottom, scholars of international relations face a twofold and paradoxical task. On the one hand they have to avoid academic snobbery and accept that they share with journalists, policy-makers and informed citizens (each group just about deserves the benefit of the doubt) a desire to create the conditions in which human beings can live free and fulfilling lives. On the other, they have to preserve a distinct sense of purpose and not relinquish their particular comparative advantages. These generalisations will be briefly developed so as to set the scene for the specific studies which make up the bulk of this book.

Firstly, it would be absurd if political scientists of any description, let alone those working in the violent and dramatic arena of international relations, took refuge in the persona of Belloc's 'remote and ineffectual don'. A concern for political realities and for change is bound to be one of the foundations of our activity. We exist on a continuum with those other groups who are also seriously 'engaged' with the fate of society in the largest sense. A few may be able to pull off the role of 'insider-academic', and a few more will draw effectively on their learning to dispense judicious policy advice in the columns of the press.[41] Others again will become powerful radical critics of governments.

But what is it we value from academics, whether directly involved in the policy world or not? In the last analysis it is unlikely to be their political roles. Who would remember Bertrand Russell as anything other than a well-meaning eccentric if his reputation rested on the activism in international affairs which occupied most of his life after

the publication of *Principia Mathematica* in 1913 at the age of 42?
Likewise E.P. Thompson may have made a contribution to society
through the European Nuclear Disarmament movement in the 1980s,
but his writings in this area were amateurish by comparison to those
which made his name as an historian of nineteenth-century Britain.
Conversely, Michael Howard was surely right in his responses to
Thompson's personal strictures when he implied that too strong an
involvement in a particular cause is damaging to intellectual health, in
the sense that it tends to reduce complexity to mono-causal simplicities.[42] It is indeed interesting that it has been people from other
disciplines like Russell, Thompson and A.J.P. Taylor who have made
the running with the Campaign for Nuclear Disarmament in Britain. The
IR professionals have kept their distance, knowing that commitment
tends to bring with it an over-simplified approach to explanation.

For the counter-argument that the International Relations community
is no less *engagé* than the radical critics, but just less visible because
supportive of the Establishment, this author has some sympathy; after
all, the main thrust of this chapter has been to warn of the dangers of
the trend towards convergence between the two worlds of policy and
academe. This brings us to the second arm of our paradoxical injunction,
namely that academics need to guard against the erosion of their own
particular comparative advantages. There seems little point in trying to
emulate what others do better in the world of policy and political
commentary. Nor is there much to be gained in accepting the inevitability of interpenetration with the state, or indeed competing elites in
general. If we accept that our work does ultimately have a political
meaning, then we should insist its impact occurs on our terms and not
of those for whom research is just another battlefield to swarm over.
This will mean holding our nerve against all the pressures, and
accepting that our academic priorities to a large extent militate against
trying to take part in the policy-making process. The academic business
centres around the notion of knowledge, not action, and if we cannot
all be Immanuel Kants, resisting all worldly blandishments so as to stay
in Königsberg and write classic theory, most of us would recognise that
one Kant is worth a thousand ephemeral commentaries on START I or
Delors 2.

The academic comparative advantage, which applies to International
Relations no less than to any other subject, is a long time-perspective
and a concern with fundamental causation. No social scientist, furthermore, can neglect the use of theory and comparisons. This means that
the subject can provide states and other actors, in the long run, with an
intellectual cartography of the world, if not the precise route-maps to

achieve particular ends. It would be tragic if International Relations, having fought so long to establish itself as a serious, indeed indispensable, area of scholarly enquiry, should at the very point of success throw it away through an inability to resist the siren song of policy relevance. Policies are in the last analysis grounded in concepts, which is where thinkers and teachers come in. The nature of the state, the causes of war, the problem of rationality in foreign policy, are all subjects which deserve extensive reflection in their own right and not simply in the margins of breathless analyses of Maastricht, the Gulf or Boris Yeltsin. There may be only one world, but we need more than one kind of approach to improving it.

NOTES

1 But even teaching is also relevant, given MI6's and the CIA's memories of what happened to idealistic undergraduates in the 1930s, and the increasing numbers of bright students destined for official careers who are now to be doing degrees in International Relations.
2 This mainly refers to broad theories of neo-functionalism, variable geometry and the like. But influence can also be more tangible. See, for example, *The Economist*'s willingness to credit Peter Ludlow's Centre for European Policy Studies with influence over the 1989 Delors report on European Monetary Union and the Commission's subsequent proposals for reform of the Common Agricultural Policy. 'The Good Think-Tank Guide: the Joys of Detached Involvement', *The Economist*, 21 December 1991–3 January 1992.
3 R. Tanter and R.H. Ullman (eds), *Theory and Policy in International Relations*, Princeton, Princeton University Press, 1972. The remainder of the relevant literature consists of insightful, but necessarily limited in scope, articles, of which it is particularly worth mentioning: Sir James Cable, 'The Useful Art of International Relations', *International Affairs* 1985, pp. 301–14; A.J.R. Groom, 'Practitioners and Academics: Towards a Happier Relationship', in Michael Banks (ed.) *Conflict in World Society*, Brighton, Wheatsheaf, 1984, pp. 192–208; T.B. Millar, 'Academics and Practitioners', in *Paradigms: The Kent Journal of International Relations*, vol. 2, no. 2, Winter 1988–89, pp. 92–101; Coral Bell (ed.) *Academic Studies and International Politics*, Canberra, Department of International Relations, Australian National University, 1982.
4 That is to say, the highly influential view, loosely based on the work of Thomas Kuhn, but also deriving from the thought of Martin Wight, that truth consists in an intellectual and moral contest between varying sets of fundamental, and fundamentally incommensurable, assumptions – such as realism, idealism and structuralism. For an elegant discussion of such an approach, see Michael Banks, 'The Evolution of International Relations Theory', in Michael Banks (ed.) *Conflict in World Society*, op. cit., pp. 3–21.
5 For a analysis of the work and impact of one of these figures see D.J. Markwell, 'Sir Alfred Zimmern Revisited: 50 years on', *Review of*

International Studies, vol. 12, no. 4, October 1986, pp. 279–92. Arnold Toynbee, although essentially unclassifiable, was also concerned to bring together historical scholarship and real-world reforms. See William H. McNeill, *Arnold B. Toynbee: A Life*, New York, Oxford University Press, 1989, and also William C. Olson, *International Relations Then and Now: Origins and Trends in Interpretation*, London, HarperCollins, 1991, pp. 56–78.

6 Olson, *International Relations*, op. cit., p. 70. The British (Royal in 1926) Institute of International Affairs was founded in 1920, and the Council of Foreign Relations in 1921.

7 See John Vasquez, *The Power of Power Politics: A Critique*, London, Pinter, 1983.

8 For a powerful attack on the spread of 'managerialism in higher education' see John Griffiths, 'Academic Freedom', a paper read to a conference of the Association of University Teachers at Edinburgh, 27 October 1990. I am indebted to Philip Windsor for drawing this piece to my attention.

9 Peter Savigear, 'Soft targets under airtime attack', *Times Higher Education Supplement*, 15 February 1991.

10 Indeed some of the tabloids in Britain went so far as to conduct 'beauty contests' of the best-known pundits, in which, inevitably, non-academic criteria were to the fore.

11 An accusation happily made – and made too much of – by Alan Sked in 'The Study of International Relations: An Historian's View', *Millennium*, vol. 16, no. 2., Summer 1987, pp. 251–62.

12 The phrase was actually first used in the 1960s of journalists, by Philip Graham in *Newsweek* magazine, but in Britain it has become indelibly associated with Peter Hennessy, particularly through his work for the Institute of Contemporary British History. See Michael Cockerell, Peter Hennessy and David Walker, *Sources Close to the Prime Minister*, London, Macmillan, 1984, p. 89.

13 This is not wholly fair on Arnold Toynbee, whose concern was with cycles of civilisation over long periods, or on Martin Wight, who in so far as he departed from a detached classificatory approach came to sympathise with the progressivist instincts of rationalism. But it remains true that the notion of cycles is inherently static, and that Wight's pessimism led him to believe that rationalism was losing out to realism and revolutionism. He also believed 'that there is very little, if anything, new in political theory, that the great debates of the past are in essence our debates'. See Martin Wight, *International Theory: The Three Traditions*, edited by Gabriele Wight and Brian Porter, Leicester, Leicester University Press for the Royal Institute of International Affairs, 1991, p. 268.

14 Adam Watson, *The Evolution of International Society*, London, Routledge, 1992. Watson acknowledges the problem all writers on the big sweep of history face, citing Elie Kedourie on Toynbee to the effect that comparative historians will necessarily find it difficult 'to discriminate between the merits of alternative specialized accounts' (p. 11, Watson's paraphrase).

15 Paul Kennedy, *The Rise and Fall of the Great Powers: Economic Change and Military Conflict from 1500 to 2000*, New York, Random House, 1987.

16 Professor Millar actually said that 'most countries' foreign policy (including Britain's and Australia's) consists of today's answers to yesterday's telegrams'. See *Paradigms*, op. cit., p. 95.

17 The term 'liberal realist' is the author's, outlined in his '1939: the Origins of Liberal Realism', in *Review of International Studies*, vol. 15, no. 4, October 1989. It refers to the fact that the realist reaction against inter-war idealism did not involve a cynical reversion to the ideas of Machiavelli or Metternich, but rather a concern to graft the development of effective international institutions onto a secure balance of power system. For the relevant works of the authors cited see Arnold Wolfers, *Discord and Collaboration*, New York, Columbia University Press, 1962, and E.H. Carr, *The Twenty Years Crisis*, London, Macmillan, 1939.

18 See in particular F.S. Northedge and M.J. Grieve, *A Hundred Years of International Relations*, London, Duckworth, 1971, and Martin Wight, *Power Politics* (first published 1946, second edn with an introduction by Carsten Holbraad, London, Penguin, 1978). Wight went to pains to stand outside his own categories, while the writings published after his death suggest that his sympathies were principally with rationalism (Wight, *International Theory*, op. cit.). But *Power Politics*, the book he did publish (1946) in his lifetime, is indubitably realist.

19 Perhaps this is why another prominent figure in the British study of international relations, the South African C.A.W. Manning, kept his support for apartheid out of his lectures and published work. I am indebted to Geoffrey Stern for discussions about the lives and beliefs of the scholars mentioned. Mr Stern himself is proud that in 30 years of LSE lectures students have never been able to guess his party politics.

20 Hedley Bull, 'Martin Wight and the Theory of International Relations', *British Journal of International Studies*, vol. 2, no. 2, 1976, p. 116, and reprinted in Wight, *International Theory*, op. cit., (p. xxiii).

21 The first quotation is from the title of James Joll's illuminating book about the experience of Leon Blum, Walther Rathenau and Filippo Marinetti when they turned from the world of ideas to praxis, *Intellectuals in Politics*, London, Chatto & Windus, 1960. The second is from Sir James Cable, 'The Useful Art', op. cit., p. 305, and continues: 'It can do harm as well as good.'

22 Cable, 'The Useful Art', op. cit., p. 305.

23 Groom, 'Practitioners and Academics', op. cit., p. 193.

24 Cited in ibid., p. 195.

25 On the problems involved in analysing power, but also on the importance of the social sources of power, see the work of Steven Lukes, particularly *Power: A Radical View*, London, Macmillan, 1974, and the 'Introduction' to his edited book, *Power*, Oxford, Blackwell, 1986.

26 See Susanne Peters, *The Germans and the INF Missiles: Getting Their Way in NATO's Strategy*, Baden Baden, Nomos Verlagsgesellschaft, 1990, pp. 61–4. The Stiftung dates back to 1962, and suggestions from Arnold Wolfers and Henry Kissinger.

27 This is not to say there is anything necessarily improper about such institutions. Indeed the author must declare an interest as a one-time Guest Scholar at the Wilson Center, which lives up to Congress's brief by its highly professional conduct of independent research. The point is rather that the institutions of the state (in this case the legislature, but usually the executive) regard academic work as of sufficient importance to the country's foreign policy as to seek to influence its agenda (only the stupid and tyrannical seek to influence its conclusions as well).

28 Hedley Bull, 'International Theory: the Case for a Classical Approach', *World Politics*, April 1966, and reprinted in Klaus Knorr and James N. Rosenau (eds) *Contending Approaches to International Politics*, Princeton, Princeton University Press, 1969. See also Oran Young, 'Professor Russett: Industrious Tailor to a Naked Emperor', *World Politics*, vol. XXI, no. 3, 1969, pp. 486–511.

29 From a very different ideological viewpoint to that of Hedley Bull, Noam Chomsky also wrote vividly on the theme of the connection between social science and US foreign policy. See his *American Power and the New Mandarins*, London, Chatto & Windus, 1969.

30 See Martin Hollis and Steve Smith, *Explaining and Understanding International Relations*, Oxford, Clarendon Press, 1990, especially Chapters 3 and 9.

31 An argument most strikingly made by Ken Booth in *Strategy and Ethnocentrism*, London, Croom Helm, 1979.

32 Mark Hoffman, 'Critical Theory and the Inter-Paradigm Debate', *Millennium*, vol. 16, no. 2, Summer 1987, pp. 231–50. Hoffman was adapting Sheldon Wolin's paraphrase of Marx's aphorism in the *Theses on Feuerbach*.

33 Ibid., p. 245.

34 The quotation is taken from the Preface of Falk Bomsdorf *et al.*, *Confronting Insecurity in Eastern Europe: Challenges for the European Community*, London, Royal Institute for International Affairs, December 1992. This publication is also available in Dutch, French, German and Italian, as it is the collaborative product of seven European research institutes, with inputs from the 'Cellule de Prospectives' of the European Commission. Since one of the seven institutes was the official Institute of Security Studies of the Western European Union, we can see that academic cooperation with policy-making in Western Europe has now gone quite a long way down the road. The argument is not that this should never happen – indeed the openness and clarity of this endeavour is to be applauded – but rather that: (i) the tendency for IR to get drawn more and more into such exercises has significant costs for basic research; (ii) the constraints imposed by time, the need for consensus, and political sensitivities produce reports which resemble bland, ephemeral shopping-lists more than penetrating treatments of the ways in which history and ideas bear on political choice.

35 The report was eventually published, despite strenuous objections from some inside the DTI, as John Sutton and Joan Pearce, *Protection and Industrial Policy in Europe*, London, Routledge & Kegan Paul, 1985. The authors state at the beginning that their work was commissioned by the DTI 'as a study of the idea that the European Community should shift towards a more strongly protectionist external-trade policy'. The book is dis-passionate and coolly analytical – except towards the DTI itself, which is never placed under the microscope.

36 Proper safeguards exist to ensure that academic criteria are employed in the selection of candidates for these positions. They did not stop a question being asked in the European Parliament about these procedures 'in order to put an end to what is doubtless idle speculation and wholly unjustified criticism'. This elicited the information that four criteria for selection had been used in 1990: 'a link with problems of European integration; the quality of the application; the academic and educational feasibility of the project; the

guarantee of continuity of the project'. Written Question No. 223/91, by Mr Victor Manuel Arbelo Muru (S), 18 February 1991 (91/C210/39).

37 Henry Nau, *The Myth of American Decline: Leading the World Economy into the 1990s*, New York, Oxford University Press, 1990. Kennedy's book was a sensation in the US, because it hit a sore nerve in comparing the United States of the 1980s with the declining Dutch, Spanish and British empires of the seventeenth, eighteenth, and nineteenth centuries. In fact Kennedy is an expatriate Englishman, and perhaps it took an outsider to have such an impact. National culture and pride can sometimes be as important as government connections in shaping outlooks. Joseph Nye, for example, another former official but high in the academic firmament for many years, was stung to reply to Kennedy, in his *Bound to Lead: the Changing Nature of American Power*, New York, Basic Books, 1990.

38 'Doctor Logic', Henry Porter's interview with Rex Brown in Washington, *The Illustrated London News*, October 1987, pp. 28–31.

39 The term 'the foreign policy executive' is used to convey the fact that foreign policy is no longer the preserve of foreign ministries, and that even at the very highest levels it will involve the head of government and possibly other Cabinet members, as well as the foreign minister and relevant advisers. See Christopher Hill, *Cabinet Decisions on Foreign Policy: the British Experience, October 1938–June 1941*, Cambridge, Cambridge University Press, 1991, especially Chapter 8.

40 Hedley Bull, *The Control of the Arms Race: Disarmament and Arms Control in the Missile Age*, London, Weidenfeld & Nicolson for the Institute for Strategic Studies, 1961; Francis Fukuyama, *The End of History and the Last Man*, New York, Free Press, 1992.

41 See today, for example, the columns of Professor Lawrence Freedman in the *Independent* (London), or Dominique Moisi (Institut français pour relations internationales, Paris) in the *European*.

42 Michael Howard, 'Two controversial pieces' in his *The Causes of Wars*, London, Unwin Paperbacks, 1984, pp. 116–50. The first of these pieces was a reply to Thompson first printed in *Encounter* in 1980. The second was an almost equally effective counter-thrust against Colin Gray and other hawks who believed in the possibility of fighting a nuclear war.

Part II
The academic perspective

2 The place of theory in the practice of human rights

John Vincent

In considering the relationship between theory and policy in any area care should be taken not to make heavy weather of the distinction itself. Theory and policy are two sides of the same coin in that they both represent *a priori* outlines which can then be tested empirically, in the first case against something called 'truth' and in the second against political practice. Some academics and policy-makers have a joint interest in broad outlines, while others form an alliance over their concern for detail. The central distinction becomes that between theory (policy) and practice (experience), a distinction akin to that between values and facts, and which has some of the same difficulties attached to it. It is difficult, for example, to have a truly content-free theory, or value, while our interpretation of the world of 'facts' is always conditioned by our theoretical assumptions.

In the case of human rights, difficulties with the common-sense distinction between theory and practice are at once obvious. The first is that what is a human rights abuse in one view may be a valuable tradition in another. There is a compelling set of problems to do with cultural relativism which occurs here.[1] On the other hand it is clearly essential for theorists to take facts seriously; events, actions, sufferings in the world of daily experience, are, after all, what incites concern over human rights in the first place. In this century, the holocaust of the Jews under Nazi Germany, the victims of the Gulag in the Soviet Union and the fate of the 'disappeared' ones in South America have all stimulated demands for human rights observance, demands which have often found international theory lagging.

A second difficulty lies, as it so often does, in the question of scope. To say how far human rights extend and what priorities should be pursued within the category invites a policy statement. Maurice Cranston's solution[2] was a league table of human rights, putting civil rights first and economic rights or aspirations in the second division;

others, including Jack Donnelly[3] and Henry Shue[4] have spent considerable effort contesting this interpretation. In this context we cannot say that we are 'just theorists' (or indeed 'unjust theorists'). Theory cannot be an intellectual exercise divorced from the requirement ultimately to deliver a position on policy. Our theories have to address painful dilemmas and, if heard in the world of politics, they can have painful consequences.

There is also the more specific question of technical problems in the theory of human rights. First, human rights thinking is often at its most coherent when it is also at its most utopian – theory in isolation from the problems of practice. It is a Herculean task to arrive at agreement on economic and political rights at the United Nations and yet another to introduce these rights into state practice or international law. Neither level can be ignored, but conceptually they need to be kept separate. Secondly, 'human rights' theory is typically most often called up when practice ignores theory. This is what Jack Donnelly called the 'possession-paradox', that is, having a right to something but not having it in the sense of enjoying the object of it. If someone steals a car and the thief is not caught, the owner still has a right to the car although he no longer has the car.[5] We are more aware of his right in the event of the car being stolen from him than we are during routine possession. The same is true of human rights. We need the concept most when the substance is absent or removed, so as to reveal the denuded rights.

Thus the paradox of possession characterises human rights. On the other hand, there is an important difference between possession in the material sense and human rights. If human beings have rights, they have them *qua* human beings and not through contractual acquisition. We have gone beyond the days of men and women buying themselves out of slavery and into citizenship. Moreover, in human rights theory, as in other areas of international relations (*pace* Tanter and Ullman, 1971[6]), theory cannot be refined incrementally in the hope of achieving limited practical improvements. There can be no compromise in the area of human rights. Fundamentally, at the levels of both theory and practice, the package has to be bought as a whole or not at all. That said, politics is also a process, and rights constantly require vigilance to prevent incremental deterioration, or to achieve hard-won particular gains.

The problem may be best explored by looking at theory in the sense of four differing usages: as vocabulary/concept, as explanation, as a guide to policy, and as justification.

THEORY AS VOCABULARY/CONCEPT

Rights in general, and human rights (that is, a minimalist claim) in particular, have entered incontrovertibly into the vocabulary of international relations. To illustrate this, we need look no further than the international law of human rights. This may be what is sometimes called 'soft law', but it is law none the less. The modern version of human rights theory is being assimilated to the concept embodied in the *ius gentium intra se* – that part of the law of nations which describes the values that nations in their domestic law have in common and that speaks to the civilised treatment of all peoples. On the other hand, one of the problems of language lies in the gap between usage and observance, and herein lies the paradox. Although the language of human rights has entered into the common parlance (if not quite yet of everyday exchanges then certainly into the conduct of relations between states), this does not mean that rights are observed. The effort has to be made, none the less, to build in language to our explanations. That is, to show how the words we use to frame our notions of rights, and to say why they can or cannot be implemented in practice, are themselves part of the 'facts' or politics of human rights in international relations. In post-modern terms, the 'discourse' employed both reflects and determines the actual possibilities in the world.[7] This kind of knowledge is 'connoisseurship' in Manning's term, or the opposite of a nationalist, 'pond-bottom', view of international relations.[8] Even realists, who seem to be immune from human rights concerns except as a possible lever against an adversary state, are thus affected despite themselves. Henry Kissinger, for example, was led over the course of his career into more and more references to human rights, because the language of international relations was not determined only by people like himself. It may have meant only a small change in his observable behaviour, but it was a significant one.

THEORY AS EXPLANATION

To bring theory into play as explanation is to give an unusual account of human rights, which is normally seen as prescriptive only. The notion of human rights is, however, now part of a conceptual framework which helps us to understand the world. As Louis Henkin says, 'Human Rights is the idea of our time, the only political moral idea that has received universal acceptance'[9] – that is, the idea of human rights is the key to our understanding of the central political debates of the late twentieth century. From one perspective, infractions of human rights can be viewed as the root of all political ills. Put another way, human rights establish the values that all political communities should start by providing. This is the position taken in the preamble to the Declaration of the Rights of Man, when it announces that 'ignorance, neglect, or contempt of human rights are the sole causes of public misfortunes and corruptions of Government'.[10] The corollary is the view that fidelity to human rights brings about political well-being, a characteristic product of the Age of Enlightenment.[11] Conversely, human rights can be seen as an excuse for irresponsible uprisings or external interventions. The argument is well-expressed in the opposing views of Tom Paine and Edmund Burke. To Paine, 'new enlightened thoughts will mean new enlightened practice'. For Burke, on the other hand, the rights of man were little more than a recipe for anarchy. According to Burke, the rights prescribed by the French Revolutionists in particular were the pretexts behind which 'pride, ambition, avarice, revenge, lust, sedition, hypocrisy, ungoverned zeal, and all the train of disorderly appetites hide'.[12] Stepping back from the debate, we might conclude that while the pursuit of human rights in the long term may turn out to be the only way of stabilising political life, in the short term it will necessarily be subversive of all authoritarian governments. To which might be added the observation that we must not neglect the issue of our historical starting-point. If we point out the ineluctable force of human rights, then we are taking a Whig, historicist view of progress. If on the other hand we talk about human rights as largely a phenomenon of the post-Nuremberg, post-1945 world, then we are limiting ourselves to more contingent statements and must be careful to avoid anachronisms when analysing other periods.

The modern scientific proposition of rights as the source of political well-being is as follows: if X (human rights) is observed then Y (order) will follow. Behind this lies the thinking which informs the idea of a contract. Huguenots in the sixteenth century needed a political theory which could provide the dissenter with a defence against the prince. This was achieved first, through a constitutionalist appeal to checks against the monarch, and secondly, through taking natural liberty as the starting-point for political society. In the seventeenth century it is Grotius who suggests that the law of nature should become 'respect for one another's rights'. Later in the same century the Huguenot theory of popular resistance to a tyrannical prince becomes, in the work of John Locke, an individual's right to resist, and the right to property becomes a right to life and liberty as well as mere possession. And from Grotius and Hobbes comes the idea of the individual as the place where political theory should begin, the ultimate purpose for the achievement of which either the prince's dominion or the social contract is then agreed. Both the concept of rights, to be so important in the evolution of Western democracy, and that of needs, central to Marxism and to modern peace and conflict theory, derive from this same root.[13]

THEORY AS A GUIDE TO POLICY

In considering the question of theory as a guide to policy, we need first to ask ourselves the scope and nature of the categorisation for which policy is being prescribed. Is it, for example, for the world as a whole: those principles which are 'self-evident' and universal, as expressed in the preamble to the Charter of the United Nations – 'we the peoples of the United Nations' and so on? Is it as a guide to 'our policy', and if so, who are the 'we' in question? Is it the demos in general, is it some amorphous grouping which we call 'the West' (which was always self-defined in terms of principles, because of its geographical vagueness), or is it (say) British foreign policy? If it is the latter, what is the advice that we (the Academy) should give to the Foreign and Commonwealth Office, or to its equivalents overseas?

After the problem of ambition comes the question, what is the function of the theory of human rights? It might be to draw the world towards respect for human rights by virtue of the strength of moral exhortation and example – a function ridiculed by Marx. Or it might be to point out the direction in which we ought to be progressing, as Kant thought, whether or not there was any prospect of this actually being achieved. At the very least it might seek to describe the moral world that confronts the statesman in order that he can make sense of human rights in foreign policy and realise the advantages which accrue from going beyond the necessary but crude obsession with survival.[14]

This will then lead us to consideration of the rules that will be needed to contain any behaviour which, as we will see, 'outrages the conscience of mankind'. And here lies the ground on which the battle between theory and practice must ultimately be fought. The requirements of action dictated by a conscience outraged by abuses of human rights, may, and frequently do, confront the conventions of international law and custom on the question of intervention in the internal affairs of states. They also run up against the problems of capability, priority and counter-productivity quite properly prominent in the minds of governments. The practitioner, pressed for a response, cannot wait while theorists and/or idealists (not of course the same thing at all) work out how to relate principles to context. His or her needs are concerned with the hour and the day. In these circumstances, such advice as can be given will probably be along the lines that if the state is to step outside the normal rules which favour non-intervention, then it had better make sure that such behaviour vindicates human rights rather than violates them. And it can show how and why this might be the case. Certainly the theory of human rights ought to be a significant input, through which practitioners can inform policy-making, both in deciding what acts to commit, and what to omit.

Let us turn to more specific considerations of the place of human rights at the level of actual national foreign policy. In the case of Britain, it should be noted that the human rights question falls to the UN desk at the Foreign and Commonwealth Office (FCO) where it occupies quite a low priority.[15] Practitioners, no doubt imbued with realist philosophy, are almost always sceptical by nature and historically it has proved difficult to get at the true significance of the issues through the cloud of disbelief that surrounds policy-making in this area. The Cold War environment made the FCO resistant to outside pressures to give human rights a higher priority. For a time, under the Labour government of James Callaghan when David Owen was foreign secretary with Evan Luard as his under-secretary, this seemed likely to change. Owen made a real effort to make EC aid dependent on human rights performance. But circumstances, as with President Carter in the USA, proved unpropitious.

Of course it might be argued that it is better to say that a state has duties – for example, not to let its people starve – and that rather than introducing the subject of rights we ought to be saying, 'let us talk to each other about the purposes of a society, and the duties of governments to their peoples'. Islam, for example, could relate to this approach more easily than to that of rights.[16] My answer to this would be to question where the idea of duties itself originates if not with the notion of rights. This is not to argue that human rights should be in the vanguard of foreign policy; that would simply provide too great an opportunity for the kind of flag-waving seen under Ronald Reagan. On the other hand, human rights should not be consigned to the bottom of the policy-maker's in-tray. Ideally, human rights questions should pass through the desk of one strategically positioned senior officer, as they had to when coming for approval to Patricia Derian in the US State Department under Jimmy Carter's presidency. This individual would then be responsible for representing human rights in the policy-making process. Practitioners in foreign offices all too often tend to see human rights as a nuisance. But arguments for human rights should create a nuisance and their consideration should be institutionalised. There is certainly no argument for down-grading them in foreign policy decision-making.

THEORY AS JUSTIFICATION

The realist posture of international law in general is of a list of legitimations, that is, base reasons dressed up in the language of theory in order to justify actions and disguise real motives. Attacking human rights abuses abroad is an attractive option for those who wish to legitimise their policies, distract from domestic difficulties, and/or create a negotiating advantage with an adversary. Arguably the Western countries played this card skilfully in the review conferences of the Conference on Security and Cooperation in Europe (CSCE) after 1975. These are only 'persuasive' reasons, as Grotius said, and not real ones. None the less, if action has to be justified before an audience (and even before one's own conscience) then it can be argued that that in itself will act as a form of constraint and legitimacy. Henkin has shown how Foreign Offices have become increasingly preoccupied with international law as they have had to defend national positions in ever-more organisations, tribunals and public debates.[17] Even when taking a narrow, interest-based view of policy, state representatives have to include considerations of prestige, reputation and domestic reaction. These elements in turn will often turn on how a government appears at the bar of international law, or what is loosely called 'world opinion'.

Human rights issues are increasingly prominent in shaping that opinion. As Walzer says, they hold the key to unlocking the whole question of ethics, which are no longer (if they ever were) a matter of parochial, national, definition.[18] The most telling characteristic of the justification of human rights is not the appeal which can be made to a particular statute or contract in municipal law. It is the justification which can be made in terms of regional international law (for example, the European Convention on Human Rights) or to global international law (for example, the International Covenants on Civil and Political Rights and on Economic, Social and Cultural Rights). The appeal then becomes one which claims that standards which are recognised at a regional or international level are prior to those of domestic practice. Such an appeal now strikes a more responsive chord than it ever has done before.

CONCLUSIONS

Human rights raise fundamental questions of a universalist nature, which is why states are so reluctant to invite precedents by admitting the force of the rights case. In this account, it is easier to see human rights as necessarily undermining rather than reinforcing the international system, built on the sovereignty of states rather than the rights of individuals. Indeed, one could argue that to admit a huge gap between theory and practice in human rights is to concede the ideological pre-eminence of the form of inter-state relations. To the contrary, however, as I have argued elsewhere, it is part of the case for better human rights that in order that international society itself may become better founded, there must be a certain minimum standard of human rights observance.[19]

Finally, let us address directly the questions posed in Chapter 1 of this book. In terms of the 'history question', or how far should we be preoccupied with the problems of the contemporary world, it is clear that the consideration of human rights draws us straight into current politics, while also providing the widest view – a view which is universalist, which draws upon the traditions of natural law, and which does not shirk the prescriptions of 'what every decent government ought to provide'. At first this might seem rather a-historical, setting absolute standards which cut across time and place. But context must always qualify abstract judgements, as a moment's thought about the passionate debates over abortion both within and across the world's Catholic countries will demonstrate. It is true that the concern for human rights is usually rooted in a sense of history in terms of being inspired by a knowledge of past atrocities (our current concern is very much fuelled by our knowledge of Auschwitz and the Gulags) but it is also sensitive to context in that we are aware that the murders of the past need assessing in terms of the standards of the past. Damiens, for example, who tried to kill Louis XV, was barbarically executed as late as 1757 by being pulled between six horses, but there is little to be gained by ritual denunciation of his executioners now.[20] Moreover, only in the present can we do good. Even recent crimes can only be remembered (as they must), not rectified. On the other hand, history has to be incorporated into the present, and not truncated. The promotion of human rights is likely to be better served by an understanding of how change must be cumulative, than by an attempt, à la 1792, to impose the new liberties at a stroke. Here a combination of Paine and Burke might be the best way.

The 'ideology question' refers to the place of normative concerns in the theory and practice of international relations. At this level it can first be said that human rights constitute an energising ideology. The rights are global rights and they speak to global politics. They force us to conceive of a community of mankind, not just of states. Secondly, human rights form an integral part of the politics of the humanist, liberal, Western tradition. Indeed it can be argued that they represent an essentially legalist approach to politics which is firmly rooted in the particularities of the French and American experiences. They are, none the less, also part of non-Western cultures, through the universal recognition of the importance of human dignity. It convinces no-one to argue for cultural relativism when discussing such things as torture, genocide and mutilation, even if there are many hard questions at the margins. At the very least, the flight of refugees from oppression, whether in British India or Tsarist Russia, Pinochet's Chile or Deng's China, in itself forces the human rights question to the forefront of international concern/relations. Whoever raises these questions, of course, academic or practitioner, cannot but accept that in doing so they are promoting a universalist paradigm with potent political implications.

As to the 'professional question', or the problem of academic independence, it seems clear that we should not endeavour to perform the role carried out by, for example, Amnesty International, however admirable. The evidence from the Soviet Union and countries in Eastern Europe in the wake of collapsing regimes at the end of the 1980s and beginning of the 1990s has demonstrated the importance to incarcerated dissidents of outside pressure concerned with human rights. None the less, members of the Academy should be no-one's agents; they should rather focus on the Rights of Everyman, and try to clarify the issues which need to be decided in the political realm. Each decade brings a new formulation of the question of rights, and it is vital to maintain a perspective on these changes. How, for example, are we to weigh the human rights of Palestinians and Jewish refugees from the Soviet Union in Israel? How can the rights of a people who might want to secede be weighed against the rights of the remaining people in the state to a peaceful life free from civil war?

However agonising the demands of particular human rights claims (and as citizens, of course, academics can be as active as the next person) these fundamental problems must not be neglected if political action is not to bounce incoherently from one single case to another. It is conceivable, for instance, that we might be able to distinguish between regions and/or cultures in terms of their different human rights traditions. But this is really starting at the wrong end of the problem, and such attempts to take short-cuts through the theoretical thicket invariably fail. Torture, for example, is either wrong or it is not, and only general theory can give us the reasons why. Anything else gets bogged down in superficial consequentialism. At the global level, moreover, the issues of political philosophy and policy analysis on which rests any conceptual framework for addressing human rights, are the special province of the academic, who has a duty to clarify and to confront them. In so doing he or she might conceivably be able to do as much good in the long term as the most strenuous pressure-group activity against this or that dictator.

NOTES

1 At this point in the presentation John Vincent expressed a wish to write his next book on the subject of cultural relativism. Chapter 3 of his *Human Rights and International Relations*, Cambridge, Cambridge University Press in association with the Royal Institute of International Affairs, 1986, contains an interesting analysis of the issues at stake.
2 Maurice Cranston, 'Human Rights, Real and Supposed', in D.D. Raphael (ed.) *Political Theory and the Rights of Man*, London, Macmillan, 1977.
3 Jack Donnelly, *The Concept of Human Rights*, New York, St Martin's Press, 1985.
4 Henry Shue, *Basic Rights: Subsistence, Affluence and U.S. Foreign Policy*, Princeton, Princeton University Press, 1980.
5 Donnelly, *Concept of Human Rights*, op. cit., pp. 16–17.
6 R. Tanter and R.H. Ullman, *Theory and Policy in International Relations*, Princeton, Princeton University Press, 1971.
7 Although John Vincent never wrote about post-modernism, and could hardly be called a post-modernist, he was interested in the emergence of the movement and sympathetic to the approach taken by, for example, James Der Derian's *On Diplomacy: A Genealogy of Western Estrangement*, Oxford, Basil Blackwell, 1987.
8 C.A.W. Manning, *The Nature of International Society*, London, Macmillan, 1975, pp. 80–1 and 194–6 (first published by Bell for the LSE, 1962).
9 Louis Henkin, *The Age of Rights*, New York, Columbia University Press, 1990, p. ix.
10 Thomas Paine, *The Rights of Man* [1791], London, Everyman edn, 1969, p. 94.
11 For an exposition of the Kantian tradition in which this view falls, see Andrew Linklater, *Men and Citizens in the Theory of International Relations*, London, Macmillan, 1982, pp. 97–120.
12 Edmund Burke, *Reflections on the Revolution in France* [1790], in *Works*, 6 vols, Bohn's British Classics edn, vol. 2, London, Bell & Daldy, 1872, p. 412.
13 On Grotius, see R.J. Vincent, 'Grotius, Human Rights and Intervention', in Hedley Bull, Benedict Kingsbury and Adam Roberts (eds), *Hugo Grotius and International Relations*, Oxford, the Clarendon Press, 1990, pp. 241–56.
14 Vincent, *Human Rights*, op. cit., Chapter 2.
15 Editors' note: events have moved on since this observation was made. In mid-1992 a Human Rights Policy Unit (now a Department) was set up in the FCO to deal with the increased salience of humanitarian questions in foreign policy. This answers to the same under-secretary as does the UN Department, but the two departments are now separate and equal.
16 This is the view of Michael Donelan, for example, as expressed during the

original seminar. See also Donelan's *Elements of International Political Theory*, Oxford, Clarendon Press, 1990 (especially Chapter 1, 'Natural Law'), which RJV had read in typescript.

17 Louis Henkin, *How Nations Behave: Law and Foreign Policy* (2nd edn), New York, Columbia University Press, 1979, especially pp. 39–87.

18 Michael Walzer, *Just and Unjust Wars: A Moral Argument with Illustrations*, London, Allen Lane, 1978.

19 R.J. Vincent, *Human Rights*, op. cit., especially pp. 150–2. Before this John Vincent had produced the edited volume *Foreign Policy and Human Rights* (Cambridge, Cambridge University Press in association with the Royal Institute of International Affairs, 1986), in which he and a team of colleagues examined varying state policies.

20 The episode opens Michel Foucault's *Surveiller et Punir: Naissance de la Prison*, Paris, Gallimard, 1975. The editors are indebted to Alan Ryan's essay 'Foucault's Life and Hard Times', in *The New York Review of Books*, April 1993, for this graphic example of RJV's general point.

3   The historian and the Foreign Office

Zara Steiner

'Historians are notoriously bad at understanding and advising on current political questions, and, as a matter of fact, the habit of following the trend of contemporary affairs and the art of writing intelligently on the subject, are outside the Foreign Office, practically confined in most countries to men who follow the profession of journalism.'[1] Coming from a man, Sir Eyre Crowe, permanent under-secretary at the Foreign Office between 1920 and 1924, who read widely in the histories of his time and who deplored the interventions of the Fourth Estate in the affairs of the Foreign Office, this is hardly a flattering view of our profession. None the less, this somewhat jaundiced view might well be greeted by nods of approval by those of us who read some of our best-known practitioners in the Sunday press. And to make matters worse, historians are more often condemned than praised for writing for the public rather than for their peers. Nor is the record of the profession, in terms of its contribution to the making of foreign policy, as positive or as respectable as some would have us believe.

THE EMPLOYMENT OF HISTORIANS BY THE FOREIGN OFFICE

The difficulty of writing about this subject is that what appears to be a simple question becomes, naturally enough in the hands of an historian, a multi-layered problem. There is the question of the Foreign Office's use of historians, either in permanent employment or as consultants on an *ad hoc* basis for a specific task. The Office has employed since 1920, with the appointment of James Headlam-Morley as historical adviser, a succession of historians in the library although the post was a personal one and not renewed on Headlam-Morley's departure. The historical adviser's inter-war memoranda and minutes are of considerable interest and importance, not only as an important source for the history of the

Paris Peace Conference and for the Foreign Office case against John Maynard Keynes's *Economic Consequences of the Peace* but for the lucid and intelligent comments on German and other European problems which clearly commanded considerable attention and respect.

In 1924, G.P. Gooch and Harold Temperley were asked to edit the *British Documents on the Origins of War*, after Kingsley Martin had been ruled out for being too bilious a personality. The Foreign Office thought it would be a three-year job and a singular, one-off effort. Instead, work begun in 1925 was not finished until 1938. The relationship between Foreign Office and editors was far from smooth and offers of resignation not infrequent. In 1927, after an altercation between the editors and the French authorities, a dispute that the Foreign Office hierarchy felt too trivial to pursue, the Foreign Office librarian, Stephen Gaselee, minuted: 'Heavy weather again. These historians' consciences are very tender.'[2] Though it was generally hoped at the Foreign Office that such a publication, particularly with inclusion of office minutes, would be a one-time affair, there followed the 1944 decision to publish the *Documents on British Foreign Policy 1919 to 1939*, admittedly some without minutes.[3] There were 64 volumes in four different series and historians such as Llewellyn Woodward, Rowan Butler, J.P.T. Bury, William Medlicott, Douglas Dakin and Margaret Lambert were involved in its production.[4] Margaret Lambert and the late Roger Bullen were subsequently engaged in the later series of *Documents on British Policy Overseas*, begun in 1973 and still proceeding.

The Foreign Office, too, has twice imported into its ranks organisations or sections composed of outsiders who had strong historical interests or were historians, though most, as was customary before the Great War, were trained in the classics. In 1918, a wartime section in Naval Intelligence was transferred to the Foreign Office as the latter's Historical Section under George Prothero, a former professor of Modern History at the University of Edinburgh and editor of the *Quarterly Review*. As part of the same wartime reorganisation aimed at strengthening the hand of the Foreign Office in the forthcoming peace negotiations, the former Intelligence Bureau attached to the Department of Information was brought into the Office as the Political Intelligence Department (PID) in April 1918. Neither of these new creations survived the economies of 1920.

These examples of major importations proved to be unique in the inter-war history of the Foreign Office. Among members of the PID were Arnold Toynbee, Lewis Namier and Alfred Zimmern, but also James Headlam-Morley, mentioned earlier, a classical scholar and historian turned educational administrator who took up the cause of enlightening the public on foreign policy issues. Some PID members actually came to Paris during the Peace Conference; others, though still in London, also had either a direct or indirect influence on the peace-making process mainly with regard to the territorial settlements. The Historical Section produced 174 Peace books involving over eighty experts. C.K. Webster, the noted diplomatic historian, wrote on the Congress of Vienna although, as he admitted, the monograph had no observable effect on the peace process. E.L. Woodward, using confidential Foreign Office papers, wrote on the Congress of Berlin. The Peace books appear to have been most widely used by the junior officials at Paris and it was the PID, the 'Ministry of All the Talents', rather than the Historical Section that left the greater imprint on the peace treaties.[5] Headlam-Morley was probably its most eminent representative, less because of what he wrote in 1918 than because Lloyd George recruited him to work on the Danzig, Saar and Upper Silesian questions in Paris and because, pressed and seconded by Louis Namier, he played a major part in the drafting of the minorities protection treaties.[6] The PID had prepared some 71 memoranda of up to 20 pages each in anticipation of questions that might be discussed at the Peace Conference. Whether these were actually read by their political masters is another story. Though Lloyd George may have been 'alert and quick', his reservoirs of historical knowledge were exceedingly shallow.

These precedents were not without influence during the Second World War when again a Political Intelligence Department was created in which historians served.[7] One section of the Royal Institute of International Affairs (Chatham House) worked for the Foreign Office, operating from its wartime headquarters at Balliol College, Oxford. Its function was to prepare a weekly digest of the foreign press, produce detailed background memoranda on foreign countries and undertake long-term planning for peace, assisting both the Cabinet War Aims Committee and the Reconstruction Committee in this respect. Some of the former members of the old PID – Webster, Zimmern and Toynbee – were members. So was R.W. Seton Watson, who had refused to join his colleagues when they moved in 1918, in part because his newly created journal, *The New Europe*, was highly critical of the way in which the Foreign Office was being run, but who continued to be consulted as the most knowledgeable expert on the needs of the new successor states. Other historians joined the Foreign Research and Press Service: Denis Brogan, Bernard Pares, G.N. Clark and C.M. Macartney. From 1 April 1943, the FRPS became the Foreign Office Research Department after 'tortuous negotiations' between the Foreign Office and Chatham House. The history of this body is still to be written. In 1940, R.A. Butler confessed that 'the good brains of Chatham House such as Professor Webster, Clark Macartney and others are dragging only small carts when they might be dragging big ones and that we should use them more than we do'.[8] Something is known of the work of Professor Webster, who helped shape the British proposals for an international organisation and participated in the later negotiations at Dumbarton Oaks and San Francisco. Many of Webster's ideas were injected into the Foreign Office and Cabinet streams through Gladwyn Jebb but he was also able to convince both Alexander Cadogan, the permanent under-secretary, and Anthony Eden, the foreign secretary, of the correctness of his views, which were not those of the prime minister.[9]

THE POST-1945 EXPERIENCE

After the war, E.J. Passant, the newly appointed Foreign Office librarian (and himself the future historian of nineteenth-century Germany) also carried the title of Head of Research, and the Research Department, divided along geographic lines, became a permanent part of the Office. Historians employed by the present-day FCO reside here, although regular diplomatic establishment officers are also assigned to the department. It is in the Research Department that the briefs or background papers are prepared for the political departments, under-secretaries, legal advisers and ministers. 'Like many of my colleagues, I have filleted the records for a straight-forward historical account of some past event. The example given here is what happened to the Chinese Embassy premises in London between 1950, when the Nationalists withdrew and 1954, where the People's Republic of China decided to open a mission in London – for those who care, not a lot and it showed.'[10] James Hoare concluded his discussion of the Research Department by noting that its most valued service was not the learned exposition of complicated issues of international relations but the finding of relevant papers. Researchers are the memory bank of the FCO servicing an office whose members are part of a rotational diplomatic service operating mainly on an *ad hoc* basis with a heavy emphasis on finding solutions to current problems. More than one diplomat assigned for work in Cornwall House has complained of 'internal exile'. Some career officers have read history as under-graduates (this hardly means they are historians) but as the FCO currently tries to attract as varied a group of entrants as possible, this, like the earlier group of classicists, is probably a shrinking proportion of the total diplomatic establishment.

POLITICIANS, OFFICIALS AND HISTORIANS: THE CASE FOR DIFFERENT FUNCTIONS

When asking the questions of how important a role historians play in the making of foreign policy and whether this role should be expanded, it is essential to keep in mind the practicalities of the British structure of government. Although it is generally accepted that British civil servants have more influence at a higher level of policy-making than in many comparable modern states, the individual officer's input into the government system is necessarily limited. Complaints that advice is ignored or that 'too many Rolls-Royces are doing the work of Fords' are not unique in the contemporary period as those of us familiar with the pre-Second World War diplomatic correspondence will know. Professor Webster, writing about Churchill's handling of the world organisation papers, noted in 1944: 'these preparations and studies will be made and then precipitate and unconsidered action by the PM will take matters entirely out of the hands of the experts. He would never even organise a small commando raid without taking some expert advice even if he did not follow it. But here he is trying to shape the whole of the future without saying a word to his Cabinet, Foreign Secretary or their officials.'[11] In another diary entry, Webster echoes the sentiments of Eyre Crowe, who refused to allow his officials to attend Cabinet meetings lest they see how matters of state were actually decided. On 7 July 1944, after weeks of anxious work to get the drafts and counter-drafts on the new world organisation ready for the Cabinet, Webster writes: 'Gladwyn [Jebb] and I coached Dick Law for three quarters of an hour before the Cabinet which was at 11.30. But it was all unnecessary. The PM walked out, said he was not much interested and the Cabinet passed the papers without discussion.'[12] On another occasion, Webster discusses the Cabinet's handling of the instructions for the Dumbarton Oaks talks: 'The old man had put local government first and they took nearly two hours over it. Only s of s insistence got our papers discussed at all. No one knew anything about them. . .It really is amazing how we are governed.'[13] Richard Crossman's diaries and Peter Hennessy's *Whitehall* are replete with examples of similar instances, some of the best found in the Hennessy volume drawn from the Thatcher era.[14]

Whether his or her advice is solicited or not, it can be argued that the historian has special talents that can be used in the foreign policy process and that they are different from those of the professional diplomat or the journalist. These come as much from the nature of the discipline as from specific expertise in any one field. Historians are taught to see problems in a continuum of time; no crisis starts today or even yesterday. He or she instinctively asks what is the story rather than what is the current problem. One looks at past landmarks that punctuate that story and notes the continuities and discontinuities in past behaviour. The historian will almost automatically place individuals and organisations within a time-stream. An understanding of the past helps with the placing of the present situation and casts light on probable outcomes. There are, for instance, patterns of personal behaviour, traditional ways of operation, and national characteristics which alert the historian to what can be expected. Or, on the contrary, familiarity with the past may lead the historian to stress the uniqueness of the current action. Because they are trained to be sensitive to the past, historians are, or should be, more attuned to the range of possible future consequences. They will view these in a different way than the policy-maker concentrating on the answer to a particular problem. In a book little noticed in Britain, *Thinking in Time: The Uses of History for Decision Makers* by Richard Neustadt and Ernest May, the authors suggest how administrators could be taught to think along historical lines.[15] This is not just one more example of a do-it-yourself handbook nor an overly optimistic tract for the times. Neither writer expects more than marginal improvements in bureaucratic behaviour to result from training public officials to make better use of the historians' tools. The book highlights, for instance, the advantages to be gained from learning how to use historical analogies so that they assist and not mislead those taking decisions. The authors do not return to the high claims once made for Clio (the success rate among contemporary historians who have become prophets does not encourage self-congratulation) but show how historians' skills can be applied to the solving of contemporary problems.

'They're too busy. Can't read what they get now. They'll glance at papers in the limousine, thumb them while someone is talking. If you do get their attention, you can't keep it. They will have to catch a plane or go to a press conference.'[16] It is hardly surprising that it was in the planning for peace that historians appear to have been most usefully employed by the Foreign Office. In the daily course of events, there is barely time to look up, digest and 'place' the subject to be studied or to have one's recommendations considered by the appropriate official. No Foreign Ministry has yet found a satisfactory way effectively to bring past memory and record as construed by the historian into the policy-making process. It was once hoped that annual reports from Foreign Office departments and from missions abroad would serve to educate the foreign secretary and become a historical memory bank for the future. Instead, the annual reviews from missions abroad have become source material for future diplomatic historians. Few policy planning staffs have succeeded in doing the kind of forward planning that would tap historical expertise outside the Office. Policy planners find it difficult enough to make future projections (five years seems to be the absolute maximum time-span) even when they are not diverted from this task by the more immediate needs of the Office. Forward planning is generally held to be an impractical and futile exercise, 'a waste of time and talent', although it is accepted that the military services and financial departments have longer lead-in times that depend on accurate foreign policy assessments.

Even in the short run, as the experience of pre-peace planning in 1918 suggests (and not just in Britain), carefully prepared position papers are not always used by the policy-makers despite the fact that individual advisers on the spot, i.e. the experts on the 1919 commissions and committees, determined those issues the politicians had neither the interest nor the time to consider. The writers of the pre-conference memoranda were specifically instructed to be as short and succinct as possible, to indicate separate points clearly and to make positive recommendation. Yet while this advice was generally followed, individual members of the PID could not be protected against the resentment of career diplomats or the indifference of the politicians.

Policy-makers often do not know exactly what they require from the historian. They clearly do not want learned disquisitions however informed or authoritative. The official historian working in the department, because of his knowledge of the office routine or the character of the questioner, or because of familiarity with past papers or the ability to find those papers, may be in a better position than the outside scholar, who knows both too much and too little, to meet the needs of the enquirer. The latter wants to have complex matters simply explained; he wants an informed recommendation without the qualifications that are almost the hallmark of our profession. If, however, the in-house historian may be of more immediate practical use to the bureaucrat there are also positive benefits from seeking outside information and advice. As all students of bureaucracies know, departments (and the Foreign Office is one of the best examples) have their own forms of 'groupthink', inherited traditions and shared assumptions which colour judgements. The outsider or the temporary appointee has the advantage of not being part of an established hierarchy.

The Webster diary is again useful in underlining this point. Mindful of the lessons of the 1930s when 'misguided idealists' spoke of collective security instead of rearmament, some of the younger officials in the Foreign Office made a point of demanding a realistic appraisal of the post-war situation. Speaking about the agenda for the Moscow conference being discussed in September 1943, Webster comments, 'The young FO men merely considered (a) what had been said in it (b) what the expediency of the moment might make us do. I once or twice ventured to point out that there was also the consideration of what was in the best interests of all the states in a permanent settlement. Strang backed me up on this and so the young men became a little less hard boiled. But they are immersed in this nauseous atmosphere and look on every negotiation as an intrigue.'[17] Webster complained that it was no use appealing to principle for the Office 'is all on the other side and opportunistic as usual. It has little sense of the long-term values.'[18] It is Webster's sense of a shared consensus that is particularly interesting. An office staffed by careerists who have served with each other in posts abroad and at home can develop a group consensus. Within the Foreign Office, departments have often become identified with a particular outlook or policy. There are mavericks but they are few. The outsider disturbs the bureaucratic routine; he or she looks at familiar material in a different way. He or she can suggest new approaches and more easily, even if unconsciously, challenge the prevailing assumptions.

In Washington, where outside appointments are far more common than in London, there has been considerable tension between the non-careerist, often a political appointee, and the permanent official. Outside advice pours in to the departments backed by the central role played by Congress in the actual formulation of foreign policy. In Britain, where the *ad hoc* adviser is rarely used and transfers between government departments or assignments to non-governmental bodies, though more frequent in recent years, are still limited, there is a tendency to operate within a closed circle of career officers. When major changes of policy do occur within the FCO, they often become tomorrow's orthodoxies, difficult to challenge or overturn. Any study of Foreign Office attitudes towards the European Community over the last three decades would make this point. P.A. Reynolds comments that 'Even a less incisive mind well versed in the history and theory of a subject coming from outside can prove to be a more innovative influence than an extremely able career officer accustomed to a certain routine and to working within a certain environment.' If he can insert his views, the outsider can have a greater impact than the career officer provided he does not outstay his welcome nor take on the coloration of the department.

The FCO has never taken kindly to the intrusion of outsiders; lateral entry procedures are not much used. It is only recently that officers have been seconded not just to other departments but to banks and business firms. In part due to the efforts of the Policy Planning Staff, officers have been sent to the universities and positive efforts been made to build bridges with the academic community. The day has passed when permanent members of the Foreign Office (though not the gentlemen of the PID) were actually forbidden to join the new British Institute for the Study of International Relations (the later Royal Institute of International Affairs), that 'dangerous band of nosey critics', but even today the continuous cross-fertilisation between the academic community and the foreign policy establishment so common in the United States still does not take place in this country.

THE CONTRIBUTIONS OF HISTORIANS OUTSIDE THE DECISION-MAKING PROCESS

We have been speaking so far of the actual use of historians by the Foreign Office. There is, however, another sense in which historians have contributed to the making of foreign policy. There are, naturally, good and bad historians. It is not always the most accomplished or the most balanced scholar who has the largest public following or the greatest influence in shaping bureaucratic attitudes. In ways not predictable, historians can create through their writings and lectures those interpretations of the 'lessons of the past' that affect the political climate. This said, historians, fortunately, do not have to take the blame for all the false historical analogies statesmen have followed. Personal experience, more often than not, has a far greater impact on the official mind than any book read or advice tendered. Although President Kennedy's reading of Barbara Tuchman's *The Guns of August* alerted him to the dangers of speeding up the diplomatic time-clock during the Cuban Missile crisis, it was Anthony Eden's own pre-1939 memories which produced his disastrous comparisons between Nasser and Mussolini: what historians do is to create pictures of the past which colour the perceptions of statesmen and bureaucrats. In particular, beliefs about recent history shape political behaviour. Occasionally a book, or series of books, radically affects the thinking of those responsible for policy decisions. One might dispute whether John Maynard Keynes should be cited as a historian but no-one can deny the impact of *The Economic Consequences of the Peace* on official attitudes towards the Treaty of Versailles and the subsequent treatment of Germany.

Manfred Messerschmidt's *Deutschland in englischer Sicht* and D.C. Watt's *Britain Looks to Germany* and other writings have called attention to the ways in which emigré and British historians of the 1930s and 1940s created a new view of German domestic history which became current orthodoxy in the post-war decade.[19] While each individual historian stressed different factors either in the German mentality or in the development of the Prussian–German state that led to the triumph of Nazism, all saw National Socialism as the inevitable product of a century of German political, social and cultural history. Assumptions about the psychology and mentality of the German people shaped official thinking about how Germany should be treated once the war was won. It was thought that a people inured to obedience would admire, even in its conquerors, severity and remoteness and would look on any attempts at conciliation as a sign of weakness and cowardice. The non-fraternisation policies supported by the Foreign Office were based on the assumption that German civilians fell into a special category of people which the British soldier should leave strictly alone. This emphasis on the ingrained characteristics of the German people is reflected in a paper on the 'German reactions to defeat' presented by Anthony Eden to the Cabinet on 10 January 1945:

> National socialism has been no more than a special form of organisation of the instincts and capacities of the German people. Other forms of totalitarian organisation almost equally unpleasant and effective may occur, for these instincts and capacities will remain largely what they were. But there is little reason to fear that national socialism will revive, and some reason to hope that the experience of it will have taught the Germans a few lessons which they will not forget. It would be superficial to regard Hitlerism as likely to remain a menace of the same order as German nationalism and German militarism.[20]

It was hardly surprising that there was an assumption that it would require a generation, some twenty to thirty years, to re-educate the German nation.

It should be pointed out that some of these historians (writers such as Rohan Butler, Lewis Namier, John Wheeler Bennett, A.J.P Taylor) were building on ideas about the nature of the German state and people that long preceded the advent of Hitler. The triumph of Bismarck, the policies of William II and the Great War had already in an earlier period convinced some contemporaries that Germany was in a special category of its own (a kind of premature version of the 'deutscher Sonderweg') and that militarism was deeply ingrained in the German psyche. One needs to look more closely at the British historical writing of the pre- and immediate post-First World War period to trace the roots of revisionism in British historiography of the Nazi era. This is not, however, to deny the special character of this later rewriting of German history with its emphasis on the power of the state, the docility and discipline of the people and the intellectual tradition that led from Potsdam to the Führer's bunker.

There were some historians who swam against this powerful current. G.P. Gooch, mentioned in Professor Watt's article, was an old man commonly known to have supported the policies of appeasement long after he had recognised the evils of Nazism.[21] There was also Herbert Butterfield, whose strong anti-Soviet (and anti-Russian) views tended to blot out the Nazi period of German history almost entirely. His quarrels with Lewis Namier were not confined to the Whig interpretation of history. It would be an interesting piece of historical analysis to see how far British historical writing about the United States created or confirmed official attitudes towards the so-called 'special relationship'. And what can be inferred about the Anglo-American partnership from the fact that Lord David Cecil's *Melbourne* was the favourite biography of both John F. Kennedy and Harold Macmillan?

THE FUTURE ROLE OF HISTORIANS IN THE FCO

The Foreign Office has made only limited use of Britain's historians, usually for special purposes and at particular times. Both the Office and the academic historians it has employed have gained in stature and reputation from the publication of the official documents. Our knowledge about the relations between the Office and its official historians is limited to the inter-war period when the editors succeeded in establishing their right to publish what they wished and in the form they wanted. Present-day historians have been assured that very few papers from the post-1945 period which have been withheld contain essential information not already available in an open file. The editors have the right to see papers that do not come into the public domain though not the right to make use of such material (special procedures are available to alert readers to withdrawals). The editors, moreover, are barred from seeing intelligence and personnel records. The high reputation of past publications series seem to have withstood the opening of the archives though the sheer number of documents and the inclusion of non-Foreign Office material make it difficult to offer a final verdict. Little is yet known about editorial practice for the inter-war series or for E.L. Woodward's wartime volumes.

Whether the electronic revolution is going to create new difficulties for the historians and other researchers employed in the Foreign Office is an open question. The problem of using the mass of information, both current and past, soon to be available for recall will inevitably affect the FCO once it has fully moved into the electronic age. The real communications revolution may transform the practice of diplomacy more radically than is assumed. It will certainly fundamentally alter the way historians will write about foreign policy. Should the Foreign Office employ more historians, and not just in the library and research departments? On the whole, I would answer in the negative though most diplomats would benefit from reading more history. It is when historians remain outside the system that they are best able to feed their ideas into the system. Their distance from the daily mechanics of policy-making is a positive advantage in their public roles as commentators, critics and Cassandras. They should be used for consultative purposes and the system made flexible enough so that they can be drawn into the FCO for specific tasks and periods of time. Eyre Crowe was at least partially correct in his belief that diplomats, historians and journalists are separate species however much or however often they try to play each other's roles.

Increased contact between career officers and historians even at the departmental level would benefit both groups. There is time available; one less inter-departmental meeting would not shake the Whitehall structure and there are few historians not flattered by an invitation to the 'corridors of power'. In a book commemorating the 200th anniversary of the Foreign Office, John Goulden suggested that in the future, diplomats will have to spend more time cultivating their domestic gardens.[22] It would not hurt if that cultivation included time spent with 'eccentric intellectuals'. There is the danger that officials who talk with historians soon think that they are themselves historians, or that historians begin to imagine themselves 'foreign policy advisers'. The record of academic historians who have actually become advisers or even, in one extraordinary American case, secretary of state, is a mixed one. It has rarely happened at the FCO. By contrast there is less doubt about the advantages for historians in seeing how business is actually conducted at King Charles Street. It is with good reason that we seek out retired officials and diplomats. The nuances of personality, hierarchy and influence are not always found in the papers. The official who wrote the longest or the most impressive memorandum may be the furthest removed from the centres of decision-making. The new posting, which turns out to be a critical assignment, might have been a way of getting rid of the departmental bore. The unrecorded but all too well-remembered gossip of the diplomatic circuit is a necessary ingredient in the diplomatic mix, even in the present day of flying circuses. The history of the Foreign Office and its establishments is part of any study of understanding of twentieth-century foreign policy. The written record gives only part of this fascinating story. Now that so many diplomats retire at sixty, perhaps a collaborative approach is in order. But better outside the FCO than in it.

NOTES

1 F.O. 366/787/II(a). Memorandum reporting the future organisation of the Treaty Department and Library of the Foreign Office, 1910.
2 Franz Eyck, *G.P. Gooch, A Study in History and Politics*, London, Macmillan, 1982, p. 361.
3 Uri Bailer, 'Telling the Truth to the People: Britain's decision to publish the diplomatic papers of the inter-war period', *Historical Journal*, vol. 26, 1963. Professor Bailer not only charts the central role of Professor E.L. Woodward, an Oxford historian serving in the wartime PID in the long struggle to get the inter-war documents published, but casts considerable light on the divisions in the Cabinet and Foreign Office over publication during the war. The first pressure for publication arose from the wish to counter the German White Book published in December 1939; the final decision had much to do with an American government publication of 1943 and the State Department's ongoing series of published diplomatic volumes. In both instances – the publication of the pre-1914 and inter-war documents – the task was left to historians recruited for the purpose from outside the Foreign Office. There is still no wartime series.
4 FCO Historical Branch, *Occasional Papers*, no. 1, p. 25.
5 This information as well as additional comments on the Political Intelligence Department comes from a Ph.D. thesis by Erik Goldstein, published in an expanded form as *Winning the Peace: British Diplomatic Strategy, Peace Planning and the Paris Peace Conference 1916–1920*, Oxford, Clarendon, 1991. See also the important articles by Keith A. Hamilton, 'The Pursuit of "Enlightened Patriotism": The British Foreign Office and Historical Researchers during the Great War and its Aftermath', *Bulletin of the Institute of Historical Research*, vol. 61, 1988, and D.C. Watt, 'Every War Must End: Wartime Planning for Post-War Security in Britain and America in the Wars of 1914–18 and 1939–1945', *Transactions of the Royal Historical Society*, Fifth Series, 28, 1978.
6 J.H. Headlam-Morley, *A Memoir of the Paris Peace Conference, 1919*, Agnes Headlam-Morley (ed.) *et al.*, London, Methuen, 1972.
7 E. Hughes and P. Reynolds, *The Historian as Diplomat, Charles Kingsley Webster and the United Nations 1939–1946*, London, Martin Robertson, 1976, p. 13.
8 Ibid., p. 13.
9 There are many examples in the Webster diary, cited in Hughes and Reynolds, *The Historian as Diplomat*, op. cit.; see, for instance, pp. 30–1, 35–7, 48–9.
10 Dr James E. Hoare, 'Present-day Records: the Prospects for Future Historians', in FCO Historical Branch, op. cit., p. 52.
11 Hughes and Reynolds, *The Historian as Diplomat*, op. cit., pp. 20–1, 70.
12 Ibid., p. 37.

13 Ibid., p. 54.
14 Richard Crossman, *The Diaries of a Cabinet Minister, 1964–70*, London, Hamilton, 1979, vol. 3, p. 402; Peter Hennessy, *Whitehall*, London, Secker & Warburg, 1989, Chapter 15.
15 Richard Neustadt and Ernest May, *Thinking in Time: The Uses of History for Decision Makers*, New York, Free Press, 1986.
16 Ibid., p. 1.
17 Hughes and Reynolds, *The Historian as Diplomat*, op. cit., p. 24.
18 Ibid., p.24.
19 M. Messerschmidt, *Deutschland in englischer Sicht*, Dusseldorf, 1955. D.C. Watt, *Britain Looks to Germany, British Opinion and Policy towards Germany since 1945*, London, Wolff, 1965.
20 WP 45(7) Cab (666/60–81528 quoted in M Steinert, 'Les Allemands vus de Londres, 1944–1945', *Relations internationales*, no. 51, autumn 1987, p. 254. The whole document is worth reading, including a reference to traces of Mongol blood which might explain Prussian behaviour. Professor Steinert develops my general argument with numerous illustrations from the Foreign Office files.
21 D.C. Watt, 'Perceptions of German History among the British Policy-Making Elite, 1930–1965 and the Role of British and German Emigré Historiography in Its Formation', in H. Kohler (ed.) *Deutschland und der Westen: Vorträge und Diskussions – beiträge des Symposiums zu Ehren von Gordon Craig*, Berlin, 1984.
22 FCO Historical Branch, op. cit., pp. 21–4. John Goulden, 'The Foreign Office and the Future', in Roger Bullen (ed.) *The Foreign Office, 1782–1982*, Frederick, Maryland, 1984, p. 139.

4   International political economy and the national policy-maker

Roger Tooze

Managing the global economy is one of the most important policy goals of the Group of Seven industrial nations that dominate world production, credit, knowledge, trade and investment. Indeed, 'how' the global economy is managed and 'who benefits' from this process is of major concern to almost every government in the contemporary global system. The level of concern is only partly explained by the traditional indicator of international economic activity – the extent, volume and intensity of international trade. The more difficult problems of understanding and policy stem from the emergence of a global *political* economy that is both more than the sum of international trade and not just the product of economic forces. The globalisation of the international economy in terms of production and services[1] has fundamentally restructured the relationship of the state (or national economy) to the international economy in political and policy terms.[2]

This altered relationship would be evident even if political institutions and frameworks had not themselves changed. As it is, the demise of the Soviet Union has transformed the global structure of international politics and economics: into what, we do not yet fully understand. At the same time, the continuing dynamics of the European Community, particularly after the Maastricht agreement, have dramatically changed the nature and process of public policy-making for its members and the policy arena for its non-members. Moreover, the USA is now attempting to reconstruct what it denotes as its economic space, with a collaborative framework for multilateral economic activity that will enable it to accrue more power in the global economy partly in reaction to the perception of 'lost hegemony' that is currently influential in US policy circles.[3] And the political role of Japan continues to be uncertain at the same time as Japanese capital contributes to and often drives a reshaping of the international division of labour. The prospect of an emerging world order that might be made up of a greatly expanded and deepened EC (including the countries of Eastern Europe), competing and/or collaborating with an enhanced North American Free Trade Area (NAFTA), which might include most of the countries of Central and South America, and with an alliance between ASEAN and Japan, is one that rightly sends shivers down the spines of all those who have to formulate foreign policy in this complex environment.

One of the reasons why policy-makers are concerned is that we are indeed moving towards a new international/global economic order. This will not be the 'NIEO' envisaged by the reformers of the 1970s, but it will still be an order which threatens to upset the norms and procedures built up over the past forty years. At the global level 'new orders' usually mean uncertainty; however, this is not the uncertainty of undefined policy outcomes within a fairly well-articulated structure of relationships and familiar issues, which is usually capable of being 'dealt with' inside existing foreign policy systems and assumptions. Now the uncertainty is that associated with new structures, processes and issues. 'Structural' uncertainty often produces hesitancy and ambiguity in policy at exactly the time when clear direction and original conceptions are the necessary prerequisites of order, progress and justice. This kind of uncertainty tests understanding, explanation and eventual policy in a very direct way. The concepts and theories currently utilised to understand, explain and analyse policy questions in the global economy are already under severe strain[4] – and a qualitative change in the nature and structure of relationships will (and should) cause a fundamental questioning of the knowledge upon which policy is based and implemented.

It is this historical conjuncture of social, political and economic forces which adds a real urgency to the evaluation of the relationship between academic knowledge and foreign policy-making that is the focus of this book. This chapter addresses a particular aspect of that relationship – that between the body of academic knowledge known as 'international political economy' (IPE) and foreign policy and foreign economic policy-making. It does so in the belief that IPE in its different forms offers a necessary framework for understanding and policy more appropriate and relevant than current economic analysis or, indeed, than an international politics which is divorced from economics. The chapter will consider the same questions as the other contributions to the volume but the line of argument may have a different starting point and involve different considerations than a more orthodox analysis of international relations.[5] In terms of the central questions identified in the Introduction to the book the argument here is unambiguous: although we should clearly be concerned with contemporary events, academic knowledge of IPE/IR is useful precisely because it offers a broader perspective. This perspective has a longer time-frame as the context for a *structural* understanding of political economy. Here, the relationship between normative and empirical concerns may be problematic but can be either accommodated within existing knowledge or becomes less significant for other forms of knowledge. In the process of the application of knowledge to policy the preservation of independence of the academic is difficult, but how difficult seems to depend upon whether the academic knowledge produced and utilised by government is supportive of the underlying structure of current policy or not. And this suggests that the notion of an 'organic intellectual' is useful in the present context.[6]

ACADEMIC KNOWLEDGE AND POLICY-MAKING

I have previously argued that the metatheoretical context of knowledge cannot be ignored when attempting to evaluate the contribution of that knowledge to understanding and explanation.[7] This argument is particularly germane to any consideration of the relationship between academic knowledge and policy because the nature, status and purpose of knowledge powerfully affects whether and how it is utilised. As will hopefully be demonstrated, this is very much the case for the knowledge constituted by IPE.[8]

Hence, before we review the substantive implications of IPE for foreign and foreign economic policy, we should consider a prior question. As indicated above this question concerns the specific nature of the relationship between academic knowledge and policy-making. An understanding of this relationship forms the *essential* basis for an investigation of the questions posed by this book and, in turn, necessitates a discussion of the nature and status of academic knowledge itself. This entails a short excursion into the philosophy of knowledge, specifically the metatheory that conditions how we know what we know – epistemology. Academic knowledge (i.e. knowledge produced by a specific social process of intellectual production), claims, and is usually granted, a particular status in the hierarchy of 'knowledges' produced in and by society. Think, for example, about the way in which we treat and receive the 'facts' or judgements contained in an advertisement or, perhaps, the claims of national politicians at election time, compared to the status that is accorded to (legitimated) academic knowledge.

Of course, much of the 'power' and status of academic knowledge comes from the perception that 'academic' in our present cultural context is often equated with 'scientific', and science still has a very special place in the social hierarchy of knowledge. Here, for knowledge to be scientific it has to be produced according to well-specified rules of 'scientific method' and it must be capable of being validated by the same rules – that is, conclusions can and should be 'tested' against an empirically verifiable reality. Until recently most academics engaged in the production of 'social' knowledge, including that which is defined as 'international political economy', did attempt to base their activities upon a set of procedures conforming to (their perception of) science and 'scientific method': this was established as the orthodox way of producing social knowledge. Such an orthodoxy meant adopting, often implicitly, a philosophical judgement on the nature of human consciousness and from this the possibility (and indeed, desirability) of 'objective' knowledge and the methodologies used to acquire such knowledge derived. This judgement forms part of the broader philosophy of positivism. The philosophical framework of positivism supports the production of a knowledge that is 'objective', a knowledge that is separate from the individuals that produce it, and a knowledge that is nomological, universally valid in time and space.[9]

Thus, the production of academic (and other) knowledge is characterised as an attempt to apply objectively generated concepts to an objectively understood external reality that is somehow separate (or can be separated) from the academic observer. This process configures the production of knowledge as the search for scientific truth and academics as nonsocial participants, thus ensuring the independence of the academic from policy as well as building in the separation of empirical from normative concerns. In this metatheoretical context 'theory' and 'concepts', as well as 'fact', have a particular definition and a specific role:

> The literature continually stresses that the social scientist is confronted with a 'sea of facts' which can be approached systematically *only* in terms of explicit analytical constructs or conceptual frameworks which, although they possess a certain arbitrary character, *are necessary as tools for description and explanation.* These frameworks. . . are to be imposed on independent data bases, to which they are linked by operational definitions.[10]

'Facts', then, exist independently of theory, and theory is instrumental (i.e. to enable us to make sense of facts). The purpose of positivist theory in particular is instrumental: to manipulate the data (say, of the international economy) in order to describe, explain and predict in as parsimonious and as logically tight a way as possible. Such theory is assumed to be applicable universally in time and space, abstracted from the conditions of its social context.[11] However, the instrumentality of positivist theory is often transposed to whole categories of knowledge when this knowledge is used for purposes of policy. Then, because the assumption is that the knowledge so produced is instrumental knowledge, and within this epistemological context assumed to be value-free and universally applicable, appropriate theories, concepts, methods and data can be used to achieve any goal, within any policy process and by any policy-maker. Although a particular body of social knowledge may be specific to a designated system or domain of activity (e.g. the international political system, or a national economy) once the problem or issue at hand is identified as belonging to that system, it is assumed that the appropriate theories and concepts can be utilised as a basis for policy.

The significance of *positivist* knowledge to the relationship between academic knowledge, academics and policy should now be clearly discernible. Because of its claims as knowledge (as opposed to any substantive empirical referents and policy concerns it may serve) positivist knowledge of society predisposes its own use over other forms of knowledge in the policy process. Positivist knowledge claims to provide policy-makers with a category of knowledge that is neutral in value: it has status, is universal, is immediately usable and can continually be refined on the basis of testing against an unproblematic 'reality'. It has status because of its claims to science and this in itself is often enough to support its use in policy. It is universal and therefore 'usable' in any appropriate issue, also because of its status as science. And it is often refined and developed over a period of time, lending support to the notion of 'progress' in understanding and policy. Moreover, because positivist knowledge separates theory from facts, the result may be to deny the broader implications of theory in the search for usable knowledge: theory is useful when it is a tool for empirical work, but not when it begins to question the edifice of society itself. The claim to value-freedom which makes positivist knowledge so attractive and useful in a policy context can also prevent that knowledge from contributing a critical perspective. Hence, the masquerade of value-free social knowledge has important political consequences in that it often tends to support the status quo.

If, as we have seen, the rules for the construction of policy-applicable knowledge have political implications, then the process by which such knowledge is selected for use by policy-makers equally has political significance. Most academic knowledge that is perceived as relevant by policy-makers, in economics, foreign policy or otherwise, is characterised by being divided into different schools of thought that not only produce different interpretations of issues and policy, but offer different facts to underpin those interpretations. For policy-makers it is not simply a question of using pre-defined tools of analysis. The existence of differing perspectives, approaches, schools of thought can be accommodated within positivism only if one accepts that empirical evidence can demonstrate that one perspective is ultimately superior to another. But this cannot be done – different basic values underpin the different interpretations rather than verification through empirical testing. The problem of selecting between and among relevant contending approaches and theories seems generic to social knowledge. The positivist resolution of this problem is the process of continually refining theory and testing this against reality in order eventually to arrive at a single explanation. However, in practice the problem of competing perspectives is resolved by forces and sentiments not considered part of 'scientific' academic knowledge at all. That is, it is resolved and choices made on the basis of the values (social, political, moral) that positivist knowledge claims to banish.[12]

The denial of the possibility of a positivist knowledge of values changes the nature of the relationship of knowledge to policy. Instead of being scientific and neutral an understanding of the *social* production of knowledge raises the possibility that positivism's claim to objectivity was and is a *political* claim. It may tell us more about the relationship between academics and policy if we understand the production of knowledge in the way that is suggested by Robert Cox when he argues that: 'Theory is always for someone and for some purpose. . .There is. . . no such thing as theory in itself, divorced from a standpoint in time or space.'[13] Cox is not saying that theory is always, or, indeed ever, part of a conspiracy, an explicit attempt to legitimate power by individuals and groups (although that sometimes may be the case), but what he is saying is that knowledge must be understood as *itself* a product of society and subject to the same forces that we take into account when we are analysing a political, economic or social event. In this conception of knowledge the important and prior questions are now: knowledge for whom and for what purpose?

Extending this argument further, it is possible to understand the notion of metatheory itself as a political statement: 'The theory, of knowledge, and knowledge construction is a dimension of political theory, because the specifically symbolic power to impose the principles of the construction of reality – in particular social reality – is a major dimension of political power.'[14] Hence, the prior consideration of metatheory ('the principles of the construction of reality') is policy-relevant in an important and direct way because it establishes what *kind of knowledge* is legitimate and *how* this knowledge will be used.

When Keynes wrote that 'The ideas of economists and political philosophers, both when they are right and when they are wrong, are more powerful than is commonly understood. . .',[15] he could well have incorporated this view of knowledge into his thoughts because the metatheoretical ideas of 'economists and political philosophers' have proved to be just as powerful, although largely hidden, as their substantive and more immediate contributions to understanding. These ideas, and the social institutions that support them, form the deeper structure of social knowledge which changes more slowly over time and which provides the legitimating context for specific knowledge both in its form and content. It is the acceptance of knowledge as a social product, and thus political, that allows some analysts of IPE to configure knowledge production as an integral part of the structure and process of political economy. Here, a distinction is made between 'organic' intellectuals, whose knowledge output broadly serves to support the prevailing structures of power, and 'critical' intellectuals who provide alternative knowledge.[16] If we accept knowledge as a social product the problem of the relationship between normative and empirical concerns for IR/IPE is removed, as all knowledge is constructed upon the basis of values and is thus 'normative' in the positivist sense.

'INTERNATIONAL POLITICAL ECONOMY' AS ACADEMIC KNOWLEDGE

'International political economy': definition and development

International political economy (IPE) is ostensibly highly relevant to contemporary foreign policy. At a minimum IPE deals with events and actions that were previously considered to be in four separate domains: politics, economics, international politics and international economics, and is defined as denoting 'an area of investigation', a particular range of questions, and a series of assumptions about the nature of the international 'system' and how we understand this 'system'.[17] IPE then brings together the four empirical domains identified above, but it does so in the context of a critical focus: a set of questions.[18]

The specific content of the set of questions that constitute the basis of IPE is, as we might expect, contentious and not generally capable of being predefined. The problematique of IPE, which gives purpose and legitimacy to IPE as a field of study, is itself a product of other values and aspirations, not all of which are either explicit or 'knowable'. For Robert Gilpin the questions concern the relationship between state and market, as '[T]he tension between these two fundamentally different ways of ordering human relationships has profoundly shaped the course of modern history and constitutes the crucial problem in the study of political economy.'[19] And Susan Strange has entitled her introduction to international political economy *States and Markets*, although she develops a different analysis of the relationship between these two social forms than does Gilpin. For her the defining characteristic of IPE is that 'it concerns the social, political and economic arrangements affecting the global systems of production, exchange and distribution, and the mix of values reflected therein'.[20] The mix of values (security, wealth, freedom and justice) within the market–authority nexus is the core of IPE for Strange, and this gives rise to a concern with structures of power in the world economy. Gilpin's problematique, however, produces a specific set of issues – 'the causes and effects of the world market economy, the relationship between economic and political change, and the significance of the world economy for domestic economies'.[21]

What these two different but overlapping conceptions of the problematique of IPE share is that, as indicated above, they are concerned with problems and issues that lie within the fusion of the previously (academically) distinct domains of international politics and economics, and domestic (national) politics and economics. The breaking down of (1) the distinction between international and domestic, and (2) the separation of politics and economics, indicates both a belated recognition of the ideological form of the original separations and the nature of the complex material changes that have taken place in the world political economy. These two changes have significant implications for our understanding of the world system of politics and economics and the processes of foreign policy within that system.

The breaking down of the distinction between domestic and international is largely the result of the growth of interdependence. Indeed one of the principal consequences of economic interdependence is to minimise the significance of this distinction in analytical and policy terms, even if national political groupings (including governments) continue to insist on its relevance and importance. Even in national political economies that are relatively autonomous, for example in the United States, a *purely domestic* economic or political policy is difficult to achieve or to imagine in the contemporary structure. In the economies of Europe, most of which are highly integrated into the international and global political economy, much 'foreign' economic policy is carried out by domestic or sub-national actors, both private and public.[22] With the deepening of the integration process within the EC and in Europe generally, this feature of interdependence has been institutionalised through the multilevel policy structures and networks that have been created. This has happened to such an extent that it is probably now meaningless for EC member states to class intra-EC relationships as 'foreign policy', and non-EC states are rapidly reaching a similar situation.

In a policy sense what this means is that one of the central theoretical and practical distinctions of classic foreign policy is itself undermined by the understanding provided by one of the key concepts of IPE. All policy can conceivably have foreign implications, and foreign policy almost certainly will have important domestic sources and repercussions. Formerly domestic agencies and ministries have more personnel involved in foreign policy than those state agencies whose prime role was and is considered foreign.

The second consequence of the coalescence of these four previously separate domains is that the separation of politics and economics is challenged. In the context of this chapter I argue that it is necessary to consider the relationship between politics and economics as itself a product of the relationship between political economy and academic knowledge. The literature concerned with this relationship (at the confluence of the four domains) embodies a particular historical interpretation of that relationship and it is therefore worth briefly exploring the dominant conception. Much of the relevant literature was produced in the historical context of the post-1945 international political economy, but has its origins in liberal and mercantilist thought from a much earlier time. The ideological and analytical frame for the dominant conception is American liberalism and this is linked to but not necessarily derived from the material conditions prevailing in the immediate post-war political economy. That is, a system whose boundaries and political dynamics were dominated by the emergence of a bipolar security/military structure, and by US capital. The ensuing 'Bretton Woods' system embodied an ideology of the separation of politics and economics within its institutions and this became the basis of orthodox thinking about the structure and operation of the international economic order. The institutionalised legitimacy of this separation came about partly as a reflection of the dominant ideology of liberalism in US policy, and partly because the resultant 'depoliticisation' of economics enabled difficult political problems to be categorised (and resolved) as *technical* issues, subject to rational economic analysis and abstract technical solutions. Nevertheless, the separation of politics and economics was real and effective – to such an extent that the late Fred Hirsch often characterised the prevailing values of the system as embodied in the maxim 'Economics is when I have it, politics is when you want it.'

However, from about 1967 onwards, the separation produced problems. Sometime between 1968 and 1971 the interests of the US government and those of the liberal system as a whole began to diverge. Economic growth in the United States began to slow. Other Western bloc countries began to overtake the United States in many fields. One OPEC member began to push up the price of oil. Finally, the US government began to abrogate responsibilities for maintaining the system as a whole. The 'formalisation' of the crisis in the Bretton Woods system by the announcement of President Nixon's 'New Economic Policy' on 15 August 1971, clearly demonstrated to scholars and practitioners alike that the world was no longer understandable in terms of the enforced separation of economics from politics.

It was initially difficult for many observers fully to comprehend these events. The difficulty can be explained, in part, as a result of the way in which the successful liberal international system had helped to reinforce the legitimacy and academic dominance of the discipline of economics. When the structures of power that underpinned the liberal system (the United States) began to have problems – partly as a result of changes in the system itself but primarily because of US domestic policy – economics, to which most scholars and policy-makers turned for an explanation, was not able to contribute that much (nor, for that matter, were political science or international relations).

What is particularly relevant, but not surprising given the above, is that the literature interpreted the ensuing (i.e. post-1971) international political conflicts as the politicisation of the international economic order, and this has often been a core assumption since: the 'pure' domain of economic relations has been corrupted by politics. The politicisation thesis is important both because it underpins so much of the policy literature and because it is so mistaken. To explore this statement would take a long discussion on the production of the discourse of political economy, but the key is in the assumption of the normality, or common sense, of the distinction. That is, that there exists in a real sense a pure, original economy, often represented by a 'market', that can be explained and understood in strictly conventional economic terms with politics as an external or 'exogenous' variable. As with many accepted categories, common sense is no guide to understanding the concepts and practice of political economy and in particular cannot be relied upon here.[23] Although it has been argued that common sense does provide a potential guide to the theory of international politics,[24] the acceptance of knowledge as a social product suggests that common sense is itself socially produced and serves particular interests. Polanyi, among others, clearly demonstrates that the separation of politics from economics in theory/doctrine as well as in practice was *created* to serve political purposes; in this case to serve the purpose of the emergent merchant class in their struggle for political legitimacy and power in the face of the totalising ideology of a mercantilism which itself legitimated the power of the state. (For mercantilism, wealth = power, and therefore, politics = economics: the affirmation of the separation of politics from economics and the claim to an autonomous realm for the economy was, and is, a political act.)[25]

As already indicated the theoretically problematic nature of the relationship between politics and economics is hardly resolved when we turn to examine the practice of 'foreign policy' – output, implementation and outcomes. Because of the complexity of global political economy (which incorporates but is not defined by *international* political economy) policy analysis faces particular levels of difficulty. Even within a simple model of the international economy (that is, one of exchange relations between national political economies, as found in traditional conceptions of commodity and manufacturing trade) the integration of key sectors of national economies into the international trade and credit system produces problems of analysis, policy and control.[26] And this integration begins to change the role and power of government, as Stanley Hoffmann and others identified some time ago:

> The international economy, manipulated by its members, operates as a constant but unpredictable system of double distribution – of incomes, jobs, status within nations, and wealth and power among nations. But the domestic victims of this redistribution do not acknowledge the legitimacy of a haphazard or shifty mechanism that is external to the nation and competes or conflicts with the internal redistribution schemes that have been legitimately, authoritatively, or imperatively set up within the confines of the nation.[27]

However, when we add to this the growth and present extent of international production and services[28] the existence of networks of international organisations (OECD, BIS, etc.) and (for its members) the authority and policy frameworks of the EC, the resulting multilevel structure demands perspectives that capture the complex and multi-layered processes that have come to characterise policy in the global political economy.

In my view IPE provides a basis for the articulation of these perspectives. IPE is not the application of an 'economic' analysis which then sets out prescriptions for politics as a separate domain of activity – that is, IPE does not accept the hierarchy of a dominant economics, in methodology or issues. It is not about the politicisation of economics. Nor is it about the economisation of international politics. It is about achieving a historical understanding of the growth and consequences of a global *political economy* through a reflexive understanding of theory and practice.

International political economy as academic knowledge

The account of the development of IPE given above is based on a non-positivist metatheory, one in which the development of IPE is understood as reflecting the principal concerns of the dominant state in the post-1945 world order – the USA. In this I do not share the views of those who see, and saw, IPE *only* as a response to material changes in the world political economy,[29] although real and profound material changes did occur and are continuing to occur. The analysis presented here locates IPE as academic knowledge firmly within the prevailing structures of power. This is not to say that other 'IPEs' have not been produced, nor that what has been produced is not 'useful', but that the dominant ideas and analyses have reflected both a methodological orthodoxy and an issue agenda that is broadly supportive of the policy interests of the USA and must be evaluated as such.

In its implications for the relationship to policy-making this analysis contrasts with a positivist-based interpretation of IPE, and, perhaps not unexpectedly, much of IPE has been offered as such positivist knowledge as purely responding to the objective changes in the reality of the world political economy. Hence for example, theories of hegemonic stability and/or hegemonic decline, and concepts such as regime and regime change are provided in response to changes in material conditions by IPE scholars who are mainly American and are principally working within a broadly positivist (but largely unacknowledged) metatheory. In this view, the needs of policy and the interests of the academic both reflect the changing circumstances and therefore complement each other. This view is clearly articulated by Stanley Hoffmann writing in 1977 about the emergence of analyses that focused on the politics of economic relations among states, 'the literature on the politics of international economic relations . . . *coincides* with what could be called the post-Vietnam aversion for force, and with the surge of economic issues to the top of the diplomatic agenda. . . Once more, the priorities of research and those of policy-making blend' (emphasis added).[30]

From a metatheoretical perspective, the problem of how to relate IPE to policy-making thus resolves itself into a simple dichotomy of views: (1) academic knowledge reflects only developments in the 'real world' and the academic search for truth; or (2) the production of knowledge (including academic knowledge) is part of the structure of power. Each of these views reflects a particular philosophical position, but more than this, each can reflect a different political view on the nature of the reality of the global political economy. And each provides us with different answers to the questions addressed in this book.

The different ontologies related to each position are fundamental to an understanding of the structures of power of the global system. Positivist IPE knowledge, whilst claiming a legitimacy derived from following a scientific process, denies the possibility that any form of (nonmaterial) intersubjective meaning be part of *the* international political economy. It denies the possibility that beliefs and values are *themselves* just as real as the material structures and powers of the global political economy.[31] For example, in the context of the Bretton Woods system, the liberal separation of economics and politics (into rational economics and non-rational politics) enabled international economic relations to be presented by the supporters of the system as technical and scientific: economic issues were resolvable on the basis of rational economic knowledge and resolution of 'technical' problems. Acceptance of the system of meaning by participants in the international economy entailed the acceptance of what constituted legitimate 'economic' knowledge and legitimate political action. Acceptance also externalised the system of meaning from the dominant state(s) into an objective part of the external reality faced by the participants: it became just as real as the material conditions facing them.[32] This point is fundamental because here a positivist IPE presents an ontology which excludes the reality of intersubjective meaning in the structure of international political economy.

INTERNATIONAL POLITICAL ECONOMY AND FOREIGN POLICY

The impact – actual and potential – of IPE upon foreign policy and foreign policy systems is difficult to assess, particularly given that much of the substantive analysis of IPE undercuts the conceptual and policy distinctions upon which traditional foreign policy is based. Moreover, before any form of political economy is able to have an impact on foreign policy content and process, it has to confront the dominance (in terms of politics defined as government) of conventional neoclassical economics. This orthodox form of economics has become the most important social science for providing both policy advice and the basis of formal frameworks for policy within any domain of government that relates to economic activity. The emergence of economics as 'the queen of the social sciences' partly reflects its success in providing policy guidance, particularly during the 1950s and 1960s, but is also a result of the perceived policy transparency of economics as an academic discipline. That is, economics developed as the closest imitator of positivist science and hence, as previously argued, provided a knowledge that could readily be translated into policy – universal and instrumental. However, for most of its intellectual history, and with certain notable exceptions,[33] neoclassical economists have propounded explanations and policies that have been based on a reductionist rational-choice model of economic activity. Despite the work of theorists like Frey, politics has largely been regarded as an exogenous variable by the neoclassicists. Analyses are developed within an ideal and rational world of economics,[34] and then 'offered' to an irrational process of politics for implementation. This often leads to the conclusion that the failure of economic policy is not in the substance of the analysis offered, but in the perversity of politics.

Yet a recent and authoritative survey of 'The Role of the Economist in Government', carried out by leading economists, clearly identifies the problem of the continued reliance upon conventional economics by policy-makers:

> Economists by and large have not reacted well to the domestic and international challenges of the 1970s and 1980s. The leading theories and writings have seldom taken much explicit account of political factors, instead exploring the consequences of economic policymaking in an abstract world where economic technicians execute policies as prescribed. . .Then, as economic policymaking became more disjointed, and economic forecasts performed poorly, members of the profession have advanced new concepts and theories, confronting the public with a welter of conflicting economic explanations.[35]

Here, Nelson identifies the same forces that prompted the development of modern IPE as those that have (not unexpectedly) proved most difficult for conventional economists to deal with. As Fred Hirsch so admirably demonstrated, economic processes *are* social and political at the same time.[36] In the context of the argument of this chapter, Nelson continues with a very pertinent set of observations:

Historically, the one greatest contribution of economics has been its vision of the competitive market, an integrative vision that gives a meaning and sets a framework for understanding diverse events that otherwise might seem purposeless or even harmful. This overarching vision of the market also emerged from a tradition of thought *that wove together economic, political, legal, philosophical and other social considerations that were deemed to be relevant* (emphasis added).[37]

The rejection of the original and broad tradition of economics, together with a sometimes astonishing intellectual arrogance, has led to a current situation in which 'too many economists are applying highly refined reasoning to draw sophisticated conclusions to questions that are not worth the effort'.[38] In other words, an economics divorced from society and polity is not useful in terms of policy and is sterile in terms of values and purpose. In opposition to this, a reflexive study of IPE is embedded in a social context and continually addresses its own (and society's) values and purpose.

The above analyses comprehensively demonstrate that, even from the viewpoint of economists, an economics separated from politics is nonsense. And, as we have seen, to separate international and domestic domains makes little sense in policy terms either. These conclusions are the starting point of IPE and modern political economy, and this inevitably challenges the dominance of a positivist-based neoclassical economics, which, until very recently, operated in a world of isolated national economies. Neoclassical economics has swamped the development of alternative 'economic' knowledge, and even when that knowledge has been produced the status of conventional economics often works against its incorporation or even its consideration. As Peter Preston argues, 'The dominant role of orthodox economics within social theorising generally must be resisted. The claims of the neoclassical theorists that they have established the core elements of a universal positive science of economic life are both false and pernicious.'[39] Preston's point is absolutely right, but resistance means power, and a consideration of power (something that economists themselves do not often acknowledge) is necessary to identify how and why economic knowledge becomes the basis of policy. What is the process whereby economic knowledge in general and certain doctrines in particular become policy?

In a wide-ranging analysis of comparative responses by governments to international economic crises Peter Gourevitch examines the role of economics and economic doctrines and suggests that 'Economic theories prevail . . . only when they have mobilized political authority, that is only if those who believe the theories get the resources that enable them to take authoritative action.'[40] This is hardly a surprising conclusion, but it does make the important point concerning power and authority. Clearly, broader historical and cultural forces are equally important here and, as suggested earlier in this argument, form the structure within which specific forms of knowledge are considered legitimate.

If this relatively simple notion explains how economic ideas are translated into policy then the instrumental aspects of knowledge become even more relevant because knowledge is presumably defined as 'useful' when it supports the purposes of those in a position to take 'authoritative action'. Ideology in its broadest sense is clearly the governing factor.[41] In the circumstances of the contemporary world order it seems particularly inappropriate not to utilise the analysis offered by IPE: an analysis which is grounded in the necessary relationship between economics and politics and moves easily between the international/global and the domestic. Moreover, IPE (even in its positivist form) provides a framework for understanding the evolution of the global political economy which puts the role of the state in a necessary historical perspective. This again is an important corrective for national policy-makers who consistently tend to overestimate the role and power of states in the global political economy.

Part of the problem for policy-makers coping with rapid change in the arena of global political economy is that because of internal formal political structures most governments are preoccupied with contemporary events. This means that, as Keynes indicated, although fundamental ideas are very powerful, these ideas are incorporated as common sense and are therefore not regarded as theoretical. Consequently, policy-makers generally constitute problems and issues in a limited, non-theoretical way, unaware that 'common sense' is indeed constituted theoretically. Here, the pressure of the immediate is very powerful and reinforces the recourse to socially embedded analyses and solutions.

In a substantive sense then, positivist and orthodox IPE offers large gains over economics or international politics for policy-makers working at the confluence of the international/domestic levels and the domains of politics/economics. It offers a systemic view that historically locates the nature and role of the state within an emerging global structure – for example, the debate over hegemony and US power. It offers both systemic and instrumental concepts, such as regime, that enable policy-makers to extend their range of influence and move towards achieving their policy goals.[42] And it offers detailed analysis of the links between economics and politics which often change the issues of policy. In this context, one of the most pertinent recent examples is the demise of the Soviet Union and the extent to which this development suggests that the relatively successful and continuing international economic cooperation between and among the non-Communist states has been largely dependent upon the security structure for its dynamism. The US-dominated security framework was based on the identity of the Soviet Union as the common enemy and this provided the external pressure for cooperation as well as the immediate context. Specific bilateral relationships, particularly between the US and Germany and the US and Japan, were predicated upon this construction of the bipolar world order. Now that this order has changed, multilateral and bilateral economic cooperation is evidently becoming more problematic.[43] A change in the security problematic clearly has long-term repercussions for the prospects of achieving a satisfactory and stable economic order.

A more critical and non-positivist IPE can provide an understanding of social forces that form the generative structures of the global order.[44] And, crucially, they can provide the framework for a more comprehensive understanding of power than that possible through orthodox IPE and orthodox economics. This is achieved partly through the repositioning of our understanding of belief systems and ideology towards a conceptualisation of material reality which includes beliefs, ideology and knowledge as core elements. It is also achieved through the constitution of theory as critical theory – theory which, unlike neoclassical economics, does not deny its necessary moral and political bases. International political economy asks: '*Cui bono*' – who benefits? Who benefits from a particular arrangement of monetary relations?, who benefits from a specific agreement between a state and a transnational corporation?, who benefits from 'free trade'?, and who benefits from particular configurations of knowledge and theory?[45]

PROBLEMS AND CONCLUSIONS

Returning to the theme of structural change and uncertainty in the management of the global political economy, what is striking is how relatively unprepared most in IR were for the speed and nature of the events that led to the demise of the Soviet Union. This observation highlights both the dangers of claiming any predictive quality in our explanations and the necessity to develop a broad historical understanding of the global system and the forces and structures producing global order. This is what, in the Introduction to this book, Christopher Hill calls 'The history question' and it is fundamental to the purpose of the academic study of IR and IPE: 'should we in International Relations be preoccupied with contemporary events?' From the point of view of IPE it is fairly clear that while much work is done that is directly located in a contemporary policy context, the real benefit of IPE is to bring to those problems and issues a wider theoretical understanding that is grounded in history. What is more, this will often be a history that is not received wisdom but critical and reflective in itself.[46]

The second and third questions identified in the Introduction are prefigured by the nature of the analysis presented in this chapter. The question concerning the relationship between normative and empirical concerns loses much of its relevance if our philosophical stance no longer accepts the existence of 'brute facts'.[47] If all facts are theoretically determined, then the metatheory we use to produce facts necessarily includes normative judgements, and 'empirical evidence' is always value-laden, although without the pejorative connotations that come from the positivist use of this phrase. A non-positivist metatheory displaces the question of the relationship between normative and empirical concerns in favour of elucidating the assumptions underpinning the analysis and articulating the values that give the analysis meaning and purpose. In this context even the claim to a 'value-free' analysis is a political claim because of the link between value-freedom in science and the social power of 'scientific' knowledge.[48]

Similarly, the nature of academic independence is also addressed through the metatheoretical position taken within this chapter. If the production of knowledge cannot be understood outside of a social context, then we as IR academics can never be totally independent. This is not to argue that individuals cannot be independent, nor to say that every idea is socially, politically or economically determined. It is to say that we must understand and accept that knowledge is a social product, and bears all the characteristics of society itself, with all that that entails. It is relatively straightforward to construct a history of the development of IPE as an academic subject that clearly demonstrates the close relationship between the principal methodologies, themes and issues of IPE and the changing concerns of US foreign policy allied to the changing position of the US economy in the global context.[49] This does not mean that all of IPE was determined by these forces.

At a 'micro' level, the question of independence relates directly to either working for government or being funded by government. The view of this author is that independence is not necessarily threatened by working for government, directly or indirectly. Indeed, in the British context, particularly when compared to the experience of academics in the US, we could do with more of us in IR being part of the larger policy community rather than less. What is important is that the frameworks, values and assumptions underpinning the theoretical understanding we bring to International Relations and International Political Economy remain clearly exposed and well articulated. It is not necessary to construct academics as 'remote and ineffectual' in order to claim independence. Real independence comes not from trying to pretend that what we do is 'value-free' but from accepting the social reality of knowledge and moving the practice of IR towards an insistent questioning of accepted explanations and authoritative actions and a consistent advocacy of the values we believe in.

The problem here is clearly one of the relationship between policy and scholarship as a whole (I take 'scholarship' to be the practice of academic knowledge). There are a number of points worth making. One, for policy-makers the imperative of this discussion of theory is relatively straightforward: there is much to be gained from casting their net for policy advice far wider than is the current practice. Politics and economics cannot be separated and neither can the domains of international and domestic policy-making. Economic analysis which only considers politics as an exogenous variable is imperfect, skewed knowledge. Moreover, states exist within historical structures that change over time and the limits of the possible as well as the nature of policy outcomes are prefigured by these historical structures. As a consequence, the apparent instrumentality of much advice that is offered as policy-relevant is chimerical.

A case in point is trade policy. One of the fixations of conventional economics is trade,[50] particularly in the place that economics gives trade at the very top of the international economic agenda. Yet it is possible, indeed desirable, to construct a different view of the structure of the world economy which does not see trade as the most important issue and does not accept that 'free trade' is necessarily always the most appropriate policy goal.[51]

The second point relates to the argument made about nonpositivist forms of knowledge. The acceptance by policy-makers of knowledge as socially constructed would not, in my view, have a fundamental impact upon the relationship between policy-makers and scholarship. This is because in their choice of advice most policy-makers and most governments *already* act as though advice is socially constructed, although this advice is normally proffered by scholars on the basis that it is, indeed, in some sense 'objective'. An interesting aspect of this acceptance would be the acknowledgement of the possibility and legitimacy of a joint policy discourse. This would situate such a discourse clearly within political and social space, with a necessary ensuing discussion of 'real' interests. The possibility of critical analysis within a joint policy discourse is potentially problematic, but is made possible through a shared sense of social purpose. However, the effectiveness of such an open discourse would probably be constrained by the imperatives of institutional power and interests as access into the policy discourse becomes the key process.

However, one important consideration that follows from the acceptance of the socially produced nature of knowledge is the necessity for policy to incorporate an understanding of the reality of ideas of political economy as constituting an integral part of the structure of IPE. It is my sense that often policy-makers are more aware of this than scholars, but the point underscores the necessity for an explicit link between ideas and institutions.

None of the foregoing makes life easier for scholars and particularly scholars of IPE. What it does is to highlight the political nature of the relationship between policy and scholarship. In so doing the possibility of a negotiated relationship is suggested, and the basis of this relationship is a consensus of values and an agreed definition of interests. On this basis some policy advice will always be ruled inadmissible, but the policy net should be and needs to be cast much wider than at present.

NOTES

1 P. Dicken, *Global Shift – the Internationalisation of Economic Activity* (2nd edn), London, Paul Chapman Publishing, 1992.
2 P.J. Katzenstein (ed.) *Between Power and Plenty: Foreign Economic Policies of Advanced Industrial States*, Madison, University of Wisconsin Press, 1978.
3 J.S. Nye Jr., *Bound to Lead: The Changing Nature of American Power*, New York, Basic Books, 1990.
4 P.R. Krugman, *Rethinking International Trade*, Cambridge, Mass., MIT Press, 1991.
5 Much of the argument that follows is developed in C.N. Murphy and R. Tooze, *The New International Political Economy*, Boulder, Lynne Rienner, 1991, but I have benefited greatly from discussions with colleagues in the ECPR 'European foreign policy group'. Our collective discussions will be published as: Walter Carlsnaes and Steve Smith (eds), *The European Community and Changing Foreign Policy Perspectives in Europe*, London, Sage, forthcoming.
6 E. Augelli and C. Murphy, *America's Quest for Supremacy and the Third World*, London, Pinter, 1988; S. Gill, *American Hegemony and the Trilateral Commission*, Cambridge, Cambridge University Press, 1990.
7 R. Tooze, 'The Unwritten Preface: IPE and Epistemology', *Millennium: Journal of International Studies*, Summer 1988, vol. 17, no. 2, pp. 285–94.

8 This statement brings the argument to the centre of the range of philosophical questions that are crucial to the future form and status of IR/IPE. For an excellent treatment of some of these issues see M. Hollis and S. Smith, *Explaining and Understanding International Relations*, Oxford, Clarendon Press, 1990.

9 Tooze, 'The Unwritten Preface', op. cit.

10 J.G. Gunnell, 'Philosophy and Political Theory', *Government and Opposition*, 1979, vol. 14, no. 2, pp. 198–216.

11 A. Sayer, *Method in Social Sciences – A Realist Approach*, London, Hutchinson, 1984.

12 T.S. Kuhn, *The Structure of Scientific Revolutions* (2nd edn), Chicago, University of Chicago Press, 1970; R.J. Bernstein, *Beyond Objectivism and Relativism*, Oxford, Basil Blackwell, 1983; and C. Taylor, *Philosophy and Human Sciences*, vol. 2, Cambridge, Cambridge University Press, 1985.

13 R.W. Cox, 'Social Forces, States and World Orders: Beyond International Relations Theory', *Millennium: Journal of International Studies*, vol. 10, no. 2, Summer 1981, p. 127.

14 P. Bourdieu, *Outline of a Theory of Practice*, Cambridge, Cambridge University Press, 1977, p. 165.

15 J.M. Keynes, reproduced in C. Huhne, *Real World Economics*, London, Penguin Books, 1991, p. 1.

16 E. Augelli and C. Murphy, *America's Quest*, op. cit; S. Gill, *American Hegemony*, op. cit.; and R.W Cox, *Production, Power and World Order: Social Forces in the Making of History*, New York, Columbia University Press, 1987.

17 R. Tooze, 'Perspectives and Theory: A Consumers' Guide', in Susan Strange (ed.) *Paths to International Political Economy*, London, Allen & Unwin, 1984, pp. 1–22.

18 There is now an enormous literature which can be considered as IPE, broadly defined. This is partly accounted for by the incorporation of much of the substance of IPE into the 'mainstream' of IR itself. For an indication of the range of literature see the bibliographies in R. Gilpin, with the assistance of Jean M. Gilpin, *The Political Economy of International Relations*, Princeton, Princeton University Press, 1987; Susan Strange, *States and Markets*, London, Pinter, 1988; J.E. Spero, *The Politics of International Economic Relations*, London, George Allen & Unwin, 1985; and R.W. Cox, *Production, Power and World Order*, op. cit.

19 Gilpin, *The Political Economy*, op. cit., p. 11.

20 Strange, *States and Markets*, op. cit., p. 18.

21 Gilpin, *The Political Economy*, op. cit., p. 14.

22 R.O. Keohane and J.E. Nye, *Power and Interdependence*, Boston, Little Brown, 1977; Dicken, *Global Shift*, op. cit.

23 Murphy and Tooze, *New International Political Economy*, op. cit.

24 J.C. Garnett, *Commonsense and the Theory of International Politics*, London, Macmillan, 1984.

25 K. Polanyi, *The Great Transformation*, Boston, Beacon Press, 1944.

26 Katzenstein, *Between Power and Plenty*, op. cit.; P. Gourevitch, *Politics in Hard Times: Comparative Responses to International Economic Crises*, London, Cornell University Press, 1988.

27 Hoffmann, quoted in L. Anell, *Recession, the Western Economies and the Changing World Order*, London, Pinter, 1981, p. 90.

28 Dicken, *Global Shift*, op. cit.; K. Ohmae, *The Borderless World: Power and Strategy in the Interlinked Economy*, London, Collins, 1990.
29 See Murphy and Tooze, *New International Political Economy*, op. cit.
30 S. Hoffmann, 'An American Social Science: International Relations', *Daedalus* 106(3), 1977, pp. 41–60.
31 J. Maclean, 'Belief Systems and Ideology in International Relations: A Critical Approach', in R. Little and S. Smith (eds) *Belief Systems and International Relations*, Oxford, Basil Blackwell, 1988, pp. 57–84; Tooze, 'The Unwritten Preface', op. cit; Cox, *Production, Power and World Order*, op. cit.
32 Maclean, 'Belief Systems', op. cit; Augelli and Murphy, *America's Quest*, op. cit; Gill, *American Hegemony*, op. cit; Cox, *Production, Power and World Order*, op. cit.
33 For example, B.S. Frey, *International Political Economics*, Oxford, Basil Blackwell, 1984; Krugman, *Rethinking*, op. cit.
34 Gilpin, *The Political Economy*, op. cit.
35 R.H. Nelson, 'Introduction and Summary', in Joseph A. Pechman (ed.) *The Role of the Economist in Government*, London, Wheatsheaf, 1989, pp. 17–18.
36 F. Hirsch, *Social Limits to Growth*, London, Routledge & Kegan Paul, 1977.
37 Nelson, 'Introduction and Summary', op. cit, p. 21.
38 Ibid., p. 22.
39 P. Preston, 'Hucksters and Dodgers', *The Higher*, 13 December 1991, p. 15.
40 Gourevitch, *Politics in Hard Times*, op. cit., p. 54.
41 The best analysis yet available of the role of ideas and ideology in policy is that by John Odell of US international monetary policy: J.S. Odell, *U.S. International Monetary Policy*, Princeton, Princeton University Press, 1982. The role and nature of belief systems in explaining economic policy is considered in Tooze, 'The Unwritten Preface', op. cit., and Maclean, 'Belief Systems', op. cit.
42 S.D. Krasner, *International Regimes*, London, Cornell University Press, 1983; R.D. Keohane, *After Hegemony*, New Jersey, Princeton University Press, 1984.
43 S. Burman, *America in the Modern World*, London, Harvester Wheatsheaf, 1991.
44 Cox, *Production, Power and World Order*, op. cit.; Augelli and Murphy, *America's Quest*, op. cit.; Gill, *American Hegemony*, op. cit.
45 Strange, *States and Markets*, op. cit.; J. Stopford and S. Strange, *Rival States, Rival Firms: Competition for World Market Shares*, Cambridge, Cambridge University Press, 1991; Murphy and Tooze, *New International Political Economy*, op. cit.
46 See particularly Polanyi, *The Great Transformation*, op. cit; Cox, *Production, Power and World Order*, op. cit.
47 Taylor, *Philosophy*, op. cit.
48 Bourdieu, *Outline*, op. cit.; Taylor, *Philosophy*, op. cit.
49 Murphy and Tooze, *New International Political Economy*, op. cit.
50 Strange, *States and Markets*, op. cit.
51 Krugman, *Rethinking*, op. cit.

Part III

The practitioner's viewpoint

5   The international lawyer
Inside and outside Foreign Ministries

*F.D. Berman**

This chapter is devoted to exploring the thesis that the governmental international lawyer[1] represents an unusual phenomenon; that in his normal dealings he crosses easily the boundary between the day-to-day practice of the law and its theoretical or scientific study; and that this state of affairs is not only congenial to the individuals concerned but very much in the public interest.

This will be done by examining two principal questions:

1 How *ought* governments to arrange to get legal advice in the international field?
2 Depending on the answer to the previous question, what should the relationship be between lawyers in government service and those outside?

These questions will be approached very much in the light of the experience of the United Kingdom. The reasons are not merely that this is the author's field of experience, but also that it seems more profitable to take one case for study in depth, rather than adopt a strictly comparative approach, which would entail trying to reconcile practices which have grown up against the background of different models of government and of public administration. Comparisons with working practices in other governments and international organisations will however be made as a means of highlighting distinctive features of the British model. United Kingdom practice is in any case worth studying if only because of the range and scope of British international relations and the influence of the British legal tradition, which has helped to shape both classical and modern international law. The United Kingdom's Foreign and Commonwealth Office is, moreover, an interesting object of study in its own right by reason of the fact that its present structure is a hybrid of different governmental functions, each with its own distinctive legal characteristics.[2] Whatever the remoter historical origins of its component parts may be, all of the legal work of the Foreign and Commonwealth Office is today the province of the FCO legal adviser and his staff, including the new European Community dimension first introduced by the negotiations which led eventually to British accession in 1972. They are therefore the governmental international lawyers with which this chapter is principally concerned.[3]

It is illuminating to start with a short description of the international law community in the United Kingdom, since the FCO legal advisers form part of it. This community is made up of four components

* in the universities and other learned institutions;
* in the practising profession;
* in government;
* in international organisations.

A substantial proportion of the institutions of higher learning in the United Kingdom offer a law degree. Most of the institutions granting a law degree offer one or more optional papers in selected topics in public international law, and in the majority of cases there is *one* international lawyer on the teaching staff to handle these courses (usually along with other subjects as well). Very few have more than one international lawyer on the teaching staff.[4] The number of Chairs in Public International Law is at present eleven.

As for the practising profession, the picture is uneven. There has been a long tradition at the Bar of specialisation, and indeed scholarship, in public international law. Professor Edwards, in his study of the law officers[5] suggests that the present-day office of legal adviser to the FCO can be seen as the lineal descendant of a third law officer of the Crown, the Queen's Advocate, whose professional base was the corps of specialist practitioners in Doctors' Commons.[6] He describes also the arrangements for securing legal advice for the government from the Doctors at a time at which the preponderance of legal advice for the government in all fields was sought from the practising profession. A large part of the base for the specialist skills in Doctors' Commons was however maritime law and the law of Naval Prize.[7] Doctors' Commons ceased to exist in 1858, and Twiss, the last Queen's Advocate, retired in 1872. As a result, while there continues to be considerable international law expertise at the English[8] Bar, it has become physically and institutionally dispersed; there is no longer any centralised nucleus.

There is however a limited number of London Chambers with a strong reputation for public international law, in much the same way as Chambers might be especially well known in particular fields of domestic law. These Chambers therefore tend to attract qualified barristers wishing to hold on to a place out in the field, including the not negligible number of university teachers who have a seat in Chambers alongside their teaching posts. All in all, though, the total number of genuine specialists in the field in current practice at the Bar is probably not in excess of a dozen.

A certain number of large City firms have established international law practices, and number foreign governments or state agencies as clients. By and large, however, solicitors have, not unreasonably, regarded public international law as a highly specialised area of work on which they would seek Opinions from the Bar when advice was needed. As more and more questions, which are pure questions of international law, find themselves being litigated before British courts, or arise incidentally in the course of litigation, the picture may change, though there is no real sign of it yet.[9] The striking fact is however that in no part of the professional examination is there even an optional paper in public international law. The position in this respect is identical in both branches of the profession.[10] It is therefore improbable that we shall see significantly greater numbers of fully fledged international lawyers on either side of the practising profession in the foreseeable future.

International organisations are inevitably also only a small part of the picture in the United Kingdom. Apart from a certain number of commodity organisations, the only two major international organisations which have headquarters in London are the International Maritime Organisation (IMO)[11] and the European Bank for Reconstruction and Development (EBRD). While the IMO has a legal staff of four professional officers under a divisional director, the EBRD has a general counsel with a personal staff only. Although the Commonwealth is not an international organisation in the strict sense of the term, its Secretariat is for present purposes similar; it has a legal division of seven under a director. By definition, not all of these lawyers will be engaged on matters of public international law.

It can thus be seen that the international law community in the United Kingdom is in fact quite a small one, and that the legal advisers in the Foreign Office, as full-time professionals in the field, form a substantial part of it, despite their modest numbers. This fact alone can be expected to show itself in their relationship with international law and lawyers outside the Office itself.

Against that background we can turn now to the first of the questions to be examined: how *ought* governments to arrange to get legal advice in the international field? It should be noted that the question is neutral as to the place of international law in foreign policy-making. It is not the intention to prescribe what place international law should have. Clearly, the position varies from one state to another.[12] Similarly, there is room for legitimate differences of opinion on the subject even within the same body politic. To return to the question of methods, however, the working arrangements used by governments throw up four basic patterns:[13]

1 A specialist cadre within the Foreign Service;
2 A department integrated into the structure of the Foreign Ministry;
3 A centralised Ministry of Justice;[14]
4 An outside professor (or professors).

These models are seldom found in a pure form. All national systems seem to partake of the features of more than one. In the British case, for example, which is one of the purest forms of model 1, matters of exceptional political importance are regularly referred to the law officers[15] for advice;[16] the submission to the law officers requesting their advice will however be drawn up by the FCO legal adviser and will incorporate a full account not only of the particular case but also of the applicable international law.

Before proceeding further it may be of help however to expand a little on the four basic models listed above. The first (a specialist cadre within the Foreign Ministry) refers to the practice of recruiting a corps of specialist professionals, who spend a full career within the same specialisation. It does not necessarily imply that they are separate or 'different' in any other sense. The FCO legal advisers, for example, are recruited into the Diplomatic Service and are subject to exactly the same conditions of service as mainstream colleagues, including the obligation to serve abroad at any post at any time.[17] The key to their practical conditions of service is, however, that they are engaged to operate in a purely advisory capacity. Their work is largely responsive and demand-driven. They are not responsible for the formation or execution of policy in any area of the United Kingdom's external relations. Their responsibility is to give accurate and objective legal advice. In operational terms this is reflected in the fact that, like barristers in Chambers, they do not 'run files'; the papers on any given subject, including the legal advice given, are registered on the files of the responsible policy department. The department is in a real sense the 'client' and the legal advice given to departments is 'theirs'. It remains the responsibility of the department how and when to request legal advice and how to use it when given (including, therefore, whether to follow it at all).[18]

A very different picture is disclosed by the arrangements in those

Foreign Ministries, like the German or French, who follow the second model (a department integrated into the structure of the Foreign Ministry). Here the legal advice is given by a 'legal department' (or division) which is given the task of handling the files on those matters classified as wholly or predominantly 'legal'.[19] On those matters, in other words, the lawyer has to make, propose or execute the policy on the basis of the legal advice which he himself has given – in all probability in answer to questions which he himself has formulated. Conversely, the lawyer will have to operate in two modes: he will have to take the lead on some subjects (those classified by the Ministry as predominantly 'legal'), while on others he will be called upon to give legal advice to another department, of an exclusively policy character, where his department and the policy department receiving his advice are of co-ordinate and equal status within the Ministry.

The final two models largely explain themselves. Where the Ministry of Justice or Attorney-General's Office is the fount of international law advice, it is normally part of an arrangement in which *all* legal advice to the government is centralised in that department. The way in which the advisory function is attended to in practice (so far as international law is concerned) will depend on how the centralised legal advisory service is staffed; it may include specialist international lawyers, it may not. Where, on the other hand, work is put out, as in the last model, to academic specialists, they may either be seconded for a period of years to full-time duties in or for the Foreign Ministry[20] or simply take on, by arrangement, cases for advice while retaining their teaching chairs.

In the present writer's opinion the first model, as represented for example by British practice, has a very great deal to recommend it; although not ideal in every respect, it approaches close to an ideal. The criteria for preference ought, however, to be made explicit, and the following are suggested. For the government, as employer, the criteria may present themselves in the form of mundane questions such as how to get the best value for money out of its specialists, or how to open up adequate career possibilities in order to retain specially skilled staff in government service. In the wider *public interest*, however, the criteria suggested are that the best systems are those which encourage *impartiality* and *breadth*.

In 1965, Sir Gerald Fitzmaurice wrote:

> The Government, it is said, ought to have completely impartial advice on international law matters, even if this advice tells against it, and how can anyone actually working in a department of government and dependent on it for his salary, give it really dispassionate advice?

Will he not tend to tell it what he thinks it wants to hear, rather than what he knows it ought to be told?

But quite apart from the fact that to give 'impartial' advice is precisely what the departmental lawyer is paid to do (and he will not long survive the difficulties his government will get into if he fails in this), the whole argument shows a radical misunderstanding of what governments want from their legal advisers. They do not, properly speaking, want 'impartial' advice, any more than private citizens or industrial concerns are looking for impartiality in their family or corporation lawyers. What governments want is accurate and judicious legal advice (which is not quite the same thing), and they want it from persons whose function is (within the limits set by professional standards and the duty of every lawyer to the law itself) to promote rather than judge the aims of government and, moreover, whose awareness of the background and *inponderabilia* of the situation enables them to give their advice with a knowledge of all its implications that no outside lawyer could normally have. In this attitude there is nothing improper or even 'hard-boiled'. It represents nothing more than what every man looks for in his lawyer and, not finding it, goes elsewhere.[21]

That remains a classic statement of the needs and wants of the government as client, which one can therefore expect will be reflected in the operational requirements of Foreign Ministries.

If Sir Gerald Fitzmaurice's remarks are true to governmental life, they enable one to suggest that the criteria of impartiality and breadth can be judged in the first instance by the degree of independence the Foreign Ministry lawyer possesses. One should not of course expect that independence to be expressed in freedom of public speech; all public service codes of behaviour demand a greater or lesser degree of public restraint on the part of government servants.[22] But the same is not true of freedom to express his mind *within* the Ministry. It should be axiomatic that the function of a legal adviser within the Ministry is the same as that of a legal adviser in private practice: to expound the law as it is, without trimming his views to suit the preconceptions of the client – or indeed the client's interests. It should be equally self-evident that independence of mind is more easily guaranteed when the exclusive, or predominant, function of the departmental lawyer is advice than when he carries also a responsibility for formulating or executing *policy*.

It might be helpful at this point to explain that the Legal Advisers in the FCO are not merely consulted on general or specific issues of international law, but also on the way in which the requirements of the law are to be translated into practice. No outgoing letter or instruction to a post abroad, which draws on legal advice, may issue without being cleared in draft by the legal adviser who gave the advice. This is in fact enshrined as a written rule of Office practice. The same applies to the terms in which legal issues are dealt with in policy submissions to Ministers. It is standard form for any such submission to recite that the responsible legal adviser concurs. The purpose is twofold: to provide a check against technical advice being inadvertently misunderstood by the lay client, but also to guard against distortions creeping in through changes in phrasing or context. The consequence is however that the Legal Advisers, over and above their function of finding and explaining the law, have acquired an important control over the way in which the law is applied to particular cases. This is a jealously guarded prerogative, the significance of which for the British government's international practice (or at least legally relevant international practice) can readily be seen.

It will be evident from the above that it is a fallacy to think of all requests for legal advice within a Foreign Ministry as if they took only one form. Using FCO practice as a guide, we can in fact distinguish three principal forms which a request to a legal adviser might take. One is for a set-piece Opinion on a question of international law. While this does occur (two obvious examples being in connection with projects being undertaken by the International Law Commission or proposals to request an Advisory Opinion from the International Court of Justice), it is very far from being the norm. By far the most common are requests in the second and third categories. Both of them have to do not or not only with finding the law, but with applying it. One is the case in which advice is sought on what the government should do (or say) in a particular situation. This might be a question of mutual rights and obligations in a particular bilateral situation, or it might be a case in which the government feels bound to take a public position (including in Parliament) on a general multilateral problem or on a situation between other states. This type may of course, depending on the circumstances, involve issues of principle, or choices of conduct of considerable political importance, and if so might (in the United Kingdom) go in due course to the law officers for more formal advice or approval.

The third type is the one mentioned in the preceding paragraph: the constant process of checking and re-checking the application of the law to the facts of particular cases – for example as a complex international crisis develops from one step to another. By definition, this third type of process (which is numerically the most common) is based on advice already given at an earlier stage on what the law is. The legal adviser may for example simply be applying a view previously taken – or the long-standing view of his government – on a particular point of international law, without re-opening the whole question *de novo*. But it also follows that, in the great majority of cases of this third type, the legal adviser is likely to be operating within the framework of a decided policy (including for this purpose as a question of policy the decision on which legal view to adopt when more than one is possible).

It is thus inescapable that, in so far as the legal adviser is called on to advise on particular conduct, he is bound to operate within the framework of established policy. This inevitably places limits[23] on how far his functions extend to the right to judge the policies and international behaviour of the government for which he works, but at the very least one would expect the right to judge between possible alternative future courses of action.

In the second instance, however, the criteria of impartiality and breadth can also reasonably be judged by reference to the nature of the lawyer's relationships with the outside world, including of course with his professional counterparts in the outside world. This leads neatly back to the second of the major questions posed at the outset: namely, what should those relations be?

There seem to the present author to be three aspects to that question. We may start with the preliminary observation that lawyers frequently claim an allegiance to the law over and above a simple loyalty to the client. In the case of lawyers in independent private practice, this is regarded as unexceptional.[24]

It would be somewhat more surprising however to assert that the same holds for the governmental lawyer in the Foreign Ministry. Yet it does. As Fitzmaurice pointed out, lawyer-advisers are bound by the rules of conduct of their profession, but also – like all lawyers – owe an allegiance to the law itself. To say this is not pious claptrap but reflects an actual reality. The reasons why have much to do with the nature of international law, which is in itself part of the international system of inter-state relations. International law has a far more fluid body of rules than its formally enacted, written, domestic counterparts, and is in a constant process of re-formation. The customary rules which (despite the surge of treaty-making of the modern epoch) continue to provide its basic core, are all in principle subject to change or modification by virtue of state practice.[25] No governmental international lawyer, who is daily engaged in the process of shaping the conduct of a state in legally relevant ways, can fail to be conscious of this fact all the time. Without a firm sense, not only of the law as it is (*lex lata*), but also of the law as it ought to develop (*lex ferenda*), this process would degenerate into a free-for-all. The development of international law (if still possible at all) would become an affair of pure power. Thus, while it is often inescapable that the governmental international lawyer deals in policy as well as law, it is equally true that the policy he deals in can be termed 'legal policy', a sense of what is fitting for the law as a coherent and principled system.

The implication behind this proposition is of course that the governmental international lawyer has his own policy choices. The extent to which this is so and the nature of the choices has long been the subject of a lively debate centred around the writings of the 'policy-oriented school' of international jurisprudence. That operates however at the level of jurisprudential abstraction, at the level of defining the rules for discovering the law applicable to the case in hand, or if one likes the rules defining what the government legal adviser *may* do. Descending from that to the mundane level of how he actually *operates* from case to case, we may immediately note that the extent to which he deals in the 'legal policy' just described is of course a function of his training, temperament and experience. There undoubtedly are differences across frontiers deriving from the role the lawyer customarily performs in particular national societies; that is hardly surprising. But the author has never over the years detected any significant differences based on different national legal systems as such. What can be said (without descending into the realms of individual psychology) is that what has been called above 'a sense of what is fitting for the law as a coherent and principled system' is something that has to be developed. There must therefore be a premium on long-term exposure to the workings of the law in real situations. One may hazard the guess (without empirical evidence) that those whose career patterns offer this are more likely to have the feel for and to deploy with confidence 'legal policy' in the sense used here; whereas those governmental lawyers whose careers move them from legal to policy jobs and back again are more likely, when bringing policy into play, to do so in terms of national interests.

In the second place, the governmental international lawyer – in the United Kingdom at least – is constantly aware of a system of interconnections which, between them, work towards binding the country's international lawyers into a genuine community. First and foremost among them is a notable interchangeability of roles. Three examples may be given. It is commonplace[26] that, for significant pieces of international litigation, such as cases before the International Court of Justice or major arbitration proceedings, the British government is represented, for the purposes of arguing its case before the tribunal, by outside professionals, sometimes by full-time practitioners but more often by academic teachers of international law who simultaneously practice at the Bar.[27] That this practice fits with current orthodoxy about the contracting out of professional work is pure chance, since it has long been the normal practice in the FCO and is based on the more general custom that the government's cases are argued in British domestic courts by independent practitioners. It goes without saying that the arrangement is dependent on briefing counsel who can be given the appropriate level of security clearance. The reason is that it would also be natural that an outsider retained to argue the case in court would previously have been consulted for advice on the substantive merits of the case or on procedural questions concerned with its conduct. In performing this function, the outside practitioner might find himself advising in effect as part of a joint team, one or more of the members of which was a serving FCO legal adviser. A similar pattern might well be followed before a voluntary submission to third-party judicial settlement, so that outside practitioners would be involved more-or-less directly in advising the British government on the *policy* question whether or not to go to arbitration (or submit a case to the ICJ).

Conversely, it is reasonably common for FCO legal advisers on final retirement to take up (or return to) private practice as specialists in international law.[28]

A second example is that of elections to high-ranking international legal bodies, notable examples being the International Law Commission of the United Nations and the International Court of Justice itself.[29] British nominations for election to both bodies ever since their original foundation have shown a remarkable mix of outsiders and (current or former) insiders. Of the seven British members of the International Law Commission, three have come from the ranks of government and four from the universities.[30] On the International Court of Justice, four of the five British judges have been outside practitioners and only one has come from government service.

A third and final example is the strong Foreign Office tradition (still maintained and encouraged in the FCO) of the government legal adviser as scholar and contributor to legal writing. The contribution in the post-war period of Sir Eric Beckett and Sir Gerald Fitzmaurice has been incomparable. More recent book-length works produced and published during government service include Sinclair's *The Law of Treaties* (1973),[31] Denza's *Diplomatic Law* (1976)[32] and *The Legal Status of Berlin* by Hendry and Wood (1987).[33] Several of the FCO legal advisers have lectured occasionally or have taught university seminars or degree courses in international law. In addition, the Office of the Legal Adviser has regarded it as part of its function to encourage and stimulate the study and teaching of international law in the United Kingdom. In recent years this activity has covered not only a regular series of visits to departments of international law at British universities, but more particularly the holding of an annual one-day seminar for teachers of international law at the FCO. This provides an opportunity to describe recent developments on the international scene of interest to lawyers and to look in greater depth at a particular theme or topic.

We may conclude by returning to the two questions posed at the beginning of this chapter. As regards the first (how should governments set about acquiring international law advice?), it will have become evident that the writer is strongly in favour of a system which combines an intimate and sympathetic understanding of the client's circumstances and needs with independence of mind on the part of the legal adviser. The British system, as epitomised in the Foreign and Commonwealth Office, is well suited to enable these criteria to be met. But it is far from being the only system capable of meeting them; and it relies, for example, on the existence of a sufficiently large number of international lawyers to permit the luxury of a sizeable cadre of international law specialists within the foreign ministry. This is a condition which will, quite evidently, only apply in a limited number of cases.

As regards the second question (what should the relationship be between these lawyers in government service and their professional counterparts outside), it will be equally plain that the writer strongly favours arrangements that recognise the adviser's professional status as *lawyer* as clearly as they embody his status as government servant. The practical embodiment of this can be seen reflected in continued subjection to the discipline and rules of conduct of the organised profession.[34] Or they can be seen in what has been termed above, rather more loftily, allegiance to the law not just to the client.

NOTES

* F.D. Berman, CMG, QC, is the Legal Adviser in the Foreign and Commonwealth Office of the United Kingdom. The views expressed in this chapter are personal and in no way should be taken to represent those of the Foreign and Commonwealth Office.

1 The term 'international lawyer' is used in both a strict and a strictly professional sense. It refers thus to the lawyer who is professionally trained and an active practitioner. And it refers to one whose field of training and practice is public international law. It therefore distinguishes at one and the

same time the practitioner loosely called an 'international' lawyer because his practice crosses national boundaries, but whose field is nevertheless private law, and the government official with training in law, notably public international law, who is employed in a Foreign Ministry in what is essentially a policy-making or administrative role.

2 The present-day Foreign and Commonwealth Office (FCO) dates from 1968. It is the product of successive amalgamations, by which separate Crown Services were brought together in stages into a unified Diplomatic Service under a single Department of State. The latest of these amalgamations were those of the Colonial Office and Commonwealth Relations Office into the 'Commonwealth Office' in 1966 and of that combined department with the old Foreign Office to form the 'Foreign and Commonwealth Office' in 1968. These steps followed the Plowden Report on Representational Services Overseas of 1962–63 (Cmnd 2276 of February 1964). HM Diplomatic Service is constituted as a separate Service under the Crown by the Diplomatic Service Order in Council of 1964 (now replaced by the 1991 Order of the same name). Both are made under Prerogative powers.

3 In addition, one of the FCO legal advisers is, at the time of writing, on loan to the Legal Secretariat to the Law Officers for England and Wales, one on loan to the Government of Hong Kong, one on temporary secondment to the Legal Services of the EC Commission and a further five are stationed at Diplomatic Service posts abroad. With the exception of the first of these, their functions are broadly similar to those of their colleagues inside the FCO, give or take the differences in the roles of the bodies to which they are assigned.

4 A typical pattern is an optional general paper at undergraduate level and a wider range of special options for a graduate degree by examination, often called LL.M. So far as specialised teaching staff are concerned, in the case of London University, with over 2,000 law students in total, there are ten to a dozen specialist teachers of international law on the permanent establishment, mostly at University College, King's College, the LSE, and Queen Mary and Westfield Colleges. Cambridge is strongly endowed with some eleven international lawyers on the teaching strength of some nine of the colleges, a University Chair in Public International Law and a Research Centre under a Director who holds no college post.

5 John Edwards, *The Law Officers of the Crown*, Sweet & Maxwell, 1964.

6 'The College of Doctors of Laws exercent in the Ecclesiastical and Admiralty Courts', established in the mid-sixteenth century to house those licensed to practice as advocates before courts operating on a base of Roman law, so including such questions of international law as prize, piracy and sovereign immunity.

7 A specialised field administered by national Prize Courts which nevertheless apply international law. The prize jurisdiction passed to the High Court in 1891, though appeals continue to lie direct to the Judicial Committee of the Privy Council. The last British Prize Courts sat at the time of the Second World War.

8 Or Scottish.

9 A much larger number of practising barristers, increasing as time goes on, will however have had experience in arguing cases before the European

Human Rights organs in Strasbourg, or the European (Community) Court of Justice in Luxembourg. The law of the former is closer to public international law, properly so called, than the latter, but in many cases is closer still to civil liberties law in domestic legal systems.

10 The optional paper for the Bar Final examination was abolished in 1979; there has never been one in the Solicitor's Finals.

11 A specialised agency within the United Nations system.

12 This is a purely empirical observation which does not touch the fact that a state's international obligations remain binding whatever its constitutional or political structure.

13 See the interesting study by H.C.L. Merillat (ed.) *Legal Advisers and Foreign Affairs*, Dobbs Henry, New York, Oceana for the American Society of International Law, 1964; although over 25 years old, this study offers a picture which continues to reflect in most respects current realities. A more recent survey, 'The Role of the Legal Advisers of Ministries of Foreign Affairs' by R.St.J. Macdonald, is published in the *Receuil des Cours* of the Hague Academy, 1977, III, pp. 381–482. See also contributions in the symposium 'The Impact of International Law on Foreign Policy-making: The Role of Legal Advisers', *European Journal of International Law*, vol. 2, no. 1, 1991; and Yachi in the *Japanese Annual of International Law*, no. 31, 1988, p. 1.

14 Or Attorney-General's Department.

15 The Attorney-General and Solicitor-General (for England and Wales), who will often be consulted, when the nature of the case makes it appropriate, in association with their Scottish colleagues, the Lord Advocate and Solicitor-General for Scotland.

16 See Merillat, *Legal Advisers*, op. cit., pp. 134–5; Macdonald, 'The Rule of the Legal Advisers', op. cit, p. 45. Also Sir Ian Sinclair, 'The Practice of International Law: The Foreign and Commonwealth Office', in Bin Cheng (ed.) *International Law: Teaching and Practice*, London, Stevens, 1982, pp. 123–34; Arthur D. Watts, 'International Law and International Relations', in *European Journal of International Law*, vol. 2, no. 1, pp. 157–64. Also the *Review of Government Legal Services*, a Report by Sir Robert Andrews, KCB, for the Cabinet Office, 1989, Ch. 10.

17 By contrast, other specialist advisers, like the economic advisers or the research cadre, are members of the Home Civil Service.

18 For a fuller exposition, see Sinclair, 'The Practice of International Law', op. cit., Watts, 'International Law', op. cit., and Andrew, *Review*, op. cit.

19 Examples might be the law of the sea, or diplomatic privileges and immunities, or treaty formalities and practice; in the FCO all of these matters would rest with policy departments, although they would, in the nature of things, work in the closest of harness with their legal advisers.

20 Commmonest where university teachers are, constitutionally, in state service.

21 59 AJIL (1965) at p. 73.

22 Often only in order to safeguard the principle that the exposition of policy is the function of elected politicians, not in order to stifle the circulation of ideas.

23 Without necessarily excluding entirely.

24 cf. 59 AJIL (1965). In British parlance it is usually described as a 'duty to the Court' and it applies both the barristers and to solicitors.
25 See article 28 of the Statute of the International Court of Justice.
26 In fact, the present writer knows of no exceptions.
27 This does not of course exclude the appearance of the FCO Legal Adviser as counsel as well as agent. Most recently Sir Ian Sinclair in the Anglo-French Arbitration on the Delimitation of the Continental Shelf, 1975–8.
28 Normally at the Bar, though there is no reason (except perhaps the practicalities) why it should not be in a solicitors' practice.
29 And its predecessor under the League of Nations, the Permanent Court of International Justice. The system for nomination to another high judicial body of an approximately 'international law' character, the European Court of Human Rights, has recently been the subject of some public discussion.
30 It would seem as if the British government is now in a small minority in nominating non-government officials to the Commission, the latest being Professor D.W. Bowett who was elected on 14 November 1991.
31 Ian Sinclair, *The Vienna Convention on the Law of Treaties*, Manchester, Manchester University Press (2nd edn), 1984.
32 Eileen Denza, *Diplomatic Law*, Dobbs Ferry, New York, Oceana, 1976.
33 I.D. Hendry and M.C. Wood, *The Legal Status of Berlin*, Cambridge, Grotius, 1987. Though one cannot fail to mention also the notable 9th edition of *Oppenheim's International Law*, Sir Robert Jennings and Sir Arthur Watts (eds) vol. I: *Peace*, Harlow, Longman, 1992.
34 Unlike earlier versions, the current version of the Bar's Code of Conduct explicitly recognises the category of 'employed barristers' as part of the practising profession, though they are subject to a somewhat different set of rules of conduct which reflect their particular duty to their employer while maintaining a broad common ground with their fellow practitioners in what is now known as 'independent private practice'.

6 Foreign policy-making
Planning or reflex?

James Cable

... the regular pattern of British foreign policy is one of reaction to international developments.

William Wallace[1]

THE BACKGROUND

In my time (1947–80) and, I dare say, even in the century's concluding decades, the principle which governed the functioning of the British Foreign Office was the conditioned reflex. A stimulating impulse – usually a message from abroad, sometimes an input from domestic politics, occasionally a spurt of initiative from a minister or senior official – evoked a response from the machine. Ideally this was one double-spaced paragraph on blue crested paper culminating in the classic sentence, 'I submit a draft telegram accordingly.' When approved, with or without modification, that telegram added a brick to the ever-growing pyramid of precedent that had conditioned the drafting and would, its contours subtly changing with each response to stimulus, not only help to shape later drafts but reflect at least a facet of that optical illusion: British foreign policy.

This system was seen at its cost-effective best in the early 1960s: before the 1968 absorption of the Commonwealth Relations Office produced an influx of under-secretaries looking for something to do and made the whole structure top-heavy;[2] before, too, the blurring of responsibilities brought about by British membership of the European Community. Ideally the pivot then was the head – a counsellor – of a busy geographical department. In 1964, for instance, the South East Asia Department had two running crises – confrontation with Indonesia and the Vietnam War – that regularly commanded the attention of ministers, as well as other problems of more intermittent importance. Waiting on one's desk when the day began were the advance copies of half a dozen immediate telegrams. Draft replies in proper form had to reach higher authority before lunch. On most days that tempo had to be maintained, even lesser matters, including many other telegrams, being swiftly handled or delegated to clear the decks for the next major engagement. Never before or since have I worked so fast or been so conscious of operating at full stretch. It was an exhilarating experience, but such a hectic routine of telegrams and telephoning and trotting to and from the offices of ministers and under-secretaries left little time for analysis, for the consideration of alternative policies, for the elaboration and submission of new initiatives. Some of those things were attempted, of course, but the efforts made might have been more systematic, less superficial, more persuasive if the constant pressure for responsive action had not so curtailed the time available. Nor, unfortunately, did greater leisure for the deliberate formulation of foreign policy exist in the higher reaches of the hierarchy, where, other responsibilities (in Whitehall as well as within the Office) apart, the number of urgent telegrams (now emanating from other sources as well) to be approved, amended or occasionally redrafted, increased with every upward step. Even when more under-secretaries arrived, no-one wishing to retain or increase his share of power could afford to stand back from the ladder of daily decisions and devote himself to wider issues and the longer term.

Lord Strang, who was permanent under-secretary from 1949 to 1953, made the classical exposition of the practice of the Foreign Office. 'Policy', he declared,

> is not a fully independent invention capable of guiding diplomatic action. It is rather, in some measure, a derivative generalization arising from within already existing diplomatic activity. . . it is a dominant or prevailing trend, established only in part, if at all, by premeditated and predetermined intention, and revealing itself through the cumulative effect of a succession of individual acts of greater or lesser moment, each decided upon in the light of practical international possibilities as they manifested themselves at the relevant time, and under the impulse of a traditional manner of behaviour characteristic of the government concerned.[3]

Strang was well aware that his conception of foreign policy as an aggregation of *ad hoc* decisions had its critics. Their numbers have increased since his time, as have the vigour and variety of their criticisms. Politicians argue that British conduct of foreign affairs is too responsive to events abroad, does not try to look ahead and takes insufficient account of political changes at home. Academics, as Strang himself remarked, complain of superficiality.[4] Many of those professing to represent public opinion deplore the absence of coherent policy that would enable Britain to influence international developments instead of always having to adapt to them. These voices have gained in volume as Britain's standing in the world has declined and the organised study of international relations has expanded.

One important source of criticism might have surprised Strang. Preoccupation with the Soviet threat, and with the need to rally and retain public support for counter-measures that became ever more sophisticated and expensive, compelled the Ministry of Defence not merely to devise a strategy and a policy, but to articulate them and, increasingly, to expound them to the general public. Year by year, the Statement on the Defence Estimates became more informative and persuasive. Relations between the Ministry and the burgeoning strategic studies establishment grew steadily closer and more cooperative. Although the extent of this commitment to a specific strategy turned out to have some practical drawbacks – undue preoccupation, for instance, with a single scenario which never arose – it was undoubtedly positive thinking and prompted both military and civilian members of the Ministry to ask why the Foreign Office could not do the same.

Within the walls of the Foreign Office (the name this chapter will stick to) there were advocates of change. In 1949 the Foreign Secretary, Ernest Bevin, authorised the establishment of a permanent under-secretary's committee of senior officials to 'identify the longer term trends in international affairs and to prepare studies on the possible bearing of these trends upon the future formulation of British policy'. Strang thought the papers produced were useful because 'they compelled the Under-Secretaries to give their minds to problems relating to other regions than those for which they were responsible'. There even 'emerged a body of thought on foreign policy' commanding substantial agreement. His conclusion was nevertheless characteristic (of the Office as much as of the man himself): 'The importance of these long-term studies should not be exaggerated. They could not help very much in the reaching of day to day decisions.'[5]

After one or two false starts in the years between, there was born in 1964 (the Office being then headed by Harold Caccia) the prototype of the modern Planning Staff: a counsellor and two or three first secretaries. This was a reform strongly recommended in the report of the Plowden Committee on Representational Services Overseas, one of whose members was Harold Caccia's predecessor as permanent under-secretary, Lord Inchyra.[6] I became aware that the Planning Staff existed when I was urged – more than once, I fear – to copy to them, ideally to discuss with them, any forward-looking policy proposal I might happen to submit. I found this, as many a head of an operational department has found it since, something of an added burden on a busy life. The Planning Staff were certainly receptive of new ideas, even of heresies, but did they have enough influence to make their support worth the extra trouble of obtaining it?

THE CASE IS ALTERED

Naturally I saw things differently when I myself became head of the Planning Staff in 1971. By then I had published three speculative books, one of them specifically concerned with the making of foreign policy.[7] I had also taken over a Planning Staff which my three distinguished predecessors, Michael Palliser, John Thomson and Percy Cradock, had equipped with a doctrine and a tradition. And there was a different permanent under-secretary, Harold Caccia having been succeeded in 1965 by Paul Gore-Booth and in 1969 by Denis Greenhill.[8]

For most practical purposes the efficacy of planning depends less on the personality of the planner than on that of his patron. Strang not only gives Bevin the credit for initiating the first approach to planning in the Foreign Office, but says that he followed the work 'with keen interest and circulated some of its papers personally and as a matter of general interest to some of his Cabinet colleagues'.[9] His enthusiasm was not matched by that of his successors, and a trudge through their memoirs does not suggest that the idea of planning ever struck a spark. By 1971, therefore, it was to the permanent under-secretary, rather than the Secretary of State, that the Planning Staff looked for guidance and protection. This was so in spite of the post-amalgamation double banking – assistant under-secretary and deputy under-secretary – between the head of the Planning Staff and the head of the Office. I was particularly fortunate in having two patrons – first Denis Greenhill, then Tom Brimelow[10] – whose genuine interest was never confined to their formal role of presiding over meetings of the permanent under-secretary's planning committee. They made full use of the Planning Staff and maintained almost daily personal contact.

Administratively this relationship was facilitated by promoting the head of the Planning Staff to be an assistant under-secretary rather than a counsellor. This not only led to the disappearance of the intervening under-secretaries and made the head of the Planning Staff directly responsible to his patron, but meant that he attended the meeting – unofficially known as 'morning prayers' – at which the permanent under-secretary discussed the day's business with the deputy under-secretaries and assistant under-secretaries, together with the private secretary to the Secretary of State and the head of the News Department (which dealt with the media). Curiously enough this morning meeting had been originated by the same head of the Office who gave the Planning Staff its modern shape.[11] Harold Caccia did not have a speculative temperament, but he was a forceful administrator whose strict regime regenerated the Foreign Office while he was its head and showed that he had not lost the capacity for innovation displayed when, as Chief Clerk, he had carried out the post-war reorganisation of the Diplomatic Service.

The tall windows of the permanent under-secretary's room on the ground floor looked west to the trees of St James's Park and north to the Horse Guards Parade, a car park for most of the year but in late spring a source of martial music as the Guards rehearsed the Trooping the Colour. At the windowless south end of the huge room was a long, shining table. For the morning meeting it was there that Denis Greenhill sat with the deputy under-secretaries and the private secretary. Chairs for lesser lights were ranged along the wall. Gore-Booth – not the first to hold such meetings, but the first to make them an established feature of the regular routine – said: 'the meeting developed arguments and attitudes and pointed the way in which the day's business should be organized for decisions, where needed, by the Secretary of State or other ministers'.[12]

Proceedings were brisk and brief. Nobody spoke, though everyone in turn was offered the chance, unless he had something to say, normally on some issue needing an early decision. From time to time I was able to interject a sentence or two to query an existing policy or to hint at an alternative. Such interventions could be hazardous, but, if really brief and not too frequent, were usually received with remarkable tolerance, and I became a kind of licensed heretic.

Alternative policies had always been a core ingredient in the work of the Planning Staff, but participation in those morning meetings provided an opportunity not hitherto available of exercising some influence, however small, on one of the informal processes of policy formation. The indulgence shown by Denis Greenhill was continued by Tom Brimelow. I left the job before the latter retired and do not know whether my successor continued the practice during his short incumbency, but the next permanent under-secretary soon decided to replace him with a counsellor, at which level the appointment of head of the Planning Staff has since been maintained, as was the case before my time. The late birth of this particular method of influencing policy formation usefully illustrates the dependence of the planner, for status and access as much as for choice of technique, on the temperament of his patron and on the personal relationship he manages to establish.

ETHOS AND STRUCTURE OF PLANNING

The paramount importance to the planner of the patron is one of the few concepts which our meetings with foreign policy planners in other countries established as universally accepted. Differences in political traditions, national temperament and governmental organisation were inevitably reflected in the objectives chosen by planners and the methods they adopted. Dual control of foreign policy in many capitals – Elysée and Quai d'Orsay, for instance; the bright young men European ministers imported to form their personal cabinets; the campaign managers, corporate lawyers and academics who flooded into the White House and the State Department: all these created both problems and opportunities for planners that differed from those posed by British professional politicians and the entrenched official hierarchy. Contributing to policy formation could be regarded as a common ambition, but the circumstances in which it had to be attempted varied so much that it was hard to make any useful comparison of methods or the results they achieved.

In London the tasks originally assigned to the Planning Staff in 1964 were 'Planning generally; PUS's Steering Committee; Contacts with other Policy Planners; Contacts with Unofficial Opinion on International Problems'.[13] By 1971 this had become 'Policy planning, PUS's Planning Committee, Planning Working Party; Contacts with other policy planners; with unofficial opinion on international problems (including Chatham House and IISS); coordination of seminars'.[14]

Such changes all had some fleeting significance, now long forgotten, in terms of office politics, but my predecessor did not much exaggerate when he assured me that, as long as the needs of the permanent under-secretary (which could sometimes be unpredictable) were promptly met, I was otherwise free to do whatever I pleased. Our charter – the internal office memorandum describing in greater detail the rights and responsibilities of the Planning Staff – was a document of symbolic rather than practical importance: a miniature Magna Carta. Nobody, curiously enough, drew my attention to the report of the Plowden Committee, some of whose precepts had actually been followed in practice. I myself came to classify our tasks as: our own business; minding other people's business; and show business.

These categories deserve, and will later receive, fuller consideration, but may now be briefly described. Our own business was everything we initiated or did at the request of the permanent under-secretary: policy papers for the Planning Committee, ideas out of the blue, analyses or anything else that might suddenly be asked for.

Minding other people's business was commenting, orally or in writing, on the proposals submitted by other departments. These two categories embraced our various attempts to contribute to policy formation. Show business was discussions with foreign planners, with academics, and with the backroom boys of British political parties, and other activities intended to enlarge our own mental horizons or to impress outsiders. These extra-mural activities were particularly popular with the bright young first secretaries who constituted the core of the Planning Staff. They also added point to a question that was often asked. Why did we not imitate some of our foreign colleagues and reinforce the Planning Staff by recruiting one or two academics? Even the Plowden Committee had suggested that this might be done for special projects.

The answer stemmed from the tension – we hoped it was a creative tension – endemic in relations between planners and operators, the latter being our name for the official hierarchy, particularly those members least inclined to welcome the interest we took in their activities. The Planning Staff, after all, was an anomaly in an office organised on the basis of defined responsibilities that broadened in scope from the bottom – perhaps a single country – to the top of the chain of command. We poked our noses in everywhere[15] and even tried to subvert the governing principle of the conditioned reflex. If we were tolerated at all, so we argued, it was because we had a familiar smell, an advantage we would forfeit if we recruited a member, however brilliant, of another species.

An academic criticism of a different order, perhaps inspired by the seminal work of Professor Northcote Parkinson, concerns the failure of the Planning Staff to achieve significant growth. There may have been an extra first secretary in my time and I managed to introduce a research assistant, but we prided ourselves on remaining small enough to operate as a collective rather than a hierarchy. One member might be assigned to write a paper, but everyone joined in discussing the principles beforehand and in criticising the draft that emerged. We thought that a good answer, but found it harder to meet the scornful eyes of some visiting Iranian officials – this was when the Shah was riding high – at our reply to their first question: how many computers did we have?

Resistance to the hierarchical principle was also reflected in our relations with the rest of the Office. If an under-secretary or head of department wished us, as occasionally happened, to remain in ignorance of what he was up to we did not invoke our charter or the thunderings of Olympian Jove. Instead one of us – Nixon needed plumbers to stop leaks,[16] but we needed well-borers – would have an obliging friend in the right department. Nobody had more friends or was better at keeping a finger on the pulse of the operators than Charlotte Rycroft, whose sadly premature death was such a loss to the Service.

This little nest of conspirators, all dreaming utopian dreams of injecting an element of predetermined intention into the derivative generalisation of British foreign policy, was accommodated in rooms along the ground-floor corridor leading from the office of the permanent under-secretary to the door at the Clive Steps end of King Charles Street. The importance in bureaucratic politics of office location is often underestimated by the detached observer. Proximity matters.

As a job, planning seldom achieved the exhilarating pace or the adrenalin charge of a busy operational department. The pleasure of seeing an immediate result, however ephemeral, was usually lacking. But the work was much more varied and it was intellectually challenging. One also met far more people and the scope for initiative had an open horizon. In its quieter, different way, the work was as enjoyable as any I did in the Office – often more so.

THE BUSINESS OF THE PLANNING STAFF

Every month the Planning Committee, comprising the deputy under-secretaries and the private secretary to the Secretary of State, met under the chairmanship of the permanent under-secretary to consider a planning paper produced by the Planning Staff. On these occasions the head of the Planning Staff and the first secretary who had done the drafting and would take the notes were allowed to sit at that shining and sacred table. The seats along the wall were occupied by those operators who were directly concerned. These papers – 15 pages is what I remember as an average length – might have been commissioned or else produced on our own initiative. They usually dealt with discrete problems of foreign policy, seldom looked more than five years ahead, often less, and employed a broad brush to suggest objectives and courses of action.

They got a vigorous discussion. We always tried to reach prior agreement with the operators, but terms could sometimes not be settled, nor was the bland courtesy of the chairman invariably matched by the deputy under-secretaries. Unexpected opinions were often forcefully expressed and sharp words occasionally spoken. When ultimately approved, sometimes only after much amendment, the papers would be submitted to ministers and, if these raised no objection, widely circulated in the Office and to posts abroad, though this practice became much less frequent after my time.

These planning papers were in direct descent from those produced under Strang and Bevin and constituted the core function of the Planning Staff. Their subjects – always agreed beforehand with the permanent under-secretary when not actually chosen by him – could range in scope and importance from official support for Chatham House to one of my favourites: The End of the Rainbow – foreign policy after North Sea oil runs out. The more limited and nitty-gritty the subject, the more likely it was that the conclusions of the paper might be reflected in decisions. The more ambitious papers met Strang's criterion of making people think about unfamiliar problems, but seldom resulted in action. I do not remember a case in which the magic formula 'I submit a draft telegram accordingly' was expressly justified by reference to a planning paper rather than to a precedent. We were sufficiently gratified when a sentence or an argument of ours passed, without attribution, into an operator's vocabulary.

I think the discussion of these papers and the circulation given to them helped to freshen what might otherwise have been a rather stagnant intellectual atmosphere, but I do not think that they constituted a sufficient response to the most damaging charge brought by Wallace:

> In contrast to the general acceptance by outsiders of the efficiency and reliability of the British foreign policy-making structure in handling immediate problems, there has been wide-spread and continued criticism of its shortcomings in anticipating international developments and in providing a coherent and realistic overall set of objectives.[17]

Nor do I think that these papers were even the most important effort made by the Planning Staff to promote a more positive approach to policy formation. We got further, ironically enough, with *ad hoc* initiatives.

The two general elections of 1974, for instance, allowed the Planning Staff to produce a fuller statement of British foreign policy than any other official formulation I can remember. On each occasion I commissioned, with the authority of the Planning Committee, some forty papers from the operational departments of the Office, each briefly – two or three sides of double-spaced foolscap – outlining the most important problems of foreign policy for which the department was responsible. While the rest of the Planning Staff edited the results –

eliminating verbosity, correcting politically tactless phraseology, combating the obstinate incredulity of the European departments concerning the attitude of the Labour Party towards British membership of the Community, insisting, where necessary, on alternative versions for different electoral outcomes – I drafted the covering paper on British foreign policy as a whole.

This and its detailed annexes were carefully considered, amended and finally approved by the Planning Committee, who devoted two sessions to the task. Irrespective of the intrinsic merits of the foreign policy described, these papers did provide a thorough exposition of what the Office regarded as British interests and objectives, together with a cautious indication of what changes might be feasible to satisfy electoral commitments or political aspirations. The Planning Staff had, of course, studied the party manifestos and endeavoured, from these and other sources, to identify the particular issues on which the views of the various parties differed from one another and from the consensus of official opinion.

I know – because I asked the various private secretaries – that the massive wads of paper that awaited ministers on their first morning in the Office were carefully read, sometimes more than once. Certainly they were in March, when Labour ministers replaced Conservative, though the perusal might have been less meticulous in October, when the same ministers returned after an electioneering interval. The influence these papers had – before all recollection of their precepts was carried away in the ebb and flow of responsive action – is a matter for future historians to determine. But nobody can complain that ministers were not, from the very outset, presented with propositions, at once comprehensive and detailed, to accept, to reject or to amend.

That was the most ambitious response made by the Planning Staff to the Wallace call, which had not then been published, for 'a coherent and realistic overall set of objectives', but there were others. Some were efforts that failed, others tackled only one aspect of foreign policy. Most were commissioned by the permanent under-secretary of the day. Proposals for an annual White Paper on foreign policy, for instance, were submitted to Conservative ministers and, later, to their Labour successors.[18] Much time was spent in trying to devise a constructive response to Kissinger's Year of Europe in 1973 and, a little later, on British options in the face of the oil weapon. Some of the doctrines we advocated – the priority for British policy of what we called the Central Triangle – Washington–Brussels–Moscow – had a certain vogue in spite of the preoccupation of the political parties with such peripheral issues as Rhodesia.

OTHER PEOPLE'S BUSINESS

Many of the problems tackled by the Planning Staff fell into that category, not least those involving the presentation of alternative policies. The opportunity for such an attempt can arise in three ways. The existing policy may be visibly failing; or the external environment may be changing; or domestic objectives may have altered. None of these premises is likely to command general acceptance. The first implies an error of judgement by those pursuing the existing policy. The second suggests that their perceptions are faulty. The third is open to the retort that the domestic proponents of change have taken insufficient account of the realities of the international situation. The operator, after all, will usually be able to argue that he knows more of the facts.

These are not the only obstacles encountered by would-be innovators. It seldom happens that there are no good arguments for continuing to apply existing policies. And these arguments, whether still valid or not, are fortified by their familiarity and by the extent to which influential people are committed to them. No planner need be disappointed by his failure to persuade the hierarchy to adopt a new policy. He will be lucky if his rebuff is eventually softened by the gradual appearance, naturally for quite unconnected reasons, of progressive, if unobtrusive, modifications of existing policy.

If the advocacy of alternative policies could be frustrating, it was never forbidden. In the 1960s, as everyone knows, the Treasury was not allowed to work on contingency plans for devaluation as long as the government's policy was to maintain the parity of the pound. In my time, the attitude of the Foreign Office was more enlightened. When circumstances seemed to the Planning Office Staff to call in question the future viability of an established policy, we were permitted to present alternatives. Their discussion might not proceed beyond that large, decorous ground-floor room, its status as the sanctum of orthodoxy emphasised by the signed photographs of royalty and of prominent politicians that adorned its many pieces of decorative furniture, but heresy had its airing.

I do not recollect an occasion when our voices were silenced because it challenged a policy that was too fundamental or politically too sensitive to be disputed. In 1974, for instance, British membership of the European Community was as acutely controversial within the political parties as it was between them. It engaged the emotional sympathies of certain senior officials to an unusual extent. But a paper by the Planning Staff on options that might have to be considered was presented and discussed.

As a rule, however, other people's business was minded on a smaller and less controversial scale: by commenting on the telegrams we saw in the distribution (three times a day) or on the proposals submitted by operational departments. This was not a very systematic process – it reached a peak when our own business was slack – and its results were rather haphazard.

One kind of involvement in other people's business brought a temptation which we usually tried to resist. That was forecasting the future. To a limited extent, of course, it was inherent in planning and could not be avoided. We considered five years to be a reasonable maximum for guesswork. Beyond that limit the geometrical progression entailed by any sensible allowance for alternative developments and their consequences made nonsense of any attempt to extrapolate what seemed to be established trends. The result resembled a typical family tree in which the branches spreading from the original ancestor and his wife produced 30 descendants in the fourth generation and ran off the largest page in the fifth.

Unfortunately, if looking even five years ahead (a maximum also chosen by the Plowden Committee) seemed to us a trifle fanciful, there were people who wanted more. The Ministry of Defence, for instance, with whom we worked a good deal, as did other departments of the Foreign Office, explained that much of their budget was devoted to equipment which took ten years to develop at a cost which could only be justified if it was expected to remain in service for ten years longer still. So what might the international situation be ten to twenty years ahead and what might British foreign policy then require of British defence policy?

SHOW BUSINESS

We also went to universities, to the contrasting luxury of weekends at Ditchley, to seminars and lectures and talks across the sandwiches at Chatham House and anywhere else, including some large commercial firms, that might offer new ideas or unfamiliar opinions. There were also encounters, a little fur-bristling, with the Central Policy Review Staff. Our major fiasco was the luncheon which I rashly persuaded the Foreign Secretary to give for twenty professors of international relations. This did not promote harmony or understanding. Otherwise we learned, from our own countrymen as from our foreign colleagues, much that was of interest to ourselves and very little that was of any service in our efforts to impart a corrective tinge of predetermined purpose to the reactive complexion of British foreign policy.

Relations with the academic community had a paradoxical element. Logically our natural interlocutors should have been the theorists and it was from their wisdom that we initially hoped to extract profitable nuggets. I learned with pleasure that my predecessor had recently commissioned a brief digest of contemporary international theory from Professor Joseph Frankel and studied it with an interest that gradually turned to disappointment. I was looking for crisp new concepts for use in argument with operators, but it scarcely seemed likely that I would find them in system analysis or interaction theory. Nor, as we discovered when attending seminars at various universities, did scholars see it as their task to fashion simple tools to serve our crude purposes. If relevance and utility were our watchwords, they preferred intellectual integrity in the pursuit of ultimate, but abstract, truth.

So the theorists, interesting though some of our discussions were, did not prove as rewarding as we had hoped. We were looking for juicy plums, but were offered what we were told was a more nutritious pudding. So we tended, almost as if we had been operators rather than planners, to prefer what we called the geographers: those scholars who specialised in particular countries or practical problems. This was the traditional attitude of the Office. In 1919 the British Delegation to the Peace Conference at Paris were fortified by handbooks commissioned from distinguished scholars, including one by Professor Webster on the Congress of Vienna. As Head of South East Asia Department I had myself commissioned memoranda from the School of Oriental and African Studies and profited by seminars conducted by their scholars for our benefit. I particularly remember Professor Patrick Honey, both for his intellectual distinction and for his favourite gambit: could his views on Vietnam, he would gently enquire, seriously be questioned by anyone lacking his own complete command of the language? His views on policy were forceful and much esteemed in Washington.

Nor did we lack expertise in-house. The Public Record Office should soon release, if they have not already done so, the masterly historical analysis of the Philippine claim to British North Borneo – an active problem in the early 1960s – prepared for us by Professor B.R. Pearn of the Foreign Office Research Department. His *tour de force*, however, was the Blue Book *Documents relating to British Involvement in the Indo-China Conflict 1945–1965*, published in December 1965 (Cmnd 2834). Hotly discussed in a seminar at Hull University, it was accepted even by that initially hostile audience – feeling on Vietnam then ran high even in British universities – as a significant contribution to knowledge. In my time, incidentally, South East Asia Department had a long list of publications to its credit.

Unfairly, perhaps, one's choice of academic contacts tended to be influenced not only by relevance and adaptability – Chatham House always scored high on those counts – but by personal distinction. Professor John Erickson was a case in point. The first time I heard him lecture I was dazzled by what seemed an entirely spontaneous torrent of free association, as compelling and as curiously coherent as Molly Bloom's soliloquy. When I went, with Charlotte Rycroft, to the seminar he organised for us at Edinburgh, I was as impressed by his extraordinary knowledge of the Soviet Army as I was by the fervour of his convictions. It is curious to reflect how often, in what should have been the predominantly intellectual atmosphere of the Planning Staff, I found myself remembering what, in a very different ambience, I used to hear in Ecuador: *'es la persona que cuenta'* – it's the person that counts.

The 'geographers' all had views of their own, but their knowledge of foreign languages and experience of living among foreigners tended to invest them with a common touch of self-confident pragmatism. Their expertise was evident and commanded respect for the advice they were happy to offer. It did not seem to worry them – as it occasionally did the theorists – that offering advice on practical problems might somehow compromise them or detract from their intellectual integrity.

On the whole, however, the pattern of our academic contacts was not systematically determined, but shaped, a little haphazardly, by personal acquaintance and preference. Certain scholars attracted us by their own eagerness to impart useful knowledge, others sought us out because they were themselves interested in the workings of the official machine. Individuals mattered more than institutions. No university department, for instance, had the same importance for the Planning Staff as Chatham House or the Institute for Strategic Studies. Nor was this simply because those two were located in London. Our contacts with the University of London were more limited than they were with several distant campuses. The two Institutes ranked high with us as houses where helpful hosts of catholic tastes could always be counted on to assemble a variety of interesting guests.

Looking back on those days I think more could have been done. It was surely inappropriate that the teaching and the practice of international relations should have been conducted in such dignified independence. There ought to have been a greater exchange, not merely of ideas, but of people, between British universities and the Foreign Office. In an article I published in 1981 (reprinted in my book *Diplomacy at Sea* – Macmillan 1985) I used the analogy of medicine, which cannot be studied or taught without the involvement of both practitioners and patients. As an academic subject, International Relations ought ideally to be a seed-bed for the breeding of practitioners and itself to be refreshed and renewed by their experience. That would entail such changes – whether on campus or in the Office – that all concerned might well prefer to keep the subject in its ivory tower as an elegant piece of show business for planners.

Planners are sometimes tempted to justify their existence by claiming special skills, but we lacked the panache to imitate our French colleagues, who called themselves the Centre d'Analyses et de Prévision. Meetings with the French planners invested show business with a distinction it usually lacked. Most of our foreign colleagues were highly intelligent, but a French intellectual, on a good day, can give discussion a sharp glitter unattainable by the best minds of more stolid nations. As only French was spoken, the opinions exchanged were almost as frank as they were meant to be – and never were with any other planners – in these avowedly unofficial and entirely non-committal talks. The idea – always solemnly agreed in advance by both sides, even the Russians – was that planners, being, in the best sense of the word, irresponsible, could broach subjects and venture views from which conventional diplomats were obliged to abstain. We talked – bilaterally as a rule, occasionally in such groups as the North Atlantic Alliance – to the planners of many nations, but only in Paris were we fascinated – and sometimes a little breathless.

One topic was always explored with our foreign colleagues: the methods used by planners and their influence on policy. The Americans, who had created their Policy Planning Staff as early as 1947, seemed to be the most successful, even if their director no longer enjoyed the remarkable ascendancy, access and freedom of expression commanded, for nearly two-and-a-half years, by George Kennan, the founding father of American planning, apostle of the Cold War and architect of the Marshall Plan.[19] It was General Marshall, incidentally, who decided to institute the process of planning when he became Secretary of State, for his many years as a soldier and a staff officer had accustomed him to regard planning as being not merely a normal, but a necessary activity. He was thus an outstanding patron.

Henry Kissinger, who became United States Secretary of State in September 1973, was another. He brought Winston Lord with him from the White House and wrote warmly of him, but as an invaluable assistant rather than an independent source of alternative ideas:

Winston Lord was largely responsible for giving an impetus to conceptual thinking as the new director of the Policy Planning Staff. . .He and his associates screened most key cables coming to me for consistency with policy and provided me with additional papers on fundamental or long-range issues that the operational bureaux often missed . . . they helped me write the speeches by which I sought to articulate the premises and goals of our foreign policy.[20]

Clearly our American colleagues were quite as much a *cabinet du Ministre* as they were planners in our sense of the word. When we visited Washington we were as impressed by their proximity to the levers of power as we were by the opulent good taste of the State Department after the dilapidated shabbiness of our own Foreign Office.

THE CASE FOR THE CONDITIONED REFLEX

Lord was close to Kissinger and normally a member of the entourage during the Secretary of State's frequent excursions to foreign parts. Kissinger was an unusual patron for a planner. Himself a most effective operator, his respect for the hierarchy of the State Department was severely qualified by criticisms that sometimes sounded a familiar note: 'the State Department machinery. . .is always on the verge of turning itself into an enormous cable machine. Too often policy filters up from the bottom in response to events, complaints, or pleas that originate abroad.'[21] Some of his other grumbles – slowness, inertia, lack of coordination, failure to comply with the known wishes of the Secretary of State – were seldom, if ever, heard in London. Perhaps the pursuit of a responsive policy demands what the State Department did not have: a strong permanent under-secretary to pull the Department together.

By his conduct of affairs, no less than by his ideas, Kissinger posed a much more fundamental challenge to the doctrine of Strang and the practice of the Foreign Office than did William Wallace. In 1972, when Kissinger was still at the White House as assistant to the President for national security affairs, the annual report to Congress on US foreign policy which he drafted for Nixon had a truly remarkable exordium:

without an understanding of the philosophical conception on which specific actions were based, the actions themselves can neither be adequately understood nor fairly judged. This account of a year of intense action, therefore, properly begins with a brief review of the intellectual foundation on which those actions rest.[22]

Both Kissinger and Nixon have their critics, who may question the sincerity of these words or complain that the later section, entitled 'The Philosophy of a New American Foreign Policy', omits considerations of electoral advantage that may have exercised at least equal influence.

These are irrelevant objections. The point at issue is that no British prime minister or foreign secretary in the second half of the twentieth century can readily be imagined as putting his name to such words. In Washington, assumptions – even if the unfriendly call them pretensions – were different.

There is too much scope for argument about the foreign policy of the United States during the last 45 years for this to be treated in the limited compass of a chapter on British foreign policy. What is obvious is that American foreign policy was more active, more positive and had greater international impact than the foreign policy of many other states, or than the foreign policy of the United States in many earlier periods of their history. But was this simply the result of the historical cataclysm that had left the United States richer and stronger, by an order of magnitude, than almost all other states? Or should some of the credit be given to an increase in the power of the President at the expense of Congress, to greatly expanded governmental resources and the systematic application of intelligence to their employment: in a word, to better *control* of foreign policy?

In London, the first explanation was usually preferred by defenders of the status quo. But the greater opportunities enjoyed by the United States provided only a single salvo in the barrage of arguments supporting the inevitability, for Britain, of a predominantly responsive foreign policy. Not only had the relative power of Britain declined, but the whole period since the end of the Second World War had been one of British withdrawal, under the pressure of external forces, from what had once been a leading role. Abroad, significant actors on the international stage had multiplied since Strang first declared, 'the number of ways in which the national interest is liable to be damaged by foreign action is legion. To find the best way to meet each of them will call for an individual exercise separately conducted.'[23] While foreign states proliferated, British membership of the European Community introduced a new dimension to a setting already complicated by the increasing emergence of non-state actors. By simple arithmetic the odds against an international development being the result of a British initiative were over a hundred to one.

There was also a qualitative factor. Some international actors had greater resources than Britain, but even more were subject to fewer constraints. Britain, dependent on allies for her security, and on trading and financial partners for her precarious economic viability, was perpetually sensitive to the views of foreigners. By comparison, Switzerland enjoyed an independence of which Britain could not afford to dream. British governments also laboured under internal handicaps, not least those imposed by a public opinion which believed it respectable to profess continued belief in the illusions of the Victorian era. Many of the options which, in foreign eyes, could be excused by success, were inhibited by the scruples British politicians thought they had to proclaim. The British government could permit itself neither the liberties of a superpower, nor the licence of Gaddafi, nor even the cynical egoism of France. It was not difficult for an informed and intelligent sceptic to argue that there could be no such thing as British foreign policy, only discrete policies directed towards particular problems. Even these were seldom fully integrated, and still more rarely were they guided by the central beacon of perceived national interest. Such policies were the mere function of domestic political reactions to external events, neither logically connected nor forming part of any coherent or deliberate whole.

This pessimistic analysis did not lack authority, but it offered an incomplete explanation. France is a power of much the same economic and military weight as Britain, has also withdrawn from most of her empire and has been longer and more deeply involved in the European Community. Ever since the inauguration of the Fifth Republic, however, French foreign policy has been characterised by 'premeditated and predetermined intention'. It has been, within the limits of the possible, positive, independent, assertive and even flamboyant. Naturally French policy has not always been successful. The captious critic might even argue that rhetoric has sometimes seemed more important than results. Nevertheless, the contrast with the low profile and responsive policy maintained until quite recently by Germany – a similarly situated but, for many years, much richer country – is striking.

No government, however clear-sighted and resolute, enjoys complete freedom to pursue the foreign policy of its choice. Not only may resource constraints be compelling, but the national character, history, institutions and current political inclinations may also exercise significant influences. Even the nature of the contemporary international system tends to inhibit national initiatives, although this is a factor that is sometimes exaggerated. Naturally there is force in the contention that foreign policy is nowadays less distinct and sharply defined, because of the infusion of domestic issues and economic relationships. The ever-expanding international movement of people, goods, ideas and fashions has even led to some blurring of national boundaries. But the rebirth of Germany is evidence that nationalism can sustain the nation-state on prosperous soil, just as, in Eastern Europe, it can disintegrate federations cemented only by ideology and the interests of the ruling class. What once seemed an obvious trend now looks more doubtful.

By the mid-1970s it was almost the conventional wisdom that foreign policy, especially in the advanced industrial countries, could not fruitfully be studied on the basis that the state was an autonomous sovereign unit in the international arena.[24]

Even in the mid-1970s this was not a view that the Foreign Office could be expected to endorse. Foreign policy, however responsive, was their *raison d'être*, just as combating the conventional wisdom belonged to the ethos of the Planning Staff.

Objectively considered, it is surely misleading to regard the nature of the international system as the most important influence on the character of British foreign policy. There had long existed a specifically British incentive to the pursuit of a responsive policy: the political culture of dependence that achieved its fastest growth after the crisis of 1940, but had originated much earlier, 'Britain's increasing resort to external assistance for the solution of problems that, to the retrospective gaze, now appear as the progressive symptoms of domestic national decline' can again be contrasted with the conduct of France after the Second Coming of Charles de Gaulle:

> France, for instance, does not rely on anyone else for her nuclear weapons; allow foreign military bases on her territory; commit her forces to foreign command;[25] run to the International Monetary Fund for loans with strings; often conform to decisions reached without her consent; or send her prime ministers and opposition leaders to kiss hands in Washington on the occasion of their appointment.[26]

Nor is the contribution made by the culture of dependence to the foreign policy of the conditioned reflex at all invalidated by the occasional assertiveness of the past decade. The rescue of the Falkland Islanders or Mrs Thatcher's campaign to reduce British contributions to the European Community may have been unexpected manifestations of national resolve, but they were still reflex actions. Moreover, it was Brussels that was defied, not Washington. As late as 25 March 1992 a leader in *The Times* gave extreme expression to the culture of dependence: 'The famous cliché remains true, that British interests are best protected by identifying them with American interests.' A departure from this doctrine occurred in 1973, when the Heath government reacted to Kissinger's Year of Europe by aligning itself with the Community rather than with the United States, and took care to distance Britain from American support for Israel during the Yom Kippur War. It was not a particularly successful experiment. European solidarity proved to be brittle and, when threatened with an Arab oil embargo, rapidly crumbled. When Labour replaced the Conservatives in 1974, they returned to the American fold, where the Thatcher and Major governments were content to remain.

If the culture of dependence helps to condition the reflexes that shape a predominantly responsive foreign policy, it is at least theoretically true that a dependent policy need not always be responsive. British believers in the 'special relationship' often emphasise the opportunities it provides for Britain to influence the policy of the United States, a task to which the Foreign Office and HM Embassy at Washington have always devoted much effort. In practice, once it is accepted that, in the last resort, the decisions taken in Washington will have to be followed in London, there is often some reluctance to strain the 'special relationship' by advocating measures which the United States government can be expected to oppose. The missionary campaign mounted by the embassy in Washington for American support over the Falklands was remarkably successful, but it was also exceptional. Known American wishes tend to bring an element of precensorship to the process of decision-making in London.

Naturally it can be argued that a more positive British foreign policy, one based on 'premeditated and predetermined intention', would be more persuasive, because it could be expounded continuously. One could pray in aid of this idea a couple of revealing sentences in Kissinger's injured account of the Year of Europe and of the Middle Eastern crisis that followed. He never really understood why an initiative he prized so highly had to turn sour.

> I find it striking that while our European allies left little doubt of their distaste for our policies, they never articulated a coherent alternative. . .one looks in vain for any attempt to present a strategy different from our own or for a serious effort at consultation.[27]

Himself an exceptionally skilful operator, Kissinger was well aware of the diplomatic advantage of persuading other players to expose their hands, but his constant emphasis on the conceptual approach suggests that he might indeed have been more receptive to a full exposition of British policy than to the polite evasions of purely tactical responses.

Whatever the immediate balance of advantage, his expectations may have been too great. So much predisposes the British to allowing their policy to evolve from the cumulative effect of decisions reached by conditioned reflex. There is the pragmatic national temperament, the distrust of theory and system, the fondness for custom and precedent, the cult of common sense. Strang even seemed to hint at direct revelation or unconscious wisdom: 'Between Minister and officials who work together, there comes into existence a large area of common ground which all can take for granted and which does not need to be explained or demonstrated.'[28]

Nothing could be more different from the attitude Kissinger, with his dedication to the conceptual approach, adopted towards his Department when he became Secretary of State: 'I insisted on thoughtful memoranda; I drove my staff mercilessly. Many could not stand the pace or my temperament and resigned. . .The analytical work of the Department improved remarkably.'[29]

Kissinger was not merely an intellectual, but one of those philosophers who unexpectedly become princes of this world. In London he seemed an altogether exotic figure, a phenomenon to whose ideas, as revealed in his published works, I devoted a memorandum for which the prime minister had asked. As George Orwell had explained a quarter of a century earlier, the British political system operated differently: 'The English will never develop into a nation of philosophers. They will always prefer instinct to logic, and character to intelligence.'[30] Strang had much the same idea when he praised 'the quality of judgment which in the Foreign Service is prized above almost all others'.[31] Judgement meant an instinctive perception of the response to external stimulus indicated by the conventional wisdom and known ministerial wishes.

POLICY PLANNING

The desirability of pursuing a purposeful policy, instead of always having to react to foreign initiatives, scarcely needs to be argued. The debatable questions are whether it can be done and, if so, how. Of course, a purposeful policy is not necessarily a successful policy, certainly not a lastingly successful policy. Kissinger pursued a purposeful American foreign policy which achieved some undoubted successes: disengagement from Vietnam, for instance, and the ending of the absurd American refusal to recognise the government of China. He has been rather unfairly criticised because some of his efforts were failures and some of his triumphs too dearly purchased or too ephemeral. 'It is hard to identify a single policy of the Kissinger years that survived intact for a decade.' The same critic complained that 'Kissinger in power claimed to act in accordance with a conceptual framework. . .the practice was less revolutionary than the promise. Kissinger often reacted to events rather than moulded them.'[32]

If even Kissinger can be thus disparaged – Kissinger who was his own planner and, as Nixon's authority crumbled, increasingly his own patron as well; Kissinger the philosopher-prince of the world's strongest power – what can we fairly expect of the subordinate officials attempting to tinge with purpose the conditioned reflexes of a dependent and declining Britain? Little more, surely, than the tokenism so far described.

Rather similar excuses, incidentally, will be found in Baroness Blackstone's apologia for that much larger, more ambitious and grandly patronised organisation, the Central Policy Review Staff (CPRS). Anxious to defend the now defunct CPRS against Denis Healey – 'I don't think it was terribly effective in my time because a group of intelligent individuals without responsibility or departmental support will very rarely persuade Ministers' – she quotes a colleague whose wistful optimism strikes a note the reader has already heard:

> specific recommendations may often have had no obvious immediate results but I believe they often continued to work in a subterranean way until at some subsequent stage – months or even years later – departments started to put them forward as departmental wisdom without acknowledgement.[33]

It would be surprising if such arguments were no longer heard in the Foreign Office of today, but we lack any scholarly study of the planning process that could provide an up-to-date pendant to the brief account in Wallace's classical work. John Dickie touches on the Planning Staff in his book *Inside the Foreign Office*, the contemporary equivalent of the earlier *The Diplomats* by Geoffrey Moorhouse, but does not treat this issue.[34] What he does indicate is that the Policy Planning Staff (the new, American-style name) has grown in numbers and has been given more attention by recent foreign secretaries, even if the main emphasis of its work now seems to be short term, *ad hoc* and even quasi-operational. A surprisingly important function – it actually appears in the Diplomatic Service List – is speech-writing. According to Dickie, this innovation was due to Callaghan, who decided that it was one feature of Kissinger's Policy Planning Staff that was worth copying. For want of fuller information on the status and methods of planning today, it may nevertheless be safer to rest the conclusions of this article on the experience of the 1970s.

Some of the lessons to be drawn from that era seem likely to prove lasting. Planners will continue to depend on their patron for more than their status. It is he who is most likely to determine the nature of their work and the extent to which it is given practical application. The most efficacious methods for planners to employ will be those that appeal to their patron. The staunchest of patrons, however, and the best advised, is still 'slave to Fate, Chance, kings and desperate men', and even superpowers can only sometimes command success for their pre-meditated intentions. Nor can they, or anyone else, escape the iron law of international relations: most decisions in foreign policy are inevitably responsive, because most of the impulses that trigger them must, by simple arithmetic, have a foreign origin. No planning will ever eliminate from the conduct of foreign policy the predominance of the conditioned reflex.

Foreign policy planning seems likely to remain the art of a small minority: its exponents a little outside the mainstream of decision-making; its preoccupations a trifle esoteric; its impact limited and intermittent. There is a case, depending on the requirements of the patron, for most of the expedients attempted at different periods and in various countries, but special emphasis ought perhaps to be laid on those least likely to be popular: asking awkward questions, for instance.

Diplomats and politicians aim to please, but planners ought often to provoke. When the Foreign Office is made the scapegoat for some international setback – invasion of the Falkland Islands, for example, though the real culprit was the Ministry of Defence – it is usually through failure to confront ministers with the awkward questions, the hypothetical ones nobody wants to answer. Next century, when the catacombs at Kew give up their dead, it will be interesting to discover what the Planning Staff had to say during the five years from 1977 (when the Callaghan government ballasted Anglo-Argentine talks with a naval deployment in the South Atlantic) to February 1982, when the Thatcher government neglected this precaution.

Heresy, alternative policies, and worst-case options will never be popular, and will often be declared a waste of time for busy ministers and senior officials. But if planners do not make a nuisance of themselves, who will? It is not enough for them to think the unthinkable, they have to say it out loud. Planners must accordingly tread a narrow path, neither falling into impotence through failure to please their patron nor abdicating their unique responsibility by fearing to provoke him. They do not justify their existence by the quality of their advice but by their choice of issues on which to offer it. To err is human: to remain tactfully silent is unworthy of a planner.

NOTES

1 William Wallace, *The Foreign Policy Process in Britain*, London, Royal Institute of International Affairs, 1975, p. 61.
2 Ibid., pp. 29–30.

3   Lord Strang, *The Diplomatic Career*, London, André Deutsch, 1962, p. 116.
4   Ibid., p. 120.
5   Ibid., pp. 110–11.
6   *Report of the Committee on Representational Services Overseas 1962–63*, London, HMSO Cmnd 2276, February 1964, paras 217–23.
7   Grant Hugo, *Britain in Tomorrow's World*, London, Chatto & Windus, 1969.
8   Sir Michael Palliser, GCMG, PC (1922–); Sir Percy John Thomson, GCMG (1927–); Sir Percy Cradock, GCMG (1923–); Lord Caccia, GCMG, GCVO (1905–90); Lord Gore-Booth, GCMG, KCVO (1909–84); Lord Greenhill of Harrow, GCMG, OBE (1913–).
9   Strang, *The Diplomatic Career*, op. cit., pp. 110–11.
10 Lord Brimelow, GCMG, OBE (1915–), Permanent Under-Secretary 1973–75.
11 Paul Gore-Booth, *With Great Truth and Respect*, London, Constable, 1974, pp. 327–8.
12 Ibid., p. 328.
13 *The Foreign Office List for 1965*, London, Harrison & Sons.
14 *The Diplomatic Service List 1971*, London, HMSO.
15 Although the administrative departments were largely closed to us (I would have loved to lay rough hands on personnel), which makes it all the odder that one academic writer lists the Planning Staff among administrative departments. See Michael Clarke, 'The Policy Making Process', in M. Smith, S. Smith and B. White, *British Foreign Policy*, London, Unwin Hyman, 1988, p. 89.
16 Henry Kissinger, *Years of Upheaval*, London, Weidenfeld & Nicolson and Michael Joseph, 1982, p. 117.
17 Wallace, *The Foreign Policy Process*, op. cit., p. 76.
18 Both parties, while in opposition, had advocated greater openness in the conduct of foreign affairs. See Wallace, ibid., pp. 280–1.
19 Walter L. Hixson, *George F. Kennan: Cold War Iconoclast*, New York, Columbia University Press, 1989, pp. 47–72.
20 Kissinger, *Years of Upheaval*, op. cit., p. 441.
21 Ibid., p. 439.
22 *US Foreign Policy for the 1970s* – A Report to the Congress by Richard Nixon, President of the United States, Washington, DC, US Government Printing Office, 9 February 1972, p. 2.
23 Strang, *The Diplomatic Career*, op. cit., pp. 115–16.
24 Steve Smith and Michael Smith, 'The Analytical Background', in Smith *et al.*, *British Foreign Policy*, op. cit., p. 14.
25 Until the Gulf War of 1991.
26 James Cable, 'Interdependence: a Drug of Addiction?', in James Cable, *Diplomacy at Sea*, London, Macmillan, 1985, pp. 55–73.
27 Kissinger, *Years of Upheaval*, op. cit., pp. 716–17.
28 Strang, *The Diplomatic Career*, op. cit., pp. 119–20.
29 Kissinger, *Years of Upheaval*, op. cit., p. 440.
30 George Orwell, *The English People*, London, Collins, 1947, p. 46.
31 Strang, *The Diplomatic Career*, op. cit., p. 40.
32 Robert D. Schulzinger, *Henry Kissinger: Doctor of Diplomacy*, New York, Columbia University Press, 1989, p. 239.

33 Tessa Blackstone and William Plowden, *Inside the Think Tank*, London, William Heinemann, 1988, pp. 215–17.

34 John Dickie, *Inside the Foreign Office*, London, Chapmans, 1992; and Geoffrey Moorhouse, *The Diplomats: The Foreign Office Today*, London, Jonathan Cape, 1977.

7   Holding policy-makers to account
The problem of expertise

Tam Dalyell

'*Chacun à son goût*', James Callaghan used to grunt, when as Foreign Secretary or Prime Minister, he took a grim view of what I was saying, during our regular Wednesday evening meetings, when I was Chairman of the Parliamentary Labour Party Foreign Affairs Group. The phrase gained in impact by being uttered by a superbly shrewd politician, whose knowledge of the French language was gained before he left school at 15 years old, half a century before. Yet, I believe Callaghan was saying something profoundly true. Those British politicians who really care about the issues of foreign policy, as opposed to being an under-secretary of state, or in a winning position, are activated in their quest to influence events by concrete personal experience or catalytic incidents in their own lives. Can anyone doubt that Ted Heath's tenacious belief in Europe was born when, as a young lieutenant-colonel in 1939–45, he witnessed the horrors of European war? Or that Julian Amery's contributions over four decades originated in his time serving with the partisans in Yugoslavia? Or that George Wigg's effective critique of the Services came out of his period as an NCO in India in the 1930s? Or that John Mendelson's education of his contemporaries on the Left in relation to Vietnam was fuelled by the experience of his family in the Warsaw ghetto? In my experience, there are things in the past of every passionate – I repeat passionate, since different criteria apply to the honourable seeking of political office – foreign-policy issue politician, which explain the present. For example, the ardent anti-apartheid campaigner, Robert Hughes MP, spent time in his youth in South Africa. Sir David Steel, who has fire in his belly on race, was brought up the son of the manse in Kenya. Bowen Wells, Champion of Development Aid on the Conservative benches was for years in the Colonial Service. We politicians are very personal creatures, popular prejudice notwithstanding.

So it is with me. When my Arabic-speaking parents were working in the Persian Gulf, I was brought up, the only child of an only child, by my maternal grandmother, Dame Mary Marjobibantes. She was obsessed by the Great War – and perhaps understandably so, since she had had twenty years of post-Gallipoli problems with my grandfather, after he returned a changed and scarred man from the Dardanelles. Moreover, she had made Sir Edward Grey of Falloden my mother's godfather, and exuded the horror and guilt of the Liberal grandees of the turn of the century. It was undoubtedly from my grandmother that I derived my fanatical opposition to war as a phenomenon which could and should be avoided. This gut feeling was reinforced by a whole range of people with whom I have had the good fortune to come into contact, from the late Lieutenant-Colonel Douglas Stewart, DSO, MC and bar, my commanding officer in the Royal Scots Greys, and an Olympic riding gold medallist, to Pastor Neimuller, with whom I spoke as an undergraduate at the Cambridge Union. I am sure that other MPs would have similar stories to relate.

Having acknowledged that there may be a constant thread, such as burning opposition to unnecessary war, it is the particular situation which triggers off any relentless campaign on which I embark – and it is not worth embarking on any campaign if one is not prepared to be relentless about it. In each of the four examples which provide the basis of this chapter, there have been certain criteria which had to be met before I was willing to raise my standard. These criteria are also fourfold:

First, that the issue should not be trivial; secondly, that I really cared about it; thirdly, that there was a likelihood of exerting influence on events, with the possibility of altering the situation; and, finally and crucially, that I should have friends in academia and journalism who cared as much, and knew as much if not more about the cause than I did. For example, the successful campaign to save Aldabra Atoll was dependent on the endless patience of the Cambridge oceanologist, Dr David Stoddart, and the late Sir Ashley Miles, FRS, then Biological Secretary of the Royal Society, who befriended me as a young MP, in the first instance because we had both, thirty years apart, been undergraduates at King's College, Cambridge. Any campaigning politician, if he is to take on Her Majesty's ministers, must have sources of information as expert as those available to HMG. Patrick Blackett told me that the Aldabra air-staging post threat was the first time ever that the Royal Society has deemed it proper to become involved in a 'political' argument.

CONFRONTATION AND BORNEO, 1965–66

I suspect it is true of all governments and most ministers – although a notable exception in my experience would be Lord Carrington, who would not stand on ceremony, and as foreign secretary would argue his point of view on its merits – that they resent challenge from their back-bench colleagues. It is understandable. You are a busy, harassed minister, trying to deal with 101 matters, to keep the Americans happy, to get permissions from the Treasury, while doing your best for government and party with the press, not to mention looking after your constituents' myriad affairs. Along comes a parliamentary colleague who you think, probably rightly, knows less than you do, to make demands on your time and energy. At the end of a long day – and it always is at the end of a long day, after any amount of Cabinet meetings, Cabinet committees, or whatever – it is all too easy to be tetchy and dismissive with those who might suppose that they are doing the very job for which the tax-payers are paying their salaries, but whom you, as minister, regard as a bloody nuisance. This was emphatically the attitude of Denis Healey (a quarter of a century later to be the author of the outstanding political autobiography of his generation), when I went to see him about my qualms over the war in Borneo.

As I've told him several times since, he is and was a political thug. In fairness, he was equally tough with other parliamentary friends, such as Frank Allaun, telling them on one celebrated occasion that they were out of 'their tiny Chinese minds' – a remark which cost Healey the leadership of the Labour Party, and perhaps the Labour Party the occupancy of 10 Downing Street in 1983. I understand Healey behaved in a more civilised way to Tory MPs who went to see him, and, obversely, I myself got an altogether better hearing from that other Balliol heavyweight, Ted Heath, than did, by their own accounts, an assemblage of distinguished Conservative MPs, when he led their party in or out of government.

For our purpose, in this volume, there are conclusions to be drawn from these salutary personal tales: don't imagine that individual MPs can hold those holding the great offices of state to account by having a quiet word in the ear of a grand personage in one's own party, and don't underestimate the metamorphosis which overtakes many chummy, pliable, agreeable, eager-to-please opposition politicians soon after they have been transformed into Ministers of the Crown.

The seeds of conflict in the Island of Borneo had been sown by the extraordinary Rajah Brooke and his descendants, who claimed Sarawak and North Borneo (Sabah) for the British Empire. Actually, Brooke's rule was not unenlightened, if paternal, and by the standards of the late twentieth century patronising. Post-1945, President Sukarno, father of the Indonesian Republic, acquiesced in his army infiltrating the British dependencies. By the early 1960s cross-border activity for Southern

Borneo, Indonesian Kalimantan, had become so widespread that a firm response was thought to be required to honour British obligations to Malaysia.

The genesis of my campaign to extricate the British Army from Borneo was relatively straightforward. It was the cold February of 1965. When in London I stayed in the house of Dick Crossman, who had been made Minister of Housing with a view to making rapid progress there, so that the Prime Minister would have something to show the electorate before going to the polls, as he would soon have to with a majority of only three. Housing programmes meant quick and substantial public expenditure. In those heady days, after languishing thirteen long years in opposition, it is strange but true that Labour did not comprehend the stringent limitations imposed by the Treasury. It was here that home and foreign policy came together. I can pin-point the exact moment, when I determined to campaign on the Borneo War. It was late one evening, when an exasperated Crossman had been told by Dame Evelyn Sharpe that his cherished proposals for quality council housing, satisfying every Parker–Norris standard, had been peremptorily turned down due to the exigencies of public expenditure. Both Crossman and I thought that the root of the trouble was the sacred obeisance which was being accorded to the defence budget. Immediately, we discussed commitments which might be cut. Surely Borneo was the next in line for cool, realistic thinking to be followed by withdrawal, the successor to Kenya and Mau-Mau, Cyprus and Eoka, Aden and the Yemenis, and a host of other post-imperial commitments, examined so effectively by John Strachey in his great book, *The End of Empire*.[1]

Now, to carry conviction in the eyes of parliamentary colleagues, it is usually necessary to have actually been oneself to a place, or, at least, to have written a book about it or about the issue involved. So, in February 1965, I went to the Ministry of Defence, hoping, in my *naïveté*, to be encouraged in my zeal to get to Sabah and Sarawak. It was a rude shock to meet not, as I thought, my friend the jovial Denis Healey of Opposition days (as he was to become again after 1979!), but a fearsome Secretary of State, whose politest observation was, 'I haven't got enough helicopters to take you around!' Undaunted – more or less! – I returned before Whitsun with the same request, more pressing than ever, that I be allowed to go to witness Confrontation at first hand, since the public expenditure situation was worse. To say that Denis Healey and Fred Mulley, his deputy, both perceived as successful ministers, sent me packing would be an unduly delicate way of describing what actually occurred. From their point of view, I was simply 'playing silly-buggers'. From my point of view, it was vital to avoid a British Vietnam in Sarawak. Don't imagine that high-minded scrutiny of the most sensitive policies of prime ministers and defence secretaries will be courteously, let alone well, received! I have noticed that when powerful ministers are even quizzed on policies, where their quizzer is perhaps more in tune with the heartstrings of the party than the minister, then the latter often resorts to a coarseness which is out of character with their day-to-day demeanour. On matters of high national importance great public figures can be breathtakingly petty. The merits or otherwise of criticism too often recede into the background.

In British politics, never even underestimate the bizarre, the comic, and the impact of chance. As a young and fit MP, I had made something of a fetish of voting in every division between October 1964 and July 1965. Track-suited, I would prance through the lobby at 5 a.m. As a result, when the selection for the annual defence visit to Borneo came before the Chief Whip, Ted Short, now Lord Glenamara, thought Dalyell had to be rewarded for physical diligence. So I was listed as one of the four Labour members to go to Sarawak and Singapore.

Truth to tell, these tours were often looked on as freebies and jaunts. However, I had friends through Crossman, Kingsley Martin and Dorothy Woodman, and as editor of the *New Statesman* and editor's consort, their imprimatur gave me a passport to the emerging states of Asia. Rather than be feted in officers' messes, I was in a position to seek out the leaders of the Chinese community, Sen-Dayaks like Mrs Tra Zender, and other contacts made by Kingsley during his inexhaustible involvement in myriad movements for colonial freedom.

From them, I derived a wholly different perspective on 'Confrontation', which was considered so righteous a war in Downing Street and Whitehall. The locals, if that be the right description of clever Chinese men of commerce, subtle Malay entrepreneurs, and proud leaders of a cultural people, told me that the borders between Sarawak and Kalimantan were ethnically and topographically artificial, and that people traded across the frontier, married across the frontier, and simply thought that borders in the island of Borneo were the creation of remote Europeans. It would be much better for all the peoples of Borneo, if the British Army went home.

Had I relied on the official briefings of the Commander-in-Chief, Air Chief Marshal Sir John Grandy (who put in an unfavourable report about me, since I asked awkward questions) and his press officers, and had not the entrée been provided by Kingsley Martin to those who cast a beady Asian eye on Pax Britannica, I could never have mounted any worthwhile critique of HMG's policy. I claim no great virtue since actually it is a politician's job to get off the military circuit and talk to non-official sources. If I recall that the delegation on return to Singapore was invited to a sixteen-course dinner by the formidable Prime Minister Lee Kuan Yew, and that after dinner I had a humdinger of an argument with him, it is only because it is instructive about what occurred later, on return to Britain.

In my supreme innocence, I fondly imagined that my senior colleagues would be all agog to hear what I had learned in South-East Asia, and eager to act on my conclusions. I soon came up against the reality. On return, I immediately asked to see the Prime Minister. To some surprise, he granted my request, I think because he liked me (at that time, though not for long, I was a bit of a blue-eyed boy), and because Harold Wilson was a very nice man. In his room in the Commons, I gave him a cascade of woeful prognostications that we were heading for a British Vietnam in Sarawak. Wilson listened, raised his eyebrows, and said he would make enquiries. Days went by, and passed into weeks. Nothing happened. I then decided to make a tour of senior members of the Cabinet. Scales fell from my eyes. Barbara Castle and Tony Greenwood, who had sat on the platform of every rally of the Movement for Colonial Freedom in the 1950s and early 1960s made it obvious that they did not want to touch me with the proverbial barge-pole. George Brown bombastically observed that I might be bloody-well right about the effect of the British Army on the peoples of Borneo, but withdrawal was not what the Americans wanted – and only the Americans could help him out with his real concern, the Gnomes of Zurich. The Chancellor, James Callaghan, said, on my entering his room, 'I supposed I had to see you, as a Labour colleague, but you are a real chump upsetting everybody. How can we make you an under-secretary if you behave like this!' Now the point is that these four ministers were not enemies – they were friends to me, and clearly I had tested their patience. There was a truth, which I believe remains a truth in the politics of the British Cabinet system. No senior Cabinet minister, even a Foreign Secretary or a Chancellor of the Exchequer, wants to get across his Cabinet colleagues by gratuitously interfering in their department business. And those Cabinet ministers with direct responsibility, in this case Michael Stewart at the Foreign Office and Denis Healey at Defence, were simply irritated by criticisms from back-bench colleagues.

I went to see Harold Wilson for a second time. He was nicer than his Cabinet colleagues, but said he thought I was wrong, and that Sukarno was bad. As I went out of his room, paradoxically the real truth emerged by accident. Seeing my King's College Cambridge tie, Harold had an afterthought, 'Tell me, Tam, do you think you have better judgement than the most gifted alumnus of your University, and trust you are a better democratic socialist?' For once, my temper got the better of me. 'That's it, Harold. You've been taken for a ride by that Westernised, attractive-to-you Cambridge intellectual, Lee Kuan Yew.' In the Westminster village, I was soon being asked by curious colleagues, 'What on earth did you say to the PM?' Dick Crossman, whose PPS I was, and my boss, was furious with me – for causing possible embarrassment between him and the Prime Minister. Weeks later, he was drily to observe, when further money for housing was not forthcoming, that at least Wilson had treated me better than he had been treated by Attlee.

On the famous occasion when Crossman returned from the Anglo-American Palestine Commission, he was given a quarter of an hour of the Prime Minister's time. After fourteen minutes of exposition, he paused for Attlee's expert reaction, and likely British government policy towards the Jewish State, and all Clem said was, 'Dick, how's your mother?' *Tout ça change.*

The fact is that the most senior politicians are not influenced by their colleague's experiences and expertise, but rather by an estimate of how courses of action will affect them and their standing. Wilson was not interested in the merits of policy towards Borneo but how what he said would impinge on his relations with Lee Kuan Yew and Lyndon Johnson. Equally, little mattered more to Mrs Thatcher than her relations with Ronald Reagan, and paramount in John Major's calculations has been his standing with George Bush and Helmut Kohl. On the other hand, prime ministers obviously have to balance out a whole range of competing considerations, within foreign policy and between foreign and domestic policies. They cannot be as monocular as a backbench critic can be, yet this does not *necessarily* mean that they are less serious or honourable.

ALDABRA ATOLL, 1967–68

Politicians who campaign on matters of foreign policy tend to get worked up when they find that authority has transgressed one of their basic beliefs. This was true for me in the case of the Aldabra Atoll, in which I became deeply involved in 1967.

Since the time of my early childhood when my father presented various animals, including a rare shox-lynx kitten, to Dr Tom Gillespie, the famous keeper of the Edinburgh Zoological Gardens, I have had a deep-seated concern for the preservation of endangered species. Thus I really did care when I heard that Wilson and Healey were solemnly proposing to build an RAF base, or 'staging-post', as they proposed to call it, on Aldabra Atoll in the British Indian Ocean Territories. The cats and the rats which would inevitably accompany an RAF base would have quickly exterminated the flightless rail, the pink-footed booby, and the young of the giant tortoise of the Indian Ocean. When I raised the ecological issue, I simply ran into the ribald comment that the East of Suez policy of Her Britannic Majesty's human government took precedence over the requirements of the pink-footed booby! This was a reflection of the fact that what are now called ecological questions were simply not part of political consciousness in the 1960s. What I would have done if I had believed in the East of Suez policy I don't honestly know, but as I thought the East of Suez commitment was a preposterous self-delusion on the part of the Wilson Cabinet, that particular dilemma did not arise. I resolved to try to scupper the scheme.

The prerequisite of effective parliamentary action in matters of non-mainstream foreign policy is to make sure that MPs of all parties know that there is an issue at stake. So I peppered the order paper with Parliamentary Questions on Aldabra, used every Prime Minister's Tuesday and Thursday Question Time, at least to have Aldabra on the Order paper, and raised it at every conceivable opportunity. Where is this place, Abra-Cadabra? That was enough. Collective political curiosity catalysed.

In my experience, luck often attends those who are pertinacious, and have a rhinoceros hide about being thought a bore by their parliamentary colleagues. It emerged that the 'planners' of this project in SW1 had assumed that the many thousands of tons of store-infilling, required as a runway base to accommodate huge Hercules-type intercontinental transport planes, could be relatively easily mined and excavated on Aldabra itself.

In the recesses of my mind, I recalled that the late Professor T.R.C. Fox, Shell Professor of Chemical Engineering, had told us that the nature of coral limestone was such, that it appeared very hard on the surface but was soft underneath. Did the Ministry of Defence know this? A couple of Parliamentary Questions established clearly that the Ministry of Defence had no notion whatsoever of the properties of coral limestone.

I therefore trundled along to the Ministry of Public Buildings and Works to see the Minister, my friend Bob Mellish. He was to be ministerially responsible for the construction of the base. I asked him cheerfully how many ore-carriers he would be chartering to carry rubble from East Africa into the middle of the Indian Ocean, and how many million tons of stone he had in mind. The visit had the desired effect. He has confirmed to me many times since, that in the direct and colourful language of Bermondsey dockland, he had asked his civil servants whether that Tam Dalyell could be right. 'Well, er, yes, Minister, we suppose that he is', came the reply.

My visit to Bob Mellish reinforced the question that parliamentary colleagues of all parties and Lobby correspondents had begun to ask – 'What on earth is Dalyell on about, when he nags on about Aldabra?' It is half the battle when the curiosity of Parliament as a collectivity has been awakened. And, the more they discovered, the less they were enchanted by the idea of this 'staging-post'. As political stones are lifted, all sorts of creepy, crawly things in the shape of awkward facts tend to crawl out.

The other half of the battle was a strategy which made Harold Wilson incandescent with anger (and for which he never forgave me, as long as he was leader of the Labour Party). With a covering letter, I sent copies of the seventy-plus Parliamentary Questions which I had put down on Aldabra to Hubert Humphrey, then Vice-President of the United States; William Carey, of the Bureau of the Budget; Glenn Seaborg, Chairman of the US Atomic Energy Authority; Ed Werk, Secretary of the Marine Sciences Council; crusty old Senator McClellan of Arkansas, then the cantankerous chairman of the powerful Senate Appropriations Committee; the young Senator Clairborn Pell, of Rhode Island, twenty-five years later to be chairman of the Senate Foreign Relations Committee; and Congressman Henry Reuss of Wisconsin, all of whom I had recently (1966) met in Washington when I had been the guest of the Bureau of the Budget. Every one of them reacted in the same way – as I had anticipated: they dispatched my correspondence to Defence Secretary, Robert A. McNamara, with a covering letter, saying in effect, 'We know this young British MP as a sincere and serious person. What is the US attitude to wrecking a unique eco-system, and has real thought been given to this? What shall we say to him?' Now, it is one thing for an American Defence Secretary to be approached by a foreign politician, who can be swotted like a fly: it is another to brush off the Bureau of the Budget and the Senate Appropriations Committee, with which the Department of Defence has to have day-to-day relations. My representations on Aldabra were taken most seriously as I later discovered.

Even so, success might not have been forthcoming had it not been for an enormous slice of luck. Passing through London at the crucial moment was Dillon Ripley, secretary and head of the Smithsonian. He agreed to see me in the Connaught Hotel at midnight (physical energy is an essential ingredient in the successful prosecution of political campaigns). Expressing extreme concern, he promised to phone Sir Ashley Miles, an old friend of his as well as mine, when he got back to

Washington the following day, and then exercise his century-old right as the representative of America's most prestigious scientific institution to go direct to the President of the United States. Ripley was as good as his word. He did contact Lyndon Johnson personally. The result was that McNamara and Johnson persuaded or told Harold Wilson what he had to do, and thus as *Hansard* reports, the Prime Minister announced, in the middle of a statement on the 'Economic Situation' that 'we have decided not to proceed with the Aldabra project [interruption] – the establishment of a staging post in the British Indian Ocean territory'.[2]

THE FALKLANDS WAR, 1982

I do not know whether it is easier or more difficult to call a government to account when the back-bench MP is in support of the government or in opposition. It is certainly different. Both in relation to Borneo and Aldabra, ministers were concerned to the extent that they feared that my views could come to be shared by a significant proportion of the Parliamentary Labour Party on whose votes they depended, and who would be the electorate for the Shadow Cabinet, should the party be defeated, and go into opposition. Equally, however, a critic is restrained to some extent by feelings of disloyalty to party, and especially if his or her Constituency Labour Party have a number of activists who frown on too much hostility of an overt nature to their government. In opposition, by contrast, the gloves might seem to be off. However, in relation to the Falklands and the Libyan Bombing, there was more front-bench disapproval than over Borneo and Aldabra. The reasons are myriad and subtle. However, the fact is that if Cabinet ministers and departments squabble over responsibilities, they are as nothing to the territorial disputes between Shadow Cabinet ministers who have more time and energy for disputes and tend to fight like Kilkenny cats. My ferocious criticism of Mrs Thatcher over the Falklands from the very beginning, Friday, 2 April 1982, greatly embarrassed my colleagues, and understandably Michael Foot was obliged to sack me from the front bench as Science Spokesman. My behaviour was justified in my own mind, because I was satisfied my opposition to government and colleagues met my criteria and justified my deviating from the party line: I knew more about the situation than my colleagues; it was a matter of central, not peripheral importance; and it was not a case of tilting at windmills, but an issue which a screeching voice in Parliament could at least hope to do something about. In my view, it is unforgivable to rebel on an issue or topic where one's colleagues know as much, if not more, than one does oneself, which ranges from the not-so-important to the trivial, and which is such that no amount of parliamentary action can do the slightest thing about it. An MP, before he or she rebels, is also wise to take into account not only whether one does know more about a subject than the collectivity of MPs, but whether one is perceived by Parliament and press to know something about the issue. In the case of the Falklands, I had been chosen by Mr Speaker Selwyn Lloyd to lead the first parliamentary delegation to Brazil in 1976. The then Governor of Rio de Janeiro, Admiral Faria Lima had told me that though Brazilians and Argentines did not get on so well at that time, nevertheless he and all politicians in Brazil believed that the Malvinas belonged to Argentina, and I, as leader of the British delegation, ought to know that South Americans shared the view that European colonial powers were not welcome to hold land in South America or its continental shelf. I remembered this conversation when, as chairman of the Parliamentary Labour Party Foreign Affairs Group, I was sent by James Callaghan, then Foreign Secretary, to observe the Foreign Office Seminar on the Falklands also in 1976. I reported back that I had never seen such intransigent, unreasonable people as the Falkland Islanders and their legal representatives. They had been to school in Argentina; some of them owned land there; they got their victuals and food there; they got any meaningful hospital treatment there; and yet they expected Britain to turn down, unceremoniously, any Argentine proposals.

It was against this background, including two years at sea between 1960–62, and my innate aversion to gung-ho simplicities, that I expressed vehement opposition to the Labour Party agreeing to the resort of force after 2 April 1982. Thus I went to John Silkin and Michael Foot to express alarm before they committed the Labour Party to support for a Task Force in the truncated three-hour parliamentary debate on Saturday, 3 April – the first occasion on which the House of Commons had sat on a Saturday since the Suez Crisis, a quarter of a century earlier. It is my experience that when the normal procedures of the House of Commons are circumvented and short-circuited by the agreement or connivance of government minsters and opposition front bench, democratic scrutiny and public accountability go out of the proverbial window. Such was certainly the case in April 1982. The bare fact of the matter, confirmed in Speaker Thomas's own memoirs, was that he (an ex-Commonwealth Office Minister, in office in the period during which crucial decisions were made in relation to the Falklands) made the judgement that the Prime Minister had to be supported.[3] As I had interrupted the Prime Minister with a hostile question during her speech, and told him in the Chair that one dissenter ought to be called, he had no excuse for not knowing. Unless minorities receive, at least, fair hearing from the Speaker, they have little chance of making an impact. As it was, the Task Force sailed with the imprimatur of Parliament, and inexorably, as the ships got nearer the Islands, war became unavoidable.

To understand the saga of the *Belgrano*, it is best to read Arthur Gavshon and Desmond Rice's *Sinking of the Belgrano*;[4] my own chapter on the *Belgrano* in *Misrule*;[5] and to view again the still oft-reported television clip of Mrs Diana Gould, that 'housewife' from Cirencester, challenging Mrs Thatcher on the course of the Argentine warship at the time of the sinking. Arguably, Mrs Gould's never-to-be-forgotten-by-those-who-saw-it contretemps was the most effective single piece of scrutiny of the 1983 General Election. On her initiative, she phoned me for information about co-ordinates, as soon as she knew she had been chosen to appear on Sue Lawley's programme. For my part, I was able to draw on the invaluable expertise of Lord (Tommy) Brimelow, the Labour Peer; Guillermo (Willy) Makin, an Argentine Ph.D. student from Cambridge; Roberto Campos, the Brazilian Ambassador and former Economics Minister; David, 2nd Viscount Montgomery of Alamein, a businessman with a special knowledge of South America; and journalists Richard Norton-Taylor of *The Guardian* and Charles Douglas-Home of *The Times*.

The conclusion to be drawn from the *Belgrano* Affair, on which Prime Ministerial misuse of information was later proved (and indeed from the whole Falkland Campaign as later the Gulf War), is that when in British politics a prime minister is faced by an opposition leader who basically concurs in the policy of war, he or she can get away with almost anything. The party system simply does not provide for any meaningful accountability in our adversarial democracy when the front benches are not basically divided on the issue. In 1956, over Suez, Hugh Gaitskell and Harold Wilson in the Labour Shadow Cabinet were divided, and that was an altogether different story.

THE LIBYAN BOMBING, 1986

Of all the causes that I have been involved in, about none have I felt more strongly than about the bombing of Tripoli on 15 April 1986 (at least until the Gulf War of 1991). I was simply appalled that huge bombers should leave the base at Fairford, Gloucestershire, on British soil, to drop bombs, inevitably maiming women and children who had not the foggiest notion about the ostensible cause of the attack – a bombing at La Belle Discothèque in Berlin, in which an American serviceman had been killed, allegedly (though wrongly as it later turned out), by Colonel Gaddafi's hit-men.

First of all there was the disproportionate nature of the response. One of St Thomas Aquinas's conditions for a just war was that the retaliatory action should not be out of response to the original hurt. Secondly, there was the fact that the action had nothing whatsoever to do with NATO, on whose behalf the B52 giant bombers were stationed in Britain; and indeed the bombers had to make a detour via Spain and Portugal, as France and Italy would not contemplate granting overflying rights for such a venture. Thirdly, Mrs Thatcher's contention that she was acting on humanitarian grounds was simply preposterous. For public consumption by an uneasy British audience, containment of terrorism became her justification.

Yet from the Pentagon came very different reasons. First, the attack on Libya provided a proving ground for weapons. *US News and World Report* carried an article by William Broyles Junior, on 12 May 1986, entitled 'The Politics of War' in which he wrote:

> The budget in short is the mission. 'It all comes back to the budget', says one ex-Pentagon analyst. 'For years we've been saying that radar, infra-red and smart bombs are the way to go. We've spent billions on night-mission avionics, so we had to try to use them, even if a daylight strike would have been better.'[6]

Equally bluntly, *Aviation Week* of 21 April 1986 asserted that the attack on Libya 'provided a good proving ground for the F1–11s to be flown in the Mediterranean, and gave the Air Force a chance to demonstrate its capabilities.' A raid of this kind was deemed to have great value in the presentation to Congress of the case for greater spending on the US Navy and US Air Force.

It became even clearer that the British government was informed, rather than consulted, about unleashing the dogs of war from British soil. Not only did British back-bench MPs have no say in the matter – British ministers had scarcely any more, and that included the then Defence Secretary, George Younger, MP, who on the very morning of the raid, 14 April, told his constituents on Radio Ayr,

> Something has got to be done. I think my colleagues and I are very dubious as to whether a military strike is the best way of doing this. It is liable to hit the wrong people, it creates other tensions in the area. There are certainly a lot of other things that can be done which my colleagues are certainly looking at very hard – further withdrawals of diplomats from offending countries, actions like reducing

trade and reducing contacts of one sort and another with those who refuse to outlaw terrorism.[7]

These are hardly the words of a man who expected action to take place that very night. The truth is that the Cabinet minister most immediately responsible was not consulted, but simply told what he had to do. This hardly reflects the working of proper Cabinet government. It was Mrs Thatcher and Mrs Thatcher alone among the British who had some say in the bombing of Libya. With the political demise of Mrs Thatcher there was the opportunity for a restoration of Cabinet government. But, as the Gulf was to show, scrutiny by Parliament has not been restored.

REFLECTIONS ON CAMPAIGNING

Where does an MP go for his information? Again, it is a question of *'chacun à son goût'*, and I can only present a personal view, without pretending to speak for my colleagues.

Above all else, an MP should go to sources who would have no hesitation in telling the MP that he was wrong, or that he was barking up the wrong tree, or that his preconceived ideas were unsupported by the facts of the situation.

In my opinion, this is one of the weaknesses of the system of MPs employing research assistants. Any amount of reading is not a substitute for the confidence that comes from first-hand knowledge. Moreover, research assistants cannot be expected to be universal experts. And, naturally, those like the Cambridge scholar, Guillermo Makin, who were extremely important to me for their expertise about Argentina during the Falklands conflict, would themselves not wish to give detailed opinions on the Middle East, Indian Ocean, or Far East. So, it is a matter of choosing experts. And, in my experience, this presents no problems for an MP who is prepared to ask for advice, in person, himself or herself. If anyone says that an expert has been unforthcoming, it is usually because that expert has been approached through a research assistant. If an MP goes to the trouble of a personal approach, cooperation is the reward.

MPs are in a position to accumulate friends for life among many different types of expert. For example, I was fortunate to be a member of the Labour Delegation to the European Parliament, 1976–79, and to find that Lord Brimelow was one of our Labour team. The most skilful drafter of a document whom I ever saw in action, he had been in charge of the Consular section of the Embassy in Moscow during the war, 'brought up', as he put it, 'under Stalin', and had risen to be permanent under-secretary at the Foreign Office. He was the most direct, and therefore valuable, of friends, in that he would identify the silly or the unwise, in any course of action or speech that I proposed. Equally, Kipling's *If* applies, in relation to 'all men counting, but none too much'.

Another example would be my intellectual debt to the Bradford School of Peace Studies. Early in the Falklands saga I heard Dr Paul Rogers of Bradford University on the radio, and was interested by the depth of his technical knowledge about weapons systems. I contacted him, and initiated what was to become a lasting friendship, covering many areas and subjects of mutual interest. As in the Falklands, so during the Gulf War I relied on Dr Rogers and his Bradford colleague, Malcolm Dando, for expertise about the policy conclusions from the deployment of weapons systems. For example, the three of us realised that as soon as the Second Squadron of Tornadoes was despatched to the Gulf, which unlike the First Squadron were deep-strike aircraft, there were aggressive intentions by the Thatcher government to invade Iraq. That wasn't clear, either to members of the Coalition such as Egypt, or to the United Nations under whose auspices the campaign was supposedly being conducted. To criticise defence policy, or certainly to mount a serious critique of it, an MP must have access to the kind of serious analysis provided by Bradford. To criticise the Foreign Office, an MP must have access to the level of expertise provided to me by Akbar Ahmed, Professor of Arabic Studies in Cambridge during the Gulf War. If an MP goes into an argument devoid of expert friends who are as committed as he is to the cause, he ought to think twice about starting. Lord Brimelow and other heavyweights of the '*surtout, pas trop de zèle*' school have their invaluable place, particularly in the prevention of own goals. But one also needs the informed enthusiast, who feels passionately about the issue and is prepared to commit time and effort. It is also necessary to take seriously what intellectual heavyweights who have a different opinion are saying in the public print, and that is why I have always carefully read the contributions of Professor Lawrence Freedman.

Finally, there is one other source of information which is priceless if it is forthcoming but must be handled with the greatest of care – that is, the 'deep-throat element'.

In any campaign, the MP involved will become a receptacle for information. Much – maybe 99 per cent – of the information will be encouraging; some will doubtless be derogatory; some will contain shrewd comment or open up new angles; the occasional letter will be crucial, if it comes from an inside source, and that really means someone in the position of a civil servant, who would get into great trouble if their identity was pin-pointed. When I received an anonymous letter, that later most of Britain was to learn came from Clive Ponting, I realised it could only have been written by someone who knew of letters I had just received from the Secretary of State for Defence about the *Belgrano*, and who was aware, as an outsider could not possibly have been aware at that time, of the role of Number 10 Downing Street. Mercifully, I thought long and hard what to do, and eschewed the temptation to give it to the press. Had I done so, I have no doubt, nor has he, that Clive Ponting would have ended up in Pentonville Jail. Because I kept the letter as a Proceeding in Parliament by giving it to the Chairman of the Select Committee on Foreign Affairs, the Jury at the Old Bailey were disposed to take a rather different view of Clive Ponting's intent than had the matter simply burst on the public through the press. The issue, which might have been seen as a cheap publicity stunt, came to be seen for what it actually was, the deceit of Parliament.

If there is to be accountability, then it is of paramount importance that the House of Commons should come to know when it is being deceived. In practice, this can only happen when a 'deep-throat' is either prepared to give information, or, at least, as Clive Ponting did, to prompt an MP to ask the right questions – questions which he might not otherwise know about, still less that they should be asked of ministers.

Of course, it could be argued – in some areas with justice – that an MP who looked at the public record carefully would not need informed outside information, let alone a 'deep-throat'. I am not sure that such a contention fits in with practice. MPs are busy people, with an itsy-bitsy day-to-day life of trying to satisfy other people, usually at short notice. We do not have the meticulous approach that we ought to, or time to reflect and ponder over answers.

So in scrutinising the public record, as set out in the official report, *Hansard*, we are often not as clever at follow-up as we should be – or as energetic. Besides, whereas very few ministerial answers actually tell lies, they are sometimes economical with the truth (in such cases, I tend to write letters to ministers which are more difficult to evade than Parliamentary Questions requiring necessarily brief answers). In the case of the *Belgrano*, there was deceit – but it needed much sweat by me, and the legitimate verbal skill of an exceedingly clever clerk in the Table Office, by training a First Class Honours Oxford philologist, to extract something like the truth from embarrassed ministers and civil servants.

The difficulty is encapsulated by a true tale. I was struggling away in the Table Office with the clerk, whose brief is to help members get what they want, provided we ourselves know what we want to ask, when in came Rt. Hon. Enoch Powell to place a question. 'Enoch,' said I, 'over the *Belgrano*, one needs a knowledge of Greek iambics to get at the truth, and untangle ministerial answers.' The response was brief, friendly, and in his opinion, factual, 'Tam, you need a knowledge of Greek iambics for everything in parliamentary life', and out he stomped.

If the clerks at the Table are clever, so are the scholars, for scholars they are, of the International Affairs Division of the Commons Library. In using the Library, I have found each individual has strengths, and therefore I go to particular members of the Library. Their particular strength is information gleaned from newspapers and periodicals of other languages. But they do not, nor should they, provide political 'ammunition' for individual MPs.

MPs who hunt as a pack or group can be most effective. And this can be, as is done, on comparatively straightforward issues, let us say, free school milk. It is much more difficult when the issue is complex, and most foreign policy issues are complex. I would like to think that my relations with other Labour (and Tory) back-bench critics were warm and friendly. But the prevailing attitude tended to be, 'We're right behind him, we will grunt our support in the House, but for God's sake leave Aldabra or the *Belgrano* to Tam Dalyell!'

Indeed, this is a rational use of time and energy. We had better not try to be universal experts, and in twenty-nine years as a Member of the House of Commons, I have never once asked a Parliamentary Question on the important issue of Housing! In promoting accountability, the important requirement is not co-ordination, but the goodwill of parliamentary colleagues.

Equally, it is no use supposing that MPs are perpetually being carried forward into combat with the government on a tail-wind of constituency outrage. These manifestations of public opinion vary, and are often more supposed than real. If there are heart-rending pictures to be seen on television, such as those of Cambodian or Ethiopian children, there will be a number of letters, and one or two telephone calls. More typical, I fear, is the attitude of a well-informed Bo'ness miner, who when I lamented that only eight people in the town of 10,000 had bothered to attend my meeting on the seemingly contentious Common Market entry issue, retorted: 'Well, what do we tax-payers pay you for, other than to make up your _ _ _ _ _ _ _ mind!'

NOTES

1 John Strachey, *The End of Empire*, London, Gollancz, 1959.
2 *Hansard*, 22 November 1967, col. 1341.
3 George Thomas, *Mr Speaker: The Memoirs of the Viscount Tonypandy*, London, Century, 1988.
4 Arthur Gavshon and Desmond Rice, *The Sinking of the Belgrano*, London, Secker & Warburg, 1984.
5 Tam Dalyell, *Misrule: How Mrs Thatcher has Misled Parliament from the Sinking of the Belgrano to the Wright Affair*, London, Hamilton, 1987.
6 William Broyles, 'The Politics of War', *US News and World Report*, 12 May 1986.
7 Quoted in Tam Dalyell, *Misrule*, op. cit. See also Terry Coleman's interview with Secretary of State for Defence George Younger, in *The Guardian*, 24 April 1986.

Part IV

Practical dilemmas and the two worlds

8   Between two worlds
Think-tanks and foreign policy

William Wallace

The origins of the academic discipline of international relations and of independent institutes of international affairs are to be found in the same revulsion at secret diplomacy among states which erupted after the Great War of 1914–18. The academic discipline and the policy research community developed from the same liberal impulse; their members moving easily between the two, and seeing no great tension between the two activities. Foreign policy and diplomacy had until 1914 remained 'matters of state', insulated from the advance of democratic accountability and detailed research over domestic social and economic policies over the previous decades. Reasoned argument and democratic control – it was hoped – would now exercise their benign influence on this most secret and central field of state sovereignty. Advice to government, while remaining independent of government; information to raise the quality of public debate, covering areas previously considered confidential; long-term thinking on international developments, without losing touch with those responsible for day-to-day policy; these were the common objectives of academics and advisers after 1918. They remain the delicate objectives which foreign policy think-tanks struggle to pursue.

As in many other areas of social science, the Anglo-Saxon model set the shape which others followed. The 'British Institute of International Affairs' was founded in 1920, and received its royal charter in 1926 – two years after the London School of Economics had appointed Philip Noel-Baker as its first professor of International Relations. The impetus to establish what was originally intended to be a single institute, with branches in London, New York, and other capitals of the British Empire, had stemmed from the group of young temporary civil servants and advisers who had been attached to the British and American delegations to the Versailles Peace Conference: a group which included the young Noel-Baker, John Maynard Keynes, Arnold Toynbee and

Philip Kerr, with Lord Robert Cecil, Harold Nicolson and others later to play leading roles also included in the British delegation. Shaken by the behaviour of their elders, they resolved 'to encourage and facilitate the study of international questions and to promote the exchange of information, knowledge and thought on international affairs' by establishing an institute independent of foreign ministries and governments, which would operate 'by means of lectures and discussions and by the preparation and publication of books, records, reports, or other works'.[1]

Independence, expertise, discussion, scholarship and publications, aimed at providing the political and social elites interested in international issues with ideas and information outside the control of the government of the day: this was the model of a foreign policy think-tank which was received in country after country for 50 years after 1919. The Council on Foreign Relations in New York was the twin of the BIIA. Members of the German delegation set up a similar body in Hamburg – which was closed in the 1930s but succeeded immediately after the Second World War by the Deutsche Gesellschaft für Auswärtige Politik in Bonn. Others followed in the 1920s in Paris and Rome; while 'branches' of the RIIA (as it became in 1926) grew into sister institutes in Ottawa, Canberra, Johannesburg and Auckland. Exiles from occupied countries who found themselves working in the Chatham House library during the Second World War, or working under Toynbee in the institute's information department (expanded and taken under Foreign Office auspices during the war) returned to their capitals to set up a second wave of national institutes of international affairs.

In the Anglo-Saxon world of the 1920s and 1930s, the distinction now firmly established between 'academic' and 'policy' research scarcely existed. Enlightened men, of learning and leisure, moved in and out of the worlds of academia, government and politics without observing too closely the boundaries between them. Arnold Toynbee began his career as a fellow of Balliol College, Oxford (in Greek and Ancient History); became a temporary civil servant in both world wars, a full-time professor at King's College London after the First World War, and Stevenson Professor at the London School of Economics while Director of Studies at Chatham House. Through his father-in-law, Professor Gilbert Murray, and Murray's mother-in-law the Countess of Carlisle, Toynbee had from the outset access to the world of London dinner parties and country house weekends through which the conventional wisdom of political ideas was still shaped.[2] The very small circles of those actively interested in ideas and international issues meant that each man (almost without exception they *were* men, though

Toynbee's second wife later contributed a great deal to his work) played many parts, and institutions and activities overlapped. Chatham House in the 1930s sponsored studies of such fundamental questions as *Nationalism* (1939), as well as more detailed studies of *The Future of Monetary Policy* (1935) and *The Problem of International Investment* (1937), commissioned volumes on such regional and national issues as the development of modern China and the interaction between Islam and Christendom, annual *Surveys of International Affairs* and a parallel series of *Documents*. Chatham House also sponsored and published David Mitrany's classic study of functionalism, *A Working Peace System* (1943), and Martin Wight's ninety-page essay on *Power Politics* (1946).

The Second World War brought renewed efforts to apply social science to policy-making. It brought, also, a second generation of academics into government service in Britain and the United States; with governments themselves setting up new planning staffs and research units to prepare for the post-war world. The impact of the great wave of exiled intellectuals from central Europe added a further dimension: leaving only a limited impression on British approaches to international relations, but making a much larger impact on American government, institutes and universities. The approach to war shattered the liberal consensus, with 'realist' critics such as E.H. Carr attacking their faith in reason and persuasion in international politics.[3] The onset of the Cold War further divided idealists from realists, with governments calling for academic 'commitment' to the struggle against Communism, and imposing tests and obligations of secrecy on those they co-opted to advise them. Idealist assumptions that reasoned argument and open debate could improve the quality of inter-governmental relations, perhaps even transform them into a more peaceful form, aroused little sympathy among those struggling with the realist dilemmas and cultural confrontations of the East–West conflict.

The post-war growth of academic analysis of military strategy and global politics in the USA fed back only slowly into Britain and other West European countries. The Institute of Strategic Studies, founded in London in 1958, was the first of a new European wave: set up to provide a focus for a debate till then dominated by American experts in and out of government, on the initiative of the Commission on International Affairs of the British Council of Churches, with the support of Labour and Liberal opposition MPs and a number of retired officers and officials, and with financial support from the Ford Foundation.[4] In the decade which followed – the optimistic years of sustained economic growth and improving East–West relations – West European governments came to appreciate the value of independent sources of advice, most particularly in responding to the ideas which spilled out of the new appointees of the Kennedy Administration about Atlantic relations, economic development, the management of nuclear strategy and East–West relations. Government funding was provided for institutes – and for policy-relevant research in universities, encouraging the growth of academic international relations as European universities themselves expanded from educating a small elite towards mass higher education. The weakening of post-war consensus politics, on foreign policy as on domestic issues, which followed in the late 1960s and 1970s, led parties and factions to establish their own intellectual 'clubs', and where funds could be found their own institutes: creating the spectrum of foreign policy think-tanks which we see today.

WHAT IS A THINK TANK?

Institutes working on foreign policy vary from the thousand-strong Academy of Sciences bodies of 1980s Moscow, through such venerable generalist entities as the Brookings Institution in Washington, to impressively titled but tiny groups operating on the fringes of political 'respectability' and financial survival. At one end of the spectrum such institutes fade into government agencies; at the other into university departments – or into campaigning groups. Classification is best attempted through a list of the central functions which policy institutes set out to fulfil. To one degree or another, these must include:

1 Intellectual analysis of policy issues; using approaches drawn from history, social science, law, or even mathematics, applied to issues relevant to government;
2 Concern with the ideas and concepts which underlie policy; examining, and questioning, the 'conventional wisdom' which shapes day-to-day policy-making;
3 Collection and classification of information relevant to policy – ranging from detailed research to provision of press reports and documents on which others can draw;
4 A longer-term perspective than that which is open to policy-makers, looking at trends rather than immediate events;
5 A degree of detachment both from government and from the immediate partisan political debate;
6 A degree of involvement with government – whether seeking to influence it indirectly through publications and through its impact on

the policy debate, or to engage in discussions with ministers or officials directly;

7 A commitment to inform a wider audience: through publication, through meetings and discussions which involve a wider and more diverse group than government or the academic community alone.

Not all foreign policy think-tanks fulfil all of these 'classic' functions. Their ability to fulfil them depends upon the national context and culture within which they operate – which will be discussed further below. Closeness to government – or distance from government – varies immensely from institute to institute and from country to country. American think-tanks are often characterised by the interchange between their staffs and government, through the 'revolving door' of political appointments (as also are the social science faculties of the major American universities, which have not yet developed the fear of contamination through contact with government which afflicts their British counterparts). But few other countries have such open or regular exchanges between government service and the intellectual world. Independence is a quality hard to maintain in many political systems; constructive criticism is not always distinguished from opposition by those in power, leaving those who seek to influence policy from the outside to strike delicate compromises in challenging the conventional wisdom without stepping too far outside it.

A useful further distinction may be made between institutes which see their task as to inform the domestic (and international) debate on foreign policy, without adopting a particular perspective, and those which set out to promote a particular perspective: between *forum think-tanks* and *committed think-tanks*. The charter of the Royal Institute of International Affairs had as a 'fundamental' principle that the Institute as such should offer no settled view; that it should act as a forum for a range of views, concerned only that they should be well argued and cogently presented. The principle is still restated in every Chatham House publication: that 'the Royal Institute of International Affairs is an unofficial body which promotes the scientific study of international questions and does not express opinions of its own. The opinions expressed in this publication are the responsibility of its authors.'

Almost all of the first wave of national institutes of international affairs adopted this Chatham House principle, along with the famous 'Chatham House rule' that discussions among officials and non-officials, between partisans of different parties and journalists from competing papers under the institute's auspices should be entirely confidential, to enable all those present to speak freely. 'Members are reminded that they are free to use the information received, but that neither the identity nor the affiliation of the speaker(s) nor that of any other participant may be revealed, nor may it be mentioned that the information was received at a meeting of the institute.'[5] The assumption underlying such rules is essentially that of liberal idealism, that reasonable people sitting round a table without their public positions to defend will find some degree of common understanding – at least, of common discourse.

For those who reject such liberal sentiments, the world of policy advice is necessarily more conflictual. As under the pressures of the Cold War international issues became more central to domestic politics, and more divisive within domestic politics, so committed groups began to set up their own think-tanks to promote their preferred approaches. Peace research institutes blossomed across Western Europe in the 1960s and 1970s, some of them sponsored by social democratic governments to challenge the conventional wisdom of their own 'foreign policy establishment' – or to satisfy the idealist sentiments of their supporters. The Institute for Policy Studies in Washington, founded in 1963 by disillusioned Kennedy appointees, linked in to this alternative network through its associated Transnational Institute, with branches in London and Amsterdam.

Suspicion of 'liberals' in the State Department and the American foreign policy establishment, and conservative reaction against the first moves towards East–West détente, led to the parallel creation of a succession of conservative think-tanks: starting with the transformation (in 1959) of the Hoover Institution from a library and resource centre on the Communist world to a focus for research committed to an anti-communist and free enterprise perspective, and the creation of the Center for Strategic and International Studies (CSIS) in Georgetown in 1962.[6] CSIS, like the American Enterprise Institute (AEI) out of which it grew, saw itself as presenting careful research and reasoned arguments from a conservative perspective, in competition with the perceived liberal perspective of the Brookings Institution's foreign policy programme. Hoover was from the outset more passionate and combative than CSIS, less willing to grant that others might have legitimate grounds for taking different positions – an institute which saw itself, in effect, as fighting the Cold War with all the intellectual weapons at its disposal. The Vietnam War, and widening differences within and between Western states about preferred policies towards the countries of the Warsaw Pact and the CMEA, led to a further surge of committed institutes in the United States and Britain: most of them on the right, financially underwritten by sympathetic American businesses and foundations.[7]

Some of the best-known American contributions to the debate on foreign policy come from 'generalist' policy institutes like Brookings and the AEI; which set out to cover a wide spectrum of issues of public policy, their foreign policy programmes overlapping and interacting with domestic economic and social research. Almost all relevant European bodies, however, specialise primarily in international issues. As from the end of the 1950s onwards policy research has expanded and institutes have proliferated; many, in Europe and North America, have cultivated 'niche' policy markets: military strategy, overseas economic development, international monetary policy and trade, or regional emphases such as Latin America or East Asia. The smallness of foreign policy elites (or 'establishments') in the inter-war years made for institutes which covered the whole spread of international issues, within which limited knowledge could be pooled. Post-war expansion, both of government and of the international agenda, has made for a compartmentalisation of the world of policy influence. Institutes of overseas development relate to aid agencies, inside and outside government, and are largely funded by them. Strategic studies institutes operate in a different network, of ministries of defence, staff colleges, defence suppliers and specialist journals. The rise of environmental issues in international politics has created another network of institutes (and of programmes within institutes), bringing expert scientists into contact with national and international agencies, specialised companies, campaigning lobbies, and the environmental press.

National and transnational networks interrelate, with specialised international organisations and regular conferences bringing national experts together. Awareness of the importance of this informal debate among foreign policy elites in feeding ideas back into policy-making within the major 'Western' states has, indeed, pushed others to create or strengthen their own national think-tanks. Publication of a joint study on *Western Security* by the Council of Foreign Relations and the foreign affairs' institutes of Britain, France and Germany, in the uncertain aftermath of the invasion of Afghanistan, the military takeover in Poland, and the Iranian revolution, provoked the Dutch foreign ministry, in cooperation with the foreign affairs spokesmen of the major parties, to reorganise several small bodies into a stronger Dutch Institute of International Affairs (Klingendaal), to strengthen the case for Dutch participation in any similar future exercise. Some institutes (like the London-based International Institute for Strategic Studies (IISS)) explicitly promote a transnational policy debate. Most aim to influence thinking in other national capitals as well as their own. The Heritage Foundation, one of the most vigorous of Washington's 'counter-establishment' think-tanks of the right, played a significant role in persuading the British government to follow the USA in withdrawing from membership of UNESCO in 1985; its involvement in international 'campaigns to attack the UN and its agencies' was criticised by the House of Commons Foreign Affairs Committee.[8]

Almost without exception, think-tanks see it as their function to draw in to their discussions people from different professions and backgrounds: to promote the exchange of ideas, to cross the conventional boundaries between types of expertise and experience. University professors sit round the table with military officers and diplomats, with journalists from the quality press, businessmen and bankers, politicians and their research assistants, professional lobbyists and the staff of campaigning groups. The character of the mix depends upon each institute's self-image and declared purpose, as well as upon the topics being studied: 'establishment' or 'counter-establishment', idealist or realist, close to government or business or critical of them.

Funding is of course a central issue – and for most institutes a central problem. Dependence on government for funding inhibits vigorous criticism of government policy; though in several countries government-funded institutes have nevertheless provided effective critiques of the conventional wisdom (as the following section will note). Finance from business or banks carries similar limitations in how far 'thinking the unthinkable' may stray from the conventional wisdom of the business community. Foundation support depends upon satisfying the priorities of each particular foundation: whether to promote market principles or world peace, to approach East–West relations (or European unity) sympathetically or unsympathetically, even to employ a sufficient proportion of women in senior positions.

Foundations – most of all American foundations, though German and Japanese foundations also became significant funders of institutes in other countries in the 1970s and 1980s – have played a crucial role in the development of think-tanks as the most easily available sources of support outside of government. The Carnegie Endowment was one of Chatham House's early major supporters. In the late 1930s a quarter of the Institute's entire income was coming from the Rockefeller Foundation; a third American foundation – Ford – was the institute's largest funder for much of the 1960s. Ford Foundation money not only assisted the development of the IISS, but also sponsored national institutes for strategic and international studies in several Mediterranean European states, in Latin America and East Asia; it played an active part in the creation of several of these, and went on to fund networking conferences with the IISS and other established institutes.

The earliest institutes, like the Council on Foreign Relations and Chatham House, built up a degree of long-term independence through initial endowments, supplemented through subscriptions from a large personal and institutional membership; though they have nevertheless needed additional grants for specific research projects to supplement this core funding. Diversity of funding sources decreases a think-tank's vulnerability to the disapproval of major funders – at the cost of condemning institute directors to constant fundraising, in contrast to those who rely on the security of subventions from government. Critics of think-tank approaches seize upon their funding patterns to argue that they are 'paid to promote' the arguments they put forward. Government-funded institutes are always open to the charge that they dare not challenge the government line. Suspicion of Japanese intentions among those promoting industrial and mercantilist policies in Washington was such by the early 1990s that the Institute of International Economics thought it wise to include in its publications a note on the modest percentage of its funding which came from Japan.[9]

There is a necessary ambivalence about the relationship between think-tanks and their sponsors. Governments, and private sponsors, are paying for intelligent criticism; but they are looking for 'constructive' criticism, within certain limits. The modern Machiavellis who staff the institutes strive to be imaginative and innovative, while couching their arguments in language which their intended audience will accept. The head of the OECD Long-term Futures Unit described the purpose of his international think-tank to a prospective OECD member government as one of living in a dangerously symbiotic relationship:

> The relationship between the academic social scientist and the policy-maker should be like that between the pilot fish and the shark. You should never get too close – for then you risk being eaten up. But equally you should never get too far away – because then the shark will no longer follow you.[10]

NATIONAL CONTEXTS, NATIONAL STYLES

Institutes – like universities – operate within distinctive national environments, and are unavoidably shaped by the need to adapt to that environment. The secrecy or openness of the policy-making process, the character of the relationship between government and opposition, the availability (or non-availability) of the press as a medium for getting across non-conventional ideas, all affect the way in which think-tanks pursue their efforts to inform and influence. The style of the national elite – intellectual or anti-intellectual, open to long-term thinking or committed to a belief in 'pragmatism' – also constrains the institutes which struggle to catch their attention.

Britain

The British political system remained throughout the 1980s – as through previous decades – dominated by an elite self-image of pragmatism, despite the incursions into domestic and foreign policy of strong ideological convictions.[11] A settled reluctance to examine received views made for easy dismissal of intellectual analysis as 'academic' and 'airy-fairy'. There was almost no demand for long-term thinking on international issues within government, within Parliament, or in the business elite – except from the handful of mineral and chemical companies whose operations necessitated long investment lead-times and exposure to political risk.[12] The chairman of one of the major clearing banks once dismissed a Chatham House draft on potential changes in the international economy over the next five years as 'an absurd attempt to second-guess the markets'.[13] Institutes which sought to influence the established elites had therefore to concentrate on detailed historical and contemporary research to catch attention, taking care not to stray too far from the conventional wisdom and lay themselves open to charges of impracticality or irresponsibility.

The tradition of secrecy in foreign policy, the weakness of parliamentary oversight of international economic, political and military policy-making, the low status of planning and analytical work within government, have all limited the ability of outside institutes in Britain to influence policy. After the wartime enthusiasms of 1939–45, post-war British governments sank back into closed patterns of incremental policy-making. Chatham House in the 1950s was the only outside body of importance; with a shrinking endowment, and without government funding to fill the gap, it was losing direction and impetus.

The Labour Opposition at the beginning of the 1960s, however, took from the Democratic US Administration an enthusiasm for what outside policy analysis might offer progressive government. Coming into office in 1964, it set up the Social Science Research Council to fund policy-relevant academic work, and underwrote the Overseas Development Institute (and the Institute of Development Studies at the University of Sussex) to apply intellectual rigour to aid policy. Within both the Foreign Office and the Ministry of Defence planning staffs and functions were upgraded.[14] Foreign Office funds began to support

Chatham House projects. The government-supported Royal United Services Institution was reorganised and refunded (from public and private sources); ministers cultivated the IISS. The 1966 Defence Review announced that the government was determined to increase intellectual interchange by encouraging 'the universities to play a more active role in higher defence studies and to stimulate academic awareness of defence problems' – by sponsoring a number of university posts and providing fellowships in universities and institutes for senior officers and officials.[15]

In retrospect the period from the mid-1960s to the mid-1970s can be seen as the golden age of forum foreign policy think-tanks in Britain. Government money flowed, both directly and through the SSRC; members of different political parties met round the table and agreed reasonably to disagree. The great exceptions were policy towards Europe, on which both major parties were divided, and defence, which divided Labour in office and in opposition; these created difficulties for Chatham House, attempting to address the broad issues of foreign policy and national interest, but affected the more specialised think-tanks very little. The Institute of Economic Affairs (IEA) and the Trade Policy Research Centre (TPRC) were to some extent on the edge of the consensus, with commitment to free trade (and scepticism about the European Community) driving their research efforts, in self-conscious contrast to the more consensual approach to international issues of the National Institute for Economic and Social Research.[16]

The challenge of the New Right to what it saw as 'consensus politics' was a challenge to the whole tradition of 'rational' social science applied to problems of government. The Social Science Research Council itself escaped abolition in 1980/81 only thanks to Lord Rothschild's robust defence – with its budget sharply cut, and the claim to 'science' removed from the retitled 'Economic and Social Research Council'.[17] Institutes specialising in development and environmental questions lost all or most of their government grants; FCO support for Chatham House, which had approached 10 per cent of the institute's funding in the 1970s, sank back to a modest corporate subscription, before recovering to around 5 per cent in the late 1980s.

The new think-tanks which sprang up alongside the IEA (and the Institute for the Study of Conflict, the earliest of the 'realist' foreign policy think-tanks) were small, passionately committed, and concerned only with providing arguments for those already half-persuaded. They drew heavily on conservative American perspectives, and benefited from transatlantic conservative funding. The Adam Smith Institute's series of 'Omega' reports in 1984 included one on foreign policy, recommending *inter alia* the creation of a 'National Security Council' in No. 10 to hold the liberal internationalism of the FCO in check. The Institute for European Defence and Strategic Studies and the International Freedom Foundation had particularly close links with like-minded Washington bodies; the former publishing robustly anti-Soviet papers, the latter sponsoring visits and lectures by leading anti-Communists from the Third World.[18]

Political patronage from the Prime Minister and those close to her ensured access to government and encouraged corporate support. *The Times*, both before and after its takeover by Rupert Murdoch, and the *Daily* and *Sunday Telegraph*, provided platforms through which to reach a wider audience. The depth of divisions within the opposition on European policy and on defence inhibited any attempt to build an intellectual alternative; perhaps the most impressive was the Alternative Defence Commission, a limited-term exercise initiated by groups concerned with peace and disarmament, with the Department of Peace Studies at Bradford University providing research support.[19]

But the weakness of Parliament and its committees as a focus for the foreign policy debate meant that private debates within the right and the left scarcely interacted with each other. The central issues of British foreign policy – relations with the USA, Germany and France, the question of European integration, defence posture and expenditure, foreign economic policy – continued to divide both British politics and British political parties throughout the 1980s; the passionately committed clashed, without greatly informing waverers or moving the debate forward. Both the Centre for Policy Studies and the Institute of Economic Affairs divided over policy towards Europe after Mrs Thatcher's resignation, with fundamentalists opposing the efforts of younger people to come to terms with an international environment which was – after 1989 – undergoing rapid and radical transformation. The role of committed think-tanks, these fundamentalists argued in effect, was to provide evidence to reinforce the beliefs of their supporters, not to re-examine those beliefs in the light of changing circumstances.

The weakness – and lack of resources – of Parliament and the political parties has also hampered the flow of people and ideas between the intellectual and policy-making worlds. The House of Commons lacked committees on either defence or foreign affairs until the 1970s; thereafter a handful of clerks held together small committees with little influence and almost no funds, with a single outside adviser retained to help in each report.[20] The Conservative Party's research department had two young men working on international issues through the 1970s – and rarely more than one during the 1980s; the Labour Party closed its International Department in the mid-1980s as one of a series of economy measures. Government initiatives to encourage exchanges between academics and officials, since the 1960s, have brought many more out of Whitehall and the armed services to spend attachments in universities and institutes than have moved from the outside in. Intermittent Foreign Office efforts have brought in a handful of outsiders over 30 years, most of them from the academic world: into diplomatic posts and into the Arms Control and Disarmament Unit in the 1960s, into the Planning Staff since 1979. The emergence of political advisers to ministers across Whitehall over the past 25 years has not fed back into institutes and universities, and only in a few instances recruited from them.

The USA

The contrast between the British and American context for think-tanks – across the whole range of domestic and international issues – remains immense. The liberalism of America's dominant political culture is much more sympathetic to the image of expertise, of rational and scientific analysis. The division of powers between President and Congress makes for a structural competition for policy analysis and proposals, spreading outwards from government agencies and Congressional committees to the lobbies which compete to catch their ear. Universities with a strongly entrenched research tradition, inherited from the German rather than the English model, have for almost a century been training social scientists to bring rational methods to bear on problems of government. Woodrow Wilson, an idealist in international relations and a rationalist in politics, moved from Princeton to the White House. The Woodrow Wilson School, with its strong international relations programme, trained generations of others to follow him from studying policy to analysing and making it: an approach which blossomed, in the 1960s and 1970s, into schools of public policy at major US universities, many of them overlapping with Washington think-tanks in their research and policy analysis.

One recent study estimates that the USA contains over 1,200 think-tanks, not counting university-based research institutes.[21] The number within the Washington area alone which include international issues within their remit, or specialise in some aspect of American foreign policy or international relations, approaches three figures – large and small, magisterial and partisan, long-established and ephemeral. They interact with (and exchange personnel with) the thousands of 'experts' within the official policy-making community: planning staffs in the State Department and the Pentagon, academics seconded to the National Security Council, foreign policy specialists in the Congressional Research Service, the Budget Office, and the Office of Technology and Assessment, committee staffs to both Houses of Congress, and staff members to senators and congressmen with particular international interests. The presence of the World Bank and the IMF in Washington, and of the United Nations in New York, further widens this market for ideas, with funds flowing out to consultancies and institutes and advice flowing in.

Dispersion of power, and funding, has created the market for ideas which think-tanks compete to supply. The rise of committed think-tanks on the right has been matched by committed think-tanks on the left; free trade proponents are countered by promoters of industrial policies and 'fair trade' – analysis fading into lobbying in the vigour with which the Heritage Foundation, the Economic Policy Institute and others press their ideas onto those they seek to influence. The arrival of each new administration is greeted by a plethora of 'agenda-setting' papers, many of whose authors move rapidly into administration positions; their places in the think-tank world then occupied by those they replace, and by younger analysts hopeful that their ideas will also help to reshape the world (and carry them into positions of influence themselves). From an outsider's perspective, Washington appears substantially over-supplied with think-tanks, in domestic as in foreign policy. Their proliferation stems from the fragmentation of power in Washington, with competing agencies and Congressional committees drawing on different institutes to support their preferred policy directions, as well as on the fragmentation of the 1960s consensus on foreign policy, defence and international economic policy.

Germany

The federal German political system is marked both by a search for consensus on foreign policy and by a respect for impartial research. Both stem from Germany's broken history. Re-establishment of democratic government in West Germany after the Second World War brought an active concern to encourage informed and reasoned debate through state support, far stronger than has been thought necessary in either Britain or France. National and regional governments have funded competing economic institutes to criticise government policy; state funds flowed into party foundations to support research and educational activities in domestic and external policy.[22] To some extent German foreign policy was conducted through the German party foundations in the 1960s and 1970s – as formally non-governmental institutions able to act independently while a still-hesitant Bonn government operated through multilateral channels. The Konrad Adenauer and Friedrich Ebert Foundations include a number of experts on foreign policy, and have close links with their parties in the Bundestag – as well as offices in a large number of third countries, and funds to support conferences, visits and publications.

The Deutsche Gesellschaft für Auswärtige Politik had re-established the tradition of reasoned debate and round-table discussions in Bonn after the war, with an active meetings programme, a library, journal (*Europa Archiv*), yearbook, and small group of researchers, largely supported by direct and indirect government funding. As Bonn moved in the 1960s towards a more confident international role it was characteristic of the continuing search for an informed consensus that the parties in the Bundestag should have agreed to establish what has become Western Europe's largest foreign policy think-tank – the Stiftung für Wissenschaft und Politik in Ebenhausen – as an independent foundation funded through the budget of the Federal Chancellor's Office. An alternative network of peace research institutes, funded by SPD-governed *Länder*, was developed in parallel, providing to a limited extent a 'non-establishment' perspective.

With a superb library and some fifty researchers, the SWP supplies advice and publications to ministries and to their critics in the Bundestag, with access under certain conditions to classified material among its sources. Its staff also play an active role in contributing to the international expert debate on defence and foreign policy across the NATO and OECD world – all the more useful to the spread of informal German influence in view of the continuing weakness of academic international relations in German universities. But its very closeness to government, its generous and guaranteed funding – and its separation by several hundred kilometres from the process of foreign policy-making in Bonn – limit its influence. Writing and researching for the public good in a political system characterised by consensus and by internal party debates has left SWP researchers uncertain for whom they are writing, or which aspects of the foreign policy debate they are trying to influence. The lack of demand from political or business elites for alternative views or non-consensual analysis, at least until the early 1990s, has inhibited the growth of policy research on international issues, leaving the quality press and its commentators as the main providers of critical views.

France

Different style and different political culture make for a contrasting picture in France. The German debate on foreign policy spreads from Bonn through Munich and Frankfurt to Hamburg and Berlin; the French debate is concentrated in central Paris. The British debate is characterised by an absence of interchange between different career paths; the French debate is dominated by a small elite, mostly trained in the École des Sciences Politiques, the École Polytechnique, and ENA (École Nationale d'Administration), moving on through the *grands corps*, ministerial cabinets and planning staffs into institutes, banks, industry and politics. Thierry de Montbrial, François Heisbourg, Pierre Lellouche, Dominique Möisi, Jean-Louis Gergorin, have marked the edges of a tight consensus on the limits of French foreign policy, which has stretched across the parties and into the small group of institutes – all close to government.

IFRI (Institut Français des Relations Internationales) was created out of the moribund post-Versailles Centre de Politique Étrangère in the mid-1970s, on the initiative of the Quai d'Orsay – as much to provide a stronger French input to the developing unofficial foreign policy debate within the NATO/OECD world as to raise the quality of the debate within France. Thierry de Montbrial, exceptional within the Quai d'Orsay in his American graduate training, moved from the ministerial planning staff he had established to direct the new institute, with substantial official funding. *Politique Étrangère*, the IFRI journal, is to be seen on official desks across Paris; the IFRI annual, *Ramses*, has rightly acquired a high reputation for its surveys of global economic and political developments. But IFRI's research – and the work of the smaller bodies funded by the Ministry of Defence – has skirted round many of the sensitive central themes of French foreign policy and defence.

To some extent the researchers of the state-funded Centre Nationale pour la Récherche Scientifique (CNRS), and in particular the 40 specialists of its Centre d'Études pour les Relations Internationales (CERI), provide a broader and more critical perspective.[23] Closely linked to Sciences Po., less prestigious and well-connected than IFRI, this constitutes the largest pool of academics working on international relations in France, and is responsible for a high proportion of the academic and informational literature – much of which is published through the official *Documentation Française*. The interpenetration of government and institutes, the geographical and social concentration of the elite debate, the weakness of critical commentary in the press, and the cross-party consensus since President de Gaulle on the *grandes lignes* of French foreign policy, make for a stifling of dissent and an unwillingness to address awkward issues which marks the Parisian foreign policy-making process out from that of any other advanced industrial country – except Japan.[24]

Japan

It is possible that the number of research institutes in Tokyo exceeds that in Washington. MITI itself supports close to twenty, fulfilling the role which research departments and planning units serve in other administrations. Most of the major banks and security companies have combined their research and planning functions into self-standing institutes, with large staffs in Tokyo and often with branches in other continents and capitals. Nomura Research Institute and its Daiwa and Mitsubishi equivalents have, for example, acquired high international reputations for the quality of their information-gathering and analytical work on international economic trends. The Japan Institute for International Affairs, sponsored by the Japanese foreign ministry, is far smaller than these, and remains dependent on seconded officials and ministerial backing. The Japan Centre for International Exchange, which developed from the Japanese secretariat for the Trilateral Commission into a clearing house for Japanese involvement in a range of bilateral and multilateral conferences and working groups, has played a leading role in linking Japanese policy 'influentials' into the informal international network of foreign policy thinkers and think-tanks. Mr Nakasone's establishment of the International Institute for Global Peace on his retirement from the prime ministership marked a further development: from direct or indirect dependence on government or company towards free-standing policy institutes working on international issues.

Yet, with very few exceptions, these many and excellent Japanese institutes avoid contentious policy issues. Working within a national culture and political system which are highly consensual, and which have preferred to pursue economic rather than political objectives in international relations, their focus is on long-term economic and technological trends rather than on more immediate policy dilemmas. As in France, critical examination of the assumptions which underpin national foreign policy is dangerous ground, to be avoided as far as possible; the long-term perspective is safer. Collaboration with think-tanks in other countries, often on Japanese initiative and with disproportionate Japanese financial support, has appeared to many observers as in part a strategy of importing the criticisms policy researchers would themselves like to make – of Japan's still passive role in international economic and political collaboration, of the need for Japan's domestic economic and political structures to adjust to their transformed international position. It is in keeping with the structure of Japanese society that the first demands for a more robust Japanese approach to international economic negotiations, and for a redefinition of Japan's sense of its international role, came not from the institute or university worlds but from that of business.[25]

The Soviet Union

The earliest policy advisers of whom we know – Aristotle tutoring the young Alexander, Seneca the young Nero, Machiavelli writing for the Medici, Thomas Hobbes for the future Charles II – addressed themselves to improving the quality of authoritarian rule. So too did the vast institutes which grew up within the USSR Academy of Sciences during the Cold War. Those which specialised on international issues were licensed to have access to Western books, journals, newspapers, radio and television within an otherwise closed society, to provide the expertise needed to understand the contradictions of the capitalist and Third Worlds: the 1,000-strong Institute of World Economics and International Relations (IMEMO), within which Donald Maclean wrote his studies of Britain, its Brezhnev-era rival the Institute for the study of the USA and Canada, the Oriental and Africa Institutes.

Entirely under the control of state and party, the most interesting aspect of the work of these think-tanks is how far they came to operate as alternative – even critical – sources of foreign policy advice in the 1980s, as the self-confidence of the Soviet leadership faltered and reforming influence grew. Privileged places to work in the 1970s, they were disproportionately staffed by children of the *nomenklatura*; IMEMO was briefly under a cloud in the early 1980s after junior staff had been apprehended for distributing alternative analyses in *samizdat* form. The director of the USA/Canada Institute, Gyorgy Arbatov, was a prominent 'kite-flyer' for Soviet foreign policy proposals under Brezhnev, operating with his staff on the edges of the informal intellectual network of foreign and defence policy specialists which had developed in the West. Gorbachev used IMEMO and other foreign policy institutes, as he used several of the economic institutes, to provide him with alternative sources of expertise to the entrenched state and party apparatus. Yakovlev, as director of IMEMO, and Yevgeny Primakov (previously director of the Oriental Institute) as his successor, moved gradually from advocates of change in foreign policy direction to become close advisers and policy-makers themselves.

SPEAKING TRUTH TO POWER: THE DILEMMAS OF INFLUENCE AND INDEPENDENCE

Truth speaks to power in many different tones of voice. The philosopher and cloistered intellectual, free of the ambition to serve a leader directly, can speak with an authority that does not need to bend the truth to justify pressing political ends. . .The policy adviser and expert, however, if they aspire to be of use, must speak to power in a political and bureaucratic context; and they must always speak a useful truth. Their claim to speak the truth must always be viewed in the light of their relationship with power.[26]

Think-tanks, like universities, are shaped by their political and social – and economic – environment; those that fail to adapt fail to survive. Think-tanks and universities interact in the study of international relations – reading each other's publications, drawing on each other's expertise.[27] The ambivalence of the relationship varies from country to country, depending upon the relativities of prestige, pay and power. By and large, however, think-tanks may be regarded – alongside government itself – as applied international relations, with universities focusing more on the theoretical and educational dimensions, at the cost of less direct contact with the international developments which they study.

Three generations ago the discipline of international relations was too rudimentary and thinly staffed for fine distinctions to be observed between categories. Theorists like E.H. Carr 'spoke truth to power directly', drawing on experience in government and developing their ideas round think-tank tables. In the professionalised complexities of the 1970s and 1980s the academic discipline largely stepped back from policy, leaving the proliferating mass of think-tanks to serve as a buffer between universities and government. American social science, with its preoccupation with the refinement of theory and methodology, has encouraged this differentiation; though American universities, much more than their counterparts in Britain or the European continent, have at the same time developed a vigorous public policy dimension of their own.

Effective policy institutes deal in 'applied theory': re-examining the concepts which guide policy-makers, which are themselves the simplified and half-remembered theories of earlier intellectuals.[28]

Thoughtful policy-makers recognise the value of turning to those who have more time and opportunity to reflect on underlying trends and their interpretation, particularly when faced with rapid international change. In the 1960s and 1970s the British Committee for International Studies, for example, brought together British (and Irish) officials and academics concerned with the broader issues of international relations to exchange ideas.[29]

The expansion of universities across the developed world in the 1960s, which brought with it in Britain and elsewhere the emergence of separate departments (or sub-departments) of international relations, overlapped with a period of relative consensus and declining international tension, during which complacent pragmatists within the British governing elite dismissed conceptualisation as academic mumbo-jumbo. At the last of the Bailey conferences which brought British students of international relations together before its replacement by the British International Studies Association, in 1972, an initiative from the FCO Planning Staff and the Royal Institute of International Affairs assembled a panel at Chatham House to discuss what insiders and outsiders could contribute to each other's work. The then Chief Inspector of Her Majesty's Diplomatic Service began his intervention by remarking that

> I am not sure what the academic discipline of international relations – if indeed there be such a thing as an academic discipline of international relations – has to contribute to the practical day-to-day work of making and managing foreign policy.[30]

The counter-establishment, launching its attack on prevailing concepts of foreign policy during the following decade, accepted the importance of ideas in shaping policy – while decrying the liberal pursuit of persuasion and dialogue in favour of conviction and confrontation.

Think-tanks can only bridge the gap between theory and practice, between academics and policy-makers, when both sides are willing to acknowledge the value of the exchange. Those in power are often reluctant to listen; particularly if they operate in a half-closed political culture, without the disciplines of an actively critical press, Parliament and opposition. Those in the academic cloister are often tempted to retreat in the higher abstractions of theory, and in the deeper recesses of historical and methodological analysis, in search of pure air and clean hands. The policy adviser struggles uncomfortably in between, living in an unavoidably ambivalent relationship with both sides. Some in British academic international relations have taken distance from policy relevance as a measure of academic standing; forgetting the deeply political roots of the discipline and the redundancy of theory which can no longer be related to contemporary developments.

Policy-makers need intellectual advisers most when they are conscious of the need to rethink the underlying assumptions of policy. Margaret Thatcher, a radical politician well aware of the importance of ideas to the flow of policy, would summon selected academics and officials to Chequers (the Prime Minister's weekend residence) for occasional re-examinations: of the conventional assumptions of Whitehall towards the Soviet Union and Eastern Europe in her early years in office; of assumptions about Germany in the Spring of 1990.[31] It was the lack of interest of the Labour opposition in re-examining its foreign policy assumptions, or in picking up ideas from outsiders for use in the public debate, which – together with the shift in political balance of the quality press – gave the British foreign policy debate in the 1980s its structural imbalance.

For all the dependence of universities on government funding, academic position gives to its holders a sense of independence from political pressures far higher than that to which think-tanks are exposed. As we have seen in reviewing different national patterns of policy influence, the freedom with which advice is given has much less to do with financial dependence or independence, and much more to do with the presence or absence of competing demands for ideas and with the prevailing political culture. The Moscow institutes operated on the edge of Soviet conventional wisdom to some effect, their staff understanding well the subtleties of presenting alternative views without the appearance of open dissent. Arguably the most radical document on British foreign policy published within the last two decades came from within the Cabinet Office itself: the 1977 Central Policy Review Staff's *Review of Overseas Representation*. Roundly attacked by the Conservative press and by most MPs who commented on its report – with the encouragement of many senior officials within the Foreign Office – the team concluded that they had been 'too intellectually honest', and that the presentation of the report had been too blunt for its recommendations to persuade.[32] No academic volume or think-tank paper in Britain has ever struck so close, or aroused such bitter antagonism within government; it is, after all, easier in a secretive political system to dismiss *outside* criticism as insufficiently informed or unaware of the 'realities' with which governments have to deal.

Conversely, financial and political independence does not spare think-tanks from pressures to conform. We have noted above the subtle pressures which operate in the Parisian environment: conditional access to close-knit circles of political and intellectual elites, the inter-connecting hierarchies of received opinion-leaders and received opinions. Withdrawal of government subventions from Chatham House did not spare it from attack from the right-wing 'counter-establishment' throughout the 1980s, as a pillar and symbol of the established consensus which they were determined to undermine. Particular scorn was poured on the Institute in the early 1980s for its attempts to promote (and fund) policy research on Soviet foreign policy, with the impli-cation that 'Mrs. Thatcher is wrong to suppose that in dealings with the Soviet Union the only justifiable form of expenditure is on defence.'[33] Later criticisms focused on the consensual liberalism of 'Chatham House man'[*sic*], and the active engagement of the Institute in research on the European Community in collaboration with its counterparts in France, Germany, Italy and the Netherlands.[34]

Both worlds of international relations – insiders and outsiders, practitioners and academics – gain from the policy institutes which help to link them together. They gain most when there is an open market for ideas among competing suppliers and demanders – and least when government secrecy or the closed character of political elites limits the questioning of conventional ideas. There are those on both sides who affect to look down on this *demi-monde*: policy-makers because of the very distance from day-to-day detail which gives outside policy research its distinctive perspective, academics because of the com-promises of presentation and understated conclusions to make think-tank arguments acceptable to those at whom they are aimed. But Thomas Hobbes and Niccolò Machiavelli wrote with the same primary aim in mind of influencing and educating those in power. What, after all, is the underlying rationale for the scientific study of international relations if this aim is omitted?

NOTES

1 Charter of the Royal Institute of International Affairs, London.
2 William H. McNeill, *Arnold J. Toynbee: a life*, Oxford, Oxford University Press, 1989.
3 Academic readers should note how much of this debate took place through Chatham House study groups rather than within the academic cloister. Carr, like most other writers on international relations before the 1950s, was as interested in changing the world as in understanding it.
4 Laurence W. Martin, 'The Market for Strategic Ideas in Britain: The Sandys Era', *American Political Science Review*, March 1962, p. 34. See also Michael Howard, 'IISS – the First Thirty Years: A General Overview', in

The Changing Strategic Landscape: Part I, London, IISS, Adelphi Paper 235, 1989.

5 *The* Chatham House Rule, as revised in 1991. The revision of this rule, over 60 years after its formulation, partly reflected the shift in the pattern of institute discussions, from closed and off-the-record discussions among members of official and non-official elites in the 1930s, 1940s and 1950s, to a more open process in the 1970s and 1980s in which most talks were on-the-record and only particularly sensitive subjects and speakers required the protection of the rule.

6 James A. Smith, in *The Idea Brokers: think tanks and the rise of the new policy elite*, New York, Free Press, 1991, p. 208, notes that the CSIS was modelled on the recently founded ISS in London. But the impetus, and the funding, came more decidedly from the centre-right than from the ISS's initial centre-left.

7 Sidney Blumenthal, *The Rise of the Counter-Establishment: from conservative ideology to political power*, New York, Times Books, 1986, traces this development in the USA; Dennis Kavanagh, *Thatcherism and British Politics: the end of consensus?*, Oxford, Oxford University Press, 1987, traces its British equivalent, though focusing more on the domestic dimension than the impact of the 'New Right' on the foreign policy debate.

8 *United Kingdom Membership of UNESCO*, London, HMSO, Fifth Report from the Foreign Affairs Committee, 1984–85, HC 461, July 1985, para. 59. Appendix 10 to this report reprints 'An Appeal from Congressman Philip M. Crane, Washington, D.C., in relation to US Funding of the UN', as part of the evidence presented to the committee. It also took note of the 'allegations' made by the Australian Permanent Delegate to UNESCO 'of attempts by the Heritage Foundation to influence the British press and opinion-leaders... [which we] have no reason to doubt'. In terms of influencing the policy debate, this should be taken as evidence of the Heritage Foundation's effectiveness.

9 Pat Choate, *Agents of Influence*, New York, Simon & Schuster, 1990, was probably the most influential of the many critical writings on Japanese (and Korean) efforts to buy friends and favourable opinions in the Washington policy-making process.

10 Dr Wolfgang Michalski, addressing a seminar at the Mexican Foreign Ministry, May 1993; my notes of the meeting, quoted with permission.

11 I recall the entrenched reluctance of an audience at the Institute of Economic Affairs in 1989 to accept the thrust of my argument that British policy towards the European Community was fundamentally ideological; the self-image was that the British were pragmatic, and that it was *other* governments (and 'Euro-enthusiasts') who took an ideological approach.

12 The largest corporate subscribers to Chatham House over the past twenty-five years have been BP and Shell, with ICI, Rio Tinto Zinc and Unilever close behind.

13 I was the author of the paper. On its presentation to a British–Japanese conference some days later a senior Japanese banker commented on the paper in his capacity as chairman of the Keidanren working party on 'The structure of the Japanese economy in the year 2010', and went on to enquire whether the Confederation of British Industry had many people working on similar long-term studies of the future of the British economy in its

international context. To the CBI's credit, it thereupon set up a working party on the structure of the British economy in 2010, composed of 'rising executives' under the age of 40. But its work and its eventual report received little attention within a British culture unaccustomed to such long-term perspectives.

14 The present-day Foreign and Commonwealth Office Planning Staff has developed from the three-person unit established under Michael Palliser in 1964. Wartime planning exercises had been halted after 1945; Ernest Bevin in 1949 established a committee within the Foreign Office to discuss longer-term trends, but it ceased to meet in the early 1950s. William Wallace, *The Foreign Policy Process in Britain*, London, RIIA, 1976, pp. 78–9.

15 Cmnd 2902, February, p. 20, London, HMSO, 1966.

16 Opposition to European integration had indeed been one of the elements which led to the establishment of the IEA in the early 1960s. Several of its founders had been prominent on the free trade wing of the Liberal Party; after vigorously opposing the leadership line on policy towards the emerging EEC at the 1957 and 1958 conferences, and failing to carry the majority of the delegates with them, they withdrew from the party and began to look for an alternative vehicle through which to promote the cause of free trade.

17 Sir Keith Joseph, then as Secretary of State for Education and Science responsible for the SSRC, reportedly regarded social science as inherently socialist; though he, and others on the right, exempted economics from general dismissal.

18 These included Chief Buthelezi, the leader of the South African Inkatha Party, and a number of Nicaraguan 'contras'.

19 *Defence without the Bomb: the report of the Alternative Defence Commission*, London, Taylor & Francis, 1983.

20 William Wallace, in Ch. 4 of *The Foreign Policy Process*, op. cit., notes the gradual evolution of these committees over this period. I recall a discussion within one of the committees as to whether in the absence of any committee budget for the purchase of documents the chairman could put the cost of purchasing copies of a relevant Chatham House Paper under food. Charles Carstairs and Richard Ware (eds) *Parliament and International Relations*, Milton Keynes, Open University Press, 1990, explains how limited is parliamentary information and influence over the whole field of international policy.

21 Smith, *The Idea Brokers*, op. cit.

22 Michael Pinto-Duschinsky, 'Foreign Political Aid: The German Political Foundations and their US Counterparts', *International Affairs*, January 1991, pp. 33–64.

23 See in particular Samy Cohen, *La Monarchie Nucléaire*, Paris, Hachette, 1986.

24 See, for example, Jack Hayward, 'Political Science, the State and Modernization', in Peter Hall *et al.*, *Developments in French Politics*, London, Macmillan, 1990; and Anand Menon, 'The Uneasy Ally: France, NATO and the limits of independence', Unpublished D.Phil. thesis, Oxford University, 1993, Ch. 6.

25 Shintaro Ishihara, *The Japan that can say no*, New York, Simon & Schuster, 1991, translated by Frank Baldwin.

26 Smith, *The Idea Brokers*, op. cit., p. xviii.

27 Critics of 'policy relevance' in British university International Relations departments in the early 1990s nevertheless included Chatham House publications on their course reading lists – without exception, in my experience; because these were in many cases the most useful studies of the subjects they wished to cover.

28 To paraphrase John Maynard Keynes's famous dictum, practical men are in international affairs the slaves of some long-dead philosopher or geopolitician.

29 The last of this committee's series of discussions emerged in published form as Hedley Bull and Adam Watson (eds) *The Expansion of International Society*, Oxford, Clarendon Press, 1984.

30 My notes of the meeting.

31 The note prepared after the 1990 Chequers discussion on Germany was 'leaked' in the *Independent on Sunday*, 15 July 1990, with extensive discussion of the meeting and those who attended in the quality press in the days following.

32 Tessa Blackstone and William Plowden, *Inside the Think Tank: advising the Cabinet, 1971–83*, London, Heinemann, 1988, pp. 176–8. See also William Wallace, 'After Berrill: Whitehall and the Management of British Diplomacy', *International Affairs*, vol. 54, no. 2, April 1978, pp. 220–39.

33 Nora Beloff, 'Golden chances that keep going West', *The Times*, 19 July 1982. Miss Beloff and others maintained their attacks on 'the triumph of wishful thinking' in the Institute's Soviet studies well into the Gorbachev era, when under Admiral Sir James Eberle (labelled 'the red admiral' by his right-wing critics) it was one of the first Western institutes to engage in joint work with IMEMO, bringing together Soviet and Western policy advisers. See, for example, her review of Stephen Shenfield's Chatham House Paper, 'Time for the West to call Gorbachev's bluff over "glasnost"', *Independent*, 23 July 1987.

34 See for example the hostile profile of 'Chatham House man' in the *Sunday Telegraph*, 15 May 1990 – the longest of a number of critical *Sunday Telegraph* pieces.

9   History and policy-makers in Argentina and Britain

Peter J. Beck

Is history 'bunk'? This much-quoted accusation reflects the temptation to regard the work of the historian as somewhat remote and esoteric, and hence to dismiss history as irrelevant to today's concerns. However, this approach is both unreal and unwise. It must be difficult for even history's strongest critic to deny the value of understanding the roots of any contemporary domestic or international issue, whether it be the rights of women, race relations in Britain, national self-determination, the Irish problem, Iraqi claims to Kuwait, the 'culture of violence' in South Africa, or Soviet–American relations. For instance, 'the only people that imagine that the Northern Irish problem can be relatively easily solved are those who know very little or no Irish history'.[1] History acts as society's memory and reference point – to quote Marc Ferro 'history marks us for life' – and a world without history is like imagining ourselves without our memories.[2]

THINKING IN TIME

In 1990 Norman Stone, Professor of Modern History at Oxford, justified his weekly journalistic contributions to the *Sunday Times*: 'this is precisely what a professor of modern history ought to do: to set contemporary matters in a historical perspective'.[3] Significantly, Stone's predecessor, Michael Howard, felt the need to employ his farewell lecture to articulate history's value to society: 'From that study we learn what we have been, understand what we are, and gain intimations of what we might become.'[4] Although one expects a historian to say this, it is undeniable that history, though focused primarily on the past, provides an invaluable, informed framework of reference for those seeking to understand the present and future policy possibilities.[5] It is difficult to look forward in an informed manner without knowing exactly where we are at the present time, how we got there, and the actual nature of the existing situation. As a result, the accuracy of any political and economic forecasting proves a function of the quality of the forecasters' understanding of the causes and nature of the current position as provided by a study of the past.

History enables us to make sense of contemporary debates as well as to assess the feasibility of varying policy options. In fact, this quality provided the rationale for a course taught by Richard Neustadt and Ernest May at Harvard University's School of Government to show decision-makers how to make practical use of history, and particularly how to treat 'thinking in time' as an input for day-to-day policy-making and management.

Thinking in time appears to have three components. One is recognition that the future has no place to come from but the past, hence the past has predictive value. Another element is recognition that what matters for the future in the present is departures from the past, alterations, changes, which prospectively or actually divert familiar flows from accustomed channels, thus affecting that predictive value and much else besides. A third component is continuous comparison, an almost constant oscillation from present to future to past and back, heedful of perspective change, concerned to expedite, limit, guide, counter, or accept it as the fruits of such comparison suggest.[6]

Obviously, history will not provide a policy-maker with *the answer*, but a historical input should improve the quality of decision-making. For example, a study of the past can explain the causes of any problem, identify the key issues to be addressed, and suggest the limitations and opportunities of certain courses of action. History can also offer reassurance at a time of crisis in terms of showing how society has survived, or muddled through, past difficulties.[7]

Neustadt and May present General Marshall, Chief of Staff of the US Army during the Second World War and later the architect of the Marshall Plan, as a prominent decision-maker seeing and thinking in 'time streams'. One example concerns civil–military relations in 1943.

He looked not only to the coming year but well beyond, and with a clear sense of the long past from which those futures would come . . . By looking back, Marshall looked ahead, identifying what was worthwhile to preserve from the past and carry into the future.[8]

Neustadt and May conclude that Marshall's judgement was generally 'better' because of his use of the past.[9] But they remind us that the process is not foolproof. Much depends on a policy-maker's sense of the past as well as the quality of the 'history' being used. Numerous examples exist showing how difficult it is to draw the right lessons from the past, particularly as we approach events which are necessarily *sui generis* – by definition, they have not happened before – as if they were merely a re-run of the past.[10] This recalls the classic jibe to the effect that all generals are fighting the last war or the last war but one. In any case, policy-makers, faced by contemporary pressures and short deadlines, have little time to survey the past in anything other than a cursory manner. Inevitably, the prime focus will be upon the accessible past defined somewhat narrowly to mean recent days or months, not years. Any history will need to be brief, selective, relevant, and readily available in a written or oral form.

THE FUNCTIONAL PAST

E.H. Carr pointed to history's nature as a dialogue between past and present. There occurs a two-way process according to which the past is often approached and interpreted according to present-day circumstances and demands. The discipline of history, albeit recognising that historians are products of their time influenced by a range of unconscious assumptions, demands an objective approach and the study of the past for its own sake. Or, at least, that is the ideal, since *in reality history is often exploited for functional reasons*. In certain cases a subjective approach is consciously adopted according to which the selection and interpretation of evidence on a topic is influenced by the desired result. This may involve an anxiety to establish a meaningful continuity with the past in order to impart an added credibility to an existing idea or policy. At times considerable distortion and manipulation of the historical 'facts', in conjunction with the perpetuation of amnesia on inconvenient points, has occurred to meet the desired policy objective. Indeed, Eric Hobsbawm employed the phrase the 'invention of tradition' to describe the use of mythologies and the creation of a past which never existed.[11]

Numerous examples of the 'functional past' can be identified. Indeed, the perceived importance of the past explains why History proved the most controversial subject in the proposed national curriculum for British schools.[12] Much of the surrounding debate was heavily politicised, as demonstrated by accusations that the Conservative government was attempting to promote national rather than European modes of thought.[13] Conversely, critics were accused of attempting to 'hijack the national curriculum as a means to promote outdated socialist ideology'.[14]

R.W. Davies has illuminated the perceived significance of history in the Soviet Union where the subject has been traditionally employed, indeed exploited, for a series of policy reasons. An active debate about history was prompted by Mikhail Gorbachev's policy of *glasnost*. Soviet citizens reinterpreted their past, while reconsidering the principles and practice of the current regime: 'the debate about history is a debate about politics. . . and a debate about the future of Soviet society'.[15] History is, and has been, utilised to promote the legitimacy of the Soviet regime, to stress the importance of class, and to foster the integration of non-Russian nationalities into the Soviet bloc.[16] However, recent events suggest that a class-based history proved unsuccessful in overriding the national identities of the Estonians, Lithuanians, Poles and others. National histories and mythologies utilised to develop and sustain a nationalist consciousness have proved more enduring. For instance, Lech Walesa, having dismissed the abstract and unreal class-based 'history' taught at school, recorded his subsequent appreciation of the subject's value in serving Polish national interests.[17]

As a result, history, albeit capable of exposing mythologies and false 'histories', is frequently used and abused to construct a functional version of the past. Objectivity is the first victim of any search for the 'functional past', and the subject frequently gives the impression of being synonymous with propaganda in the sense that, say, a specific interest group (e.g. nation, feminists) or government writes, and then rewrites, the past according to individual prejudices and contemporary policy requirements.[18]

Against this background, one history professor has complained that 'There is no limit to the historical nonsense that is believed especially when propagated by professors of history when they venture to make history serve the interests of the state.'[19]

In these circumstances, the historian's search for objectivity, including his imposition of the sceptical mind, may be compromised by the demands made upon the subject.

HISTORY AND THE 1982 WAR

The recent debate about the National Curriculum in History concentrated in part on the alleged mis-match between its focus upon British history and the fact that pupils are growing up at a time when Europe is becoming a more central feature of their lives, as highlighted by forthcoming moves towards a single European market. At present, the year 1992 is viewed primarily in terms of either its European significance or perhaps the quincentennial of Columbus's voyages to the New World. However, this year witnesses also the tenth anniversary of the Anglo-Argentine war fought over the Falkland Islands with the loss of nearly 1,000 lives. The Falkland islanders, though celebrating their liberation from Argentina, plan to commemorate also John Davis's *alleged* discovery of their archipelago in 1592.[20] This 400th anniversary will serve as a vivid reminder of the manner in which Argentina and Britain remain divided and imprisoned by history. The Argentine view of the Falklands past, or rather the Malvinas past (the islands are called the 'Islas Malvinas' therein), means that 1992 possesses no other historical significance apart from marking the tenth anniversary of defeat. Argentina, denying Davis's claims, possesses an entirely different version of prior discovery.

The British House of Commons Foreign Affairs Committee's post-1982 enquiry on the Falklands question devoted considerable time to history because 'an assessment of the claims of Argentina and the United Kingdom depends critically on their interpretation of the early history of the Islands, particularly between 1811 and 1833'.[21] Clearly, the sovereignty question remains a central focus for Anglo-Argentine relations. Both disputants, attaching considerable significance to the presentation and relative strength of their respective historical and legal cases, view sovereignty in rather black-and-white terms.[22] The Falkland islanders have assumed an equally dogmatic view of the question.

On 1 April 1982 Sir Anthony Parsons, speaking for the British government at the time of an escalating Argentine threat to the Falklands, informed other delegates in the UN Security Council that 'My Argentine colleague and I could debate endlessly the rights and wrongs of history, and I doubt whether we would agree.'[23]

Nicanor Costa Mendez, the Argentine Foreign Minister, responded in a predictable fashion, even if his assertion that 'the facts of history are absolutely indisputable' overlooked the marked contrast between the Argentine and British versions of the 'facts'.[24] Argentinians believe that 'going back in history, the Malvinas were Argentina's, are Argentina's'.[25]

The Argentine armed forces proceeded to occupy the disputed islands. Their action gave effect to Argentina's 'indisputable' historical and legal rights to sovereignty over a territory depicted hitherto on maps in an act of cartographical wish-fulfilment as belonging to Argentina and named the Islas Malvinas. One Argentine conscript looked back to these events: 'We'd been lectured a lot about the *Malvinas,* the importance of their recovery. . .they talked a lot about the English as invaders of something that is ours. We felt that we were going to the *Malvinas* to defend something that was ours.'[26]

From this perspective, military action terminated Britain's 'illegal' occupation and allowed the archipelago and Port Stanley to be re-named on-the spot as the Islas Malvinas and Puerto Argentino respectively. Significantly, Costa Mendez resorted to history, when he addressed the UN Security Council again on 3 April 1982:

> Argentine territory . . . was illegally occupied by the United Kingdom by an act of force which deprived our country of that archipelago. . . Since 1833, the Republic of Argentina has been claiming reparation from the United Kingdom for the great wrong done.[27]

This official emphasis upon the 'Malvinas past' was reinforced subsequently by Admiral Destefani, whose book was translated into several languages and widely distributed – it must be assumed with official support and encouragement – 'to enable the wider world to better understand how substantial our rights are'.

> The simple geographical, historical and legal truths constitute the best defence of our rights of sovereignty over the three southern archipelagos (the *Malvinas, * South Georgia and South Sandwich Islands). . . The fighting still continues. . . Whatever the cost may be and however long it may take, the three archipelagos must be ours, because our cause is just. The Malvinas are Argentine.[28]

Margaret Thatcher, speaking to the House of Commons on the day after the Argentine invasion, stressed the strength of the British position:

> We have absolutely no doubt about our sovereignty, which has been continuous since 1833. . . The lawful British government of the islands had been usurped. . . I must tell the House that the Falkland Islands and their dependencies remain British territory. No aggression and no invasion can alter that simple fact.[29]

The despatch of 'Operation Corporate', the task force sent to recapture the islands, was presented to domestic and international audiences primarily in terms of defending Britain's historical and legal rights reinforced by a period of continuous occupation lasting nearly 150 years. During the 1982 war the strength of the British claim to the Falklands was taken for granted by ministers, MPs, the media and public opinion. Official statements attempted to convince the British people of the rights and wrongs of history. Britain was right and Argentina, despite its protestations to the contrary, was wrong.

The Thatcher government, though citing international law and the right of self-defence, concentrated upon the historical and legal 'facts' supporting British sovereignty over the islands.[30] A widely available government publication entitled *The Falkland Islands. The Facts* – the very title reassured readers – made a strong appeal to history to prove that 'British sovereignty over the Falkland Islands rests on a secure historical and legal foundation'.[31] Soon afterwards, another official publication called *The Disputed Islands* reaffirmed the British position: 'successive British governments have had no doubt about British sovereignty over the islands'.[32]

Policy reasons deriving from the enhanced post-war commitment to the islands meant that a desire to press the British case survived the end of the war. History figured prominently in the background briefs published in 1983 and 1986 by the Foreign and Commonwealth Office, as well as in the latter's submissions to the House of Commons Foreign Affairs Committee (1982–4).[33] Inevitably, the official view of the past, together with the lack of alternative British accounts, encouraged the media and wider opinion to conclude, like the *Daily Telegraph*, that British sovereignty 'satisfies every known test of international law'.[34]

THE FALKLANDS PAST

In 1983 Mary Cawkell was presented as 'the historian of the Falkland Islands', 'whose passion for accuracy' was accompanied by a passionate belief in the Islands and their sturdy people'![35] The title of her book, *The Falkland Story 1592–1982*, typifies the tendency of most British histories to gloss over deliberately alleged Spanish sightings in the *sixteenth* century. According to this view the islands' story commences in the closing decade of the sixteenth century, when the archipelago was 'discovered' by John Davis (1592) and Sir Richard Hawkins (1594).[36] However, in practice, the length, continuity, effectiveness and peaceful nature of the post-1833 British occupation became the key part of British title deeds, especially as British governments have attempted increasingly to move on beyond history. This is shown by the contemporary emphasis placed upon self-determination, including the 'paramountcy' assigned to the islanders' freely expressed wishes to 'Keep the Falklands British'.[37]

For Britain, the islanders' views take priority over Argentina's 'abstract' historical claim: 'we cannot allow the democratic rights of the Islanders to be denied by the territorial ambitions of Argentina'.[38] This approach was given renewed significance after 1982 in order to validate Britain's increased post-conflict role in the islands. Recent Queen's Speeches in Parliament, plus annual Christmas messages broadcast to the islanders by both Margaret Thatcher and John Major, have stressed popular rather than territorial sovereignty. Thus, the

British government 'will honour the commitment to *the people of the Falkland Islands*', that is, 'their right to live in peace and security under a government of their own choosing'.[39]

Self-determination, though normally interpreted as a legal concept, has frequently been exploited for policy purposes. In reality, self-determination is primarily 'a political axiom. . .it has no strength in international law but great strength in international relations'.[40] Paradoxically, Argentinian denials regarding the principle's applicability to the islanders as compared to a dispossessed Argentine population, forced the British government back on history to establish the 'scattered' and 'impermanent' nature of the pre-1833 Argentine settlement.[41]

The continuing Argentine challenge, in conjunction with changing international political and legal considerations, prompted successive British reappraisals about the nature and validity of the sovereignty claim. After 1910 the *public* image of certainty offered by British governments was qualified by a series of *private* doubts expressed in official discussions on the subject. During 1910 the Foreign Office produced a substantial Falklands 'history', which became an accepted British point of reference on the dispute together with subsequent revisions (e.g. 1928, 1946).[42] This memorandum pressed the length of British occupation, but cast doubt upon certain 'facts' (e.g. 'ancient rights' based on prior British discovery and settlement) traditionally employed to justify the British claim. However, official doubts prompted no visible alteration in British policy.[43] Successive governments, treating sovereignty as non-negotiable, continued to argue publicly that 'we are not in any doubt about our title to the Falkland Islands and we never have been'.[44]

The British case has been characterised by a reasonable degree of stability, even if recent decades have witnessed a subtle downgrading of so called 'ancient rights', like prior discovery, alongside a growing stress upon self-determination and the long period of occupation. Emphasis has been placed increasingly upon post-1833 rather than pre-1833 criteria. At present, Britain's case rests upon a rationale embodying a clear historical component.

> The United Kingdom title to the Falkland Islands is derived from early settlement, reinforced by formal claims in the name of the Crown and completed by effective occupation for nearly 150 years. The exercise of sovereignty by the United Kingdom over the Islands has, furthermore, consistently been shown to accord with the freely expressed wishes of the people who form their permanent population.[45]

Foreign Office versions of the Falklands past have been produced internally. No attempt has ever been made to engage in a dialogue with the historical profession on the history of the Falklands dispute, although perhaps this was difficult, given the fact that historians, attracted by more mainstream topics, have rarely studied the question in any detail. During the 1920s Julius Goebel, an American lawyer, examined historical and legal issues in a work possessing a strong anti-British theme. Paradoxically, his book, though generally perceived as hostile to the British case, reaffirmed the *private* doubts fostered by the 1910 Foreign Office memorandum.[46] Within the Foreign Office, Goebel's book came to be used as a respectable source capable of elaborating or clarifying gaps in existing accounts; in fact, the 1928 rewrite of the Falklands history cited it as the only additional source book consulted since the 1910 memorandum version.[47] At this time, Wilfred Down, a research student, was writing a history of the dispute, but his work was hampered by the unavailability of key archival sources. In any case, he was not the type of historian to shake up the official line, as evidenced by the manner in which he meekly returned without using closed files inadvertently made available to him.[48] More recently, several relevant files have been released under the Thirty Year Rule, but the extended closures of file is still a problem for the historian studying the sovereignty problem.[49]

Historians and diplomats have different interests and priorities. Today, opportunities for meaningful exchanges between historians and diplomats are rare. My discussions with British diplomats on the Falklands past have proved largely a by-product of contacts – these have occurred on both an individual basis and as part of the Royal Institute of International Affairs framework of Study Groups – primarily concerned with contemporary and future events. The Foreign and Commonwealth Office (FCO) appears to be reluctant actually to solicit academic expertise on historical topics; for example, only Argentine, Brazilian and Chilean diplomats have ever consulted me specifically on the history of the Falklands dispute. This example recalls the FCO's apparent failure at the time of the outbreak of the 1982 war to take up an offer made by several academics to come together and offer expertise on the Latin American dimension of the conflict.[50]

THE MALVINAS PAST

In 1982 Argentina's attempt to give effect to the country's historical and legal rights to the Malvinas ended in defeat, the loss of the islands, the fall of the military regime, and democratisation. Subsequent Argentine governments, whether led by Raul Alfonsin (1983–9) or Carlos Menem (from 1989), maintain the claim as a policy priority. Dante Caputo, Alfonsin's foreign minister, reaffirmed the enduring power of history in 1987, when informing the UN about 'the sound historical and legal arguments that support the Argentine claim'.[51] Subsequently, Menem, a Peronist, employed his first UN address to remind the international community about Argentina's undoubted 'historical' rights to sovereignty over the Malvinas. 'We have extended our hand showing our willingness to enter into dialogue, in no way doubting our historical and inalienable rights to sovereignty over those usurped South Atlantic islands.'[52]

An acknowledgement of UN support for 'our just claim' was accompanied by an assertion that 'we will fight unstintingly and peacefully to recover our Malvinas Islands with reason and per-severance'. It was vital to 'bring to an end an obsolete colonial situation that is *historically unsustainable*'.

The Argentine claim is rooted in history, being 'founded on priority of discovery, priority of occupation, possession entered into and exercised, tacit and explicit recognition, and the acquisition of the titles belonging to Spain'.[53] Rights inherited from Spain, Argentina's mother country, appertaining to sixteenth-century discoveries and subsequent settlement on East Falkland (1760s–1811) were allegedly reinforced by Argentine occupation during the 1820s and early 1830s. Naturally, the events of 1833 are interpreted in a manner favourable to Argentina. 'In 1833, Great Britain, having no right on her side, could only resort to force in order to occupy the Islands. . . Force is still the cornerstone of Britain's presence . . . and cannot generate nor create any rights for Great Britain.'[54]

During the mid-1980s Caputo, the Argentine foreign minister, re-minded the UN that 'more than a century and a half ago, the United Kingdom forcibly stripped my country of its sovereignty over those islands'.[55] The repetitive and emotive use of certain words and phrases like 'force' have characterised Argentine accounts of this episode, thereby conveying a picture of Britain's occupation as illegal.[56]

During and after 1833 the Argentine government, lacking power, was forced to rely upon diplomacy and international law to press for the return of 'its islands'. International legal principles, for what they were worth, offered a small country in dispute with a larger state a means of partially compensating for a power imbalance. Diplomatic statements have relied heavily upon history to expose the 'illegal' British claim – this was presented as basically a function of British expansionism and imperialism rather than of law – and to record Argentina's 'indisputable rights' to the islands.

The changed international context of the 1960s, most notably, India's exploitation of anti-colonialism to justify the use of force against Portuguese Goa in December 1961, fostered an alternative strategy of presenting the 'facts' in a form designed to appeal to the growing Third World audience represented at the UN. The UN Committee of Twenty Four on Decolonisation took up the dispute in 1964, when the Argentine delegation utilised history to deny the islanders' right of self-determination.

The *Malvinas* Islands are in a different situation from that of the classic colonial case. *De facto* and *de jure*, they belonged to the Argentine Republic in 1833 and were governed by Argentine authorities and occupied by Argentine settlers. . .they were evicted by violence. . .and replaced by a colonial administration and a population of British origin. . .The population is basically a temporary population. . .and cannot be used by the colonial power in order to apply the principle of self-determination.[57]

This attack upon 'an outstanding example' of British colonialism struck a chord with newly emerging nations represented at the UN, and gave new life to the Argentine campaign. 'At that time, advantage was taken of a country that was in the throes of organisation and struggling, as many new countries in Africa and Asia today, to achieve political and economic progress.'[58]

The resulting link between the Malvinas issue and the UN's anti-colonialism campaign enabled the Galtieri regime to justify military action in April 1982 on the grounds that colonialism was an 'act of force' and a state of 'permanent aggression'.[59] In addition, the Argentine claim draws strength from other factors, most notably geopolitical modes of thinking, which have proved traditionally influential in military circles, where the Malvinas are interpreted as part of one claim extending to Antarctica.[60]

The claim, though possessing considerable merit in such respects as 'effective occupation' prior to 1833, is obscured by nationalist mythologies transmitted by 'a self-perpetuating process of indoctrination through the educational system and the mass media'.[61] On 10 June of each year all Argentines are reminded of the claim through the 'Day of Affirmation of Argentine Rights over the *Malvinas*' commemorating the 1829 proclamation of an Argentine political and military command over the islands.[62] Similarly, Argentine maps, whether used for postage stamps, atlases, or textbooks, are required by law to depict the islands as 'Las Islas Malvinas' governed by Argentina.[63]

Official authorisation of school textbooks, notably those for geography, history and social science, ensures that education implants, and then reinforces, the claim to the Malvinas in the Argentine consciousness from a very early age.[64] For example, *Manual Estrada*, a Fourth Grade school text, devotes considerable attention to history in order to explain why '*las islas Malvinas nos pertenecen*' (the Malvinas islands belong to us).[65] Looking back to the 1982 conflict, *Manual Estrada* asserts that the justifiable restitution of '*nuestra soberanía*' (our sovereignty) merely prompted '*una agresiva reacción de Gran Bretaña*' (an aggressive reaction by Great Britain). Similarly, history textbooks mention the dispute in some detail – it is, of course, rare for any history text used in British schools even to mention the Falkland Islands – and refer to the topic in terms of the '*usurpación*' of Argentine rights by Britain.[66]

These entrenched attitudes, in association with policy considerations, explain why minimal effort has been made within Argentina to examine either the country's version of the Malvinas past in a critical and balanced manner or the extent to which the historical dimension constitutes a realistic rationale for current policy. A sense of patriotic commitment rather than of reason has determined thinking on the subject. Argentine writers tend to work within a narrow framework designed to establish the strength of '*nuestro derecho*'; indeed, this preordained objective dominates publications. Critiques are neither sought nor welcomed, while domestic political pressures create a difficult environment for accounts failing to highlight the country's 'superior historical rights'. The work of historians, including those working in other countries, has been incorporated into official statements upon a selective basis related to the confirmation and strengthening of the existing position. In this sense, the Argentine Foreign Ministry has established better and more continuous linkages with historians, whether based in Argentina or elsewhere, than its British counterpart. The historian is encouraged to believe that Argentine diplomats care more about his work, or at least about the sections commenting favourably upon aspects of their country's claim.

Carlos Escudé has proved one of the few Argentines prepared to expose the chauvinistic and self-perpetuating mythologies taken to be unquestionable 'facts' of history:

These myths have perpetuated themselves, becoming deeply rooted in every stratum of Argentine society. . .and transmitted principally through the educational system. Thus, a vicious cycle is generated by which these untruths become more firmly entrenched, are taken for granted by rulers and ruled alike, and lead to the implementation of self-defeating policies.[67]

Escudé, conforming to the demands of his subject and refusing to write a functional history, concluded that 'the matter is not obvious'.[68]

Who is right and who is wrong is not an obvious matter. . .In the final instance it is very difficult to say objectively whose rights are better, and it is therefore a case in which fanaticism is by no means warranted and much less so the recourse to force.[69]

However, Escudé, though acting like an academic historian, has proved a lone voice in Argentina, thereby illustrating the limitations of history's policy role when the version of the past presented was out of step with government objectives. On the Malvinas question, Argentine governments remain imprisoned by the conviction that history is on their side. The sovereignty claim is treated – to quote Oscar Camilion, a former foreign minister – as 'a very important priority. . .something that is beyond any kind of discussion'.[70] Argentina, refusing to go away even after defeat in 1982, continued to challenge the British position and to reject rival histories. Indeed, the wartime occupation gave substance, at least for a few weeks, to Argentine territorial aspirations and created images – these included television pictures of the Argentine flag flying over their islands and letters postmarked '*Islas Malvinas, Republica Argentina*' – outlasting the restoration of British control.

The impact of 'official' history as a force for policy inertia and intransigence should not be discounted. The traditional stress upon 'how substantial our rights are' has hindered any engagement in a rational discussion regarding the real nature of Argentina's Malvinas interests.[71] The automatic, even unthinking, stress upon title deeds indicates a mere desire to recover a lost possession usurped by force. Successive governments, viewing current policy as primarily a logical extension of past events, imply that the restoration of the *status quo ante* 1833 is all that matters. Policy-makers and others seem content to articulate a series of platitudes regarding the claim without defining the country's actual interests and priorities regarding the Malvinas. The tendency has been to look backwards to the pre-1833 period rather than forward to the needs of Argentina in tomorrow's world. This dogmatic, myopic attitude qualifies Argentina's ability to conduct meaningful negotiations on the Malvinas with the British government. Opinion polls, illustrating that Argentinians care significantly more about sovereignty to the islands than Britons, suggest that it might prove politically difficult, if not impossible, to sell any compromise solution (e.g. leaseback) to a people taught to believe in the unquestioned validity of the country's rights to the islands.

At present, it is easier to pose questions than to provide answers. Are outsiders liable to over-exaggerate the historical and legal inertia characterising the attitudes of Argentine policy-makers and opinion? What is the current policy priority of the sovereignty claim? How enduring are schoolday versions of the Malvinas past? Does the man in the Buenos Aires street really care about the Malvinas claim? What scope exists for pragmatism rather than dogmatism, given the realism displayed by Menem during his initial period of office? How much time is required for re-education to disrupt the tyranny of the Malvinas past in the light of the static nature of Argentine thinking towards a claim apparently embedded deeply through all levels of society? The evidence is mixed. Whereas certain Argentinians claim that outsiders are over-impressed with the influence of the historical dimension, it remains difficult to ignore the continuing input of history. On 2 April 1991, the ninth anniversary of the Argentine military 'deployment' – this word is naturally preferred to 'invasion' – was marked by a series of official ceremonies and rallies involving politicians, the military and others. Vice-President Eduardo Duhalde employed the occasion to state that the Argentine flag 'will wave again one day in the Malvinas Islands . . . What we Argentine people feel is the absolute certainty that the Malvinas are ours.'[72] At the same time, Galtieri, who headed the military junta in 1982, went on record as saying that 'if the circumstances were the same, I'd do it again'.[73] Perhaps more revealing was the message from General Martin Bonnet read out to all army units. Bonnet, denying that the 1982 war ended in defeat, pointed out that 'we are still moved by the same reasons which led us to seek the military defence of our fatherland'.[74] Two months later, on 10 June 1991, the 'Day of Affirmation' of Argentine rights to the islands prompted a foreign ministry statement indicating that the country 'will recover the islands'.[75] Few appeared to disassociate themselves from such sentiments.[76]

PERCEPTIONS OF NATIONAL ROLES IN THE WIDER WORLD

A further historical element operates on a more general level, where it serves to influence national perceptions of global roles. In this vein, it is necessary to allow for the persistent Argentine exaggeration of the country's role on the international stage. Traditionally, Argentinians have seen their country as a 'powerful land' destined to be another USA. For example, in 1888 Domingo Sarmiento, a former Argentine president, predicted that 'We shall be the United States', while soon afterwards, *La Prensa* pressed Argentina's reluctance to conform to a small state mentality: 'This powerful land is destined to undertake in the southern continent a mission as great as that of the country in Washington.'[77] Unrealistic perceptions have prompted numerous policy errors, most notably the gross miscalculations in 1982 regarding the likely British and United States responses to the invasion of the Falklands/Malvinas, as noted by Joseph Tulchin:

> The Argentine leaders lived in a world of dreams created in the course of a century of distorted perceptions of the world. . .In the case of the Malvinas war, their misperception proved tragic. The soldiers who lost their lives on the islands or who went to the bottom with the *General Belgrano* paid the consequences.[78]

In 1982 these mistakes were compounded by a mis-reading of history, which led the Argentine military to expect 'another Suez' (i.e. withdrawal of the task force) on the part of Britain.[79]

In 1962 Dean Acheson remarked that Britain had 'lost an Empire but not yet found a role' to replace her 'played out separate power role'. Within this context, the Falklands dispute can be seen against the background of Britain's long-standing reluctance to accept the loss of world power status. Speaking at Cheltenham a few weeks after Britain's 'great victory' over Argentina, Margaret Thatcher drew freely upon history when arguing that the 'spirit of the South Atlantic' embodied the 'real spirit of Britain'.

> When we started out there were the waverers and the fainthearts . . . Those who believed that our decline was irreversible – that we could never again be what we were. . .Well they were wrong. The lesson of the Falklands is that Britain has not changed and that this nation still has those sterling qualities which shine throughout history.[80]

In many respects, British policy towards the Falklands was a code for something else – that is, the country's role in the contemporary world and underlying desire to revive past glories. In turn, the nauseating wartime 'Gotcha-type' jingoism displayed by British politicians, media and opinion led Raphael Samuel and others to look to history.

> It seemed that the country had gone mad. The drowning of 500 Latin American sailors was treated as a national triumph, the sacrifice of British lives as a restoration of national greatness. . .Rather than treating this as an aberration we wanted to make sense of it in terms of the national past, and to account for the resilience of those

sentiments on which history had seemed to turn its back ie. to explain patriotism and jingoism through reasoned and historical enquiry.[81]

IMPRISONED AND DIVIDED BY HISTORY

National stereotypes, though relevant to the area of debate, are beyond the scope of this study. In the meantime, any consideration of the rights and wrongs of the sovereignty dispute depends upon the availability of relevant information. But what are the 'facts' of the Falklands/Malvinas past? Both governments agree about the importance of the historical dimension, but disagree profoundly regarding the precise nature of the islands' history. Rival versions of the past remain a principal cause and effect of Anglo-Argentine controversy. The two disputants display confidence in the rightness of their respective views of 'history', which prove a function of the demands of politics and law rather than of historical scholarship. Indeed, the constant references to historical 'truths' reveal the unhistorical nature of this process, since no responsible historian accepts the possibility of ever arriving at a definitive version of the past. This emphasis on 'truths' is shared by the islanders, like Sydney Miller, formerly editor of *The Falkland Islands Journal*:

> I probably know more of the true facts of the history of these Islands than anyone else as I have made it my business to ascertain the true facts of the early discovery by British seamen and certainly the facts of the absurd and unfounded Argentine claims.[82]

The resulting impasse, both causing and surviving the 1982 war, merely exacerbates the prospects for a resolution of the dispute.

The 1982 war was followed by a period when the continuing impasse over the ownership of the islands and the absence of diplomatic relations rendered it difficult for Argentina and Britain to make any progress even on practical matters like air transport, fishing conservation, and trade. British governments, rejecting the rival claim, asserted sovereignty's non-negotiable character.[83] The resulting non-relationship was suddenly transformed at the close of the 1980s, when the new Argentine president, Carlos Menem, seeking to build bridges for the sake of improved relations with Europe, confounded British pessimism arising from his Peronist affiliations and strident election pronouncements on the dispute.

In 1989 the two governments, meeting at New York, accepted a 'sovereignty umbrella' protecting their respective legal positions regarding the Falkland Islands as well as South Georgia and the South Sandwich Islands. This formula provided a basis for the *Joint Statements* agreed at Madrid on 19 October 1989 and 15 February 1990 enabling the restoration of diplomatic relations, the withdrawal of the post-war Protection Zone, and the start of meaningful discussions on urgent practical questions, most notably the conservation of South West Atlantic fish stocks.[84] In this vein, Domingo Cavallo, the Argentine foreign minister, stated that 'We are certain we have sovereign rights over the *Malvinas*, but the subject can be put in parenthesis and discussed when circumstances permit.'[85]

A few months later Margaret Thatcher informed the islanders of the unaltered British position: 'we will not negotiate on sovereignty. That will remain our position, and we shall uphold our commitments and responsibilities to you, the people of the Islands.'[86] Inevitably, during November 1990 most attention focused upon the implications of Thatcher's departure as prime minister for domestic, European and Gulf affairs. By contrast, Argentinians, like the Falkland islanders, were preoccupied with its consequences for Anglo-Argentine relations in general and the Falklands/Malvinas question in particular. Although Thatcher was often presented as a prime obstacle to closer links between London and Buenos Aires, her resignation was generally interpreted, even by Menem and Cavallo, as bringing about no significant change of course.[87] It is often forgotten that the Anglo-Argentine *détente* occurred during the last year or so of her premiership, and John Major, her successor, soon took the opportunity to stress policy continuities. Significantly, he became prime minister on 28 November 1990 – that is, the very day on which an Anglo-Argentine Joint Statement on the Conservation of Fisheries in the South West Atlantic was accepted.[88] In December 1990 Major, pointing to his predecessor's close identification with their future, reassured the islanders that their interests were 'equally close to mine'.

> I do assure you that we achieved these agreements with Argentina without in any way compromising our position on British sovereignty. You need be in no doubt that we will continue to honour our commitments to you.[89]

The intransigent attitude of the islanders towards Argentine reinforced the unchanging situation. In March 1986 a Marplan opinion poll based upon a 90 per cent plus response rate recorded the islanders' unanimous support to 'Keep the Falklands British'.[90] Recent Falklands Legislative Council debates, like statements delivered at the UN by islanders' representatives, reaffirmed this point, as evidenced in August 1990 when Lewis Clifton reminded the UN Committee of Twenty Four that:

Without exception, Falkland Islanders do not wish to see a change of British sovereign status. . . For so long as Argentina pursues her sovereignty claims to my homeland, Islanders will be ever more determined to remain forceful in their wish to maintain the *status quo*. . . We want no cultural, political, education or social relationship with Argentina.[91]

CONCLUSIONS

In 1982 a short, sharp war had a decisive outcome, even if the restoration of British control failed to resolve the fundamental cause of the Falklands dispute. A difficult period of Anglo-Argentine relations, or rather non-relations, ensued. Diplomatic relations were not restored until 1990. Today, both disputants, relying on a 'sovereignty umbrella' to protect their respective positions, press their rival claims based upon conflicting 'histories'. Argentina and Britain, though displaying confidence in the rightness of their respective versions of the 'facts', agree to differ over the precise nature of the islands' story.

As a result, it remains important to look backwards when going forwards into the 1990s and beyond in order to understand both the nature of the dispute and the influences upon current and future policy possibilities. During 1990 Sir Geoffrey Howe, defining the concept as 'a flexible, organic notion' rather than some pre-defined absolute, presented sovereignty as 'a resource to be used, rather than a constraint that inhibits or limits our capacity for action'.[92] However, in South Atlantic affairs sovereignty has proved hitherto the master rather than the servant of events. The tendency of both disputants to project their respective black-and-white versions of the Falklands/Malvinas past for policy purposes merely polarises, complicates and aggravates their relationship. Neither party is prepared to admit publicly the historical uncertainties to the effect that in reality claims are a grey and 'finely balanced' area. Marc Ferro, having conducted a detailed study about the use and abuse of history in general, concluded that: 'It is high time to confront these differing presentations of the past. . . Our differing views of the past have, more than ever, become one of the factors in conflict between states, nations, cultures and ethnic groups.'[93]

But there exists little prospect that Argentine and British historians will ever arrive at an agreed version of the Falklands/Malvinas past.[94] Recently, Sir Anthony Parsons, who represented Britain at the UN during the 1982 war, observed that 'time, long time, must be allowed to do its work on the attitudes of all concerned'.[95]

In the meantime, history continues to divide and imprison the disputants. But does history matter? The events of 1982, like those of 1833, confirmed that, in the last resort, power and will constitute the decisive factors. There seems a certain futility in relying too heavily upon historical and legal argumentation in sovereignty disputes – in such cases history and the law prove a function of policy considerations – when the prime focus should be placed upon the matter of advancing arguments and policies which are politically reasonable, convincing and relevant to contemporary and future national interests.

In both Argentina and Britain historians and policy-makers, inhabiting separate worlds, have experienced an uneasy relationship. Opportunities for dialogue and exchanges of views have proved few and far between. The widely reported exchange on Germany's past and present in July 1990 between Margaret Thatcher and a small group of historians, though a revealing episode, was very much the exception proving the rule.[96] Most academic historians, believing in the intrinsic historical value of their work, place the requirements of policy-makers low down their list of priorities. Little or no effort has been made to produce material quickly in a form relevant to policy issues and capable of being used by governments. The detailed academic monograph or article has little attraction to a diplomat working to a deadline and seeking a clear, concise summary of relevant points. Policy-makers, influenced by pragmatic and non-academic considerations, have neither the time nor inclination to incorporate a significant historical dimension into their work. The historian, excepting those prepared to produce functional histories, is not usually made to feel welcome in government circles, which regard with irritation academic scepticism of, say, the historical basis for sovereignty claims.

These conclusions reflect the impressions of the historian. Whether or not policy-makers, even those entering the FCO with history degrees, are depicted correctly is a matter for judgement. Perhaps the extent to which history is valued by British diplomats today will only become clear in thirty years' time, when this year's archives become available. Of course, this assumes that history-related policy documents are adjudged worthy of preservation, given the fact that only about 5 to 10 per cent of documents survive the weeding process!

NOTES

1 Michael Bentley, in P. Collinson, M. Bentley and R. Samuel, 'The History of Nations', *PUSH Newsletter*, vol. 3, no. 1, 1991, p. 16.
2 Marc Ferro, *The Use and Abuse of History*, London, Routledge & Kegan Paul, 1981, p. vii. See also Peter J. Beck, 'Has History a Future?',

Contemporary Review, vol. 249, no. 1450, 1986, pp. 264–7; Christopher Thorne, 'International Relations and the Promptings of History', *Review of International Studies*, vol. 9, 1983, pp. 123–31; F.S. Northedge, 'Russia and the Lessons of History', *Millennium*, vol. 11, no. 1, 1984, pp. 50–1.

3 *Sunday Times*, 15 April 1990.

4 Michael Howard, 'Structure and Process in History', *The Times Literary Supplement*, 23–9 June 1989, p. 689.

5 Northedge, 'Russia', op. cit, p. 50.

6 Richard E. Neustadt and Ernest R. May, *Thinking in Time: the uses of history for decision makers*, New York, Free Press, 1986, p. 251.

7 Susan Strange, 'Looking back – but mostly forward', *Millennium*, vol. 11, no. 1, 1984, p. 38.

8 Neustadt and May, *Thinking in Time*, op. cit., p. 248.

9 Ibid., p. 251.

10 See Collinson, Bentley and Samuel, 'The History of Nations', op. cit., pp. 7–10.

11 Eric Hobsbawm and Terence Ranger (eds) *The Invention of Tradition*, Cambridge, Cambridge University Press, 1983, p. 14. See also Raphael Samuel and Paul Thompson (eds) *The Myths we live by*, London, Routledge, 1990.

12 Richard Aldrich (ed.) *History in the National Curriculum*, Kogan Page, London, 1991.

13 For example, see Martin Jacques, 'Tories launch their biggest takeover bid – for history', *Sunday Times*, 1 April 1990. Jacques edited *Marxism Today*. Thatcher's interest was highlighted in 'Interview: Margaret Thatcher', *Sunday Telegraph*, 15 April 1990.

14 See letters column, *Sunday Times*, 8 April 1990.

15 R.W. Davies, *Soviet History in the Gorbachev Revolution*, London, Macmillan, 1989, p. vii, p. 187.

16 Ibid., pp. 1–6.

17 Lech Walesa, *Path of Hope*, London, Collins, 1987, p. 36.

18 Arthur Marwick, *The Nature of History*, London, Macmillan, 1970, p.11. Peter Novick's, *That Noble Dream: The 'Objectivity Question' and the American Historical Profession*, Cambridge, Cambridge University Press, 1988, stimulated considerable and continuing debate within the profession on the ideal of objectivity.

19 J.A.S. Grenville, *Europe Re-Shaped 1848–78*, London, Fontana, 1976, p. 349.

20 W.H. Fullerton, Governor of the Falklands, *Record of the Falklands Legislative Council* (hereafter *Legco*), 19 May 1990, p. 15. There are other claimants for prior discovery: see Peter J. Beck, *The Falkland Islands as an International Problem*, London, Routledge, 1988, pp. 35–8. For recent bibliographical studies of the dispute, see Peter Beck, 'The Conflict Potential of the Dots on the Map', *International History Review*, vol. 13, no. 1, 1991, pp. 124–33; Alex Danchev, 'Life and Death in the South Atlantic', *Review of International Studies*, vol. 17, 1991, pp. 305–12.

21 House of Commons Foreign Affairs Committee (HCFAC) 1982–83, *Report*, p. xxiii.

22 See pro-Argentine advert in *New York Times*, 18 April 1982.

23 Sir Anthony Parsons, British representative, 1 April 1982, quoted in *Britain*

and the Falklands Crisis: a Documentary Record, London, HMSO, 1982, p. 24.

24 Raphael Perl (ed.) *The Falkland Islands Dispute in International Law and Politics: a Documentary Sourcebook*, New York, Oceana, 1983, p. 438.

25 Roberto Guyer, quoted in Michael Charlton, *The Little Platoon: Diplomacy and the Falklands Dispute*, Oxford, Blackwell, 1989, p. 103.

26 Daniel Kon, *Los Chicos de la Guerra*, London, NEL, 1983, pp. 46–7.

27 Costa Mendez, 3 April 1982, in Perl, *The Falkland Islands Dispute*, op. cit., p. 433.

28 Laurio H. Destefani, *The Malvinas, the South Georgias and the South Sandwich Islands, the conflict with Britain*, Buenos Aires, Edipress, 1982, p. 5.

29 *Hansard Parliamentary Debates: House of Commons*, vol. 21, col. 25, 3 April 1982.

30 *Hansard (Commons)*, vol. 21, col. 633, 3 April 1982.

31 *The Falkland Islands: The Facts*. London, HMSO, 1982, p. 3.

32 *The Disputed Islands*, London, HMSO, 1982, p. 29.

33 FCO, *Background Brief: The Falkland Islands – Early History*, London, FCO, 1983, p. 1; FCO, *Background Brief: Claims to the Falkland Islands*, London, FCO, 1986 and see p. 179 below.

34 *Daily Telegraph*, 27 April 1982. See also letter from Sir Miles Clifford (former Governor of the Falkland Islands), *The Times*, 12 November 1982.

35 B.W. Hunter Christie, 'Foreword', in Mary Cawkell, *The Falkland Story 1592–1982*, Oswestry, Anthony Nelson, 1983. Sydney Miller has also praised Cawkell as a 'very accurate historian' whose work contrasts with the 'nonsense contributed by the Argentine government', S. Miller to the author, 22 March 1989.

36 Beck, *The Falkland Islands as an International Problem*, op. cit, pp. 35–8.

37 FCO, *HCFAC 1982–83*, 10 November 1982, p. 1.

38 Cranley Onslow, *HCFAC 1982–83*, 21 February 1983; Thatcher, *Hansard (Commons)*, vol. 21, col. 633, 3 April 1982; *HCFAC 1982–83*, 10 November 1982, p. 1.

39 Queen's Speech, *Hansard (Commons)*, vol. 162, col. 5, 21 November 1989; *Hansard (Commons)*, vol. 158, col. 435, 24 October 1989; John Major, Christmas message to the Falkland Islands, 12 December 1990, London, Prime Minister's Dept., 1990; *The Times*, 8 November 1990.

40 Fawcett and Sinclair, *HCFAC 1982–83*, 17 January 1983, pp. 142–3; Michael Akehurst, *A Modern Introduction to International Law* (5th. edn), London, Allen & Unwin, 1984, pp. 296–7.

41 *The Falkland Islands: The Facts*, op. cit., p. 8.

42 Memorandum by G. de Bernhardt, 7 December 1910, F0371/824/44753, Public Record Office, Kew, London; Lord Sherfield, *Hansard (Lords)*, vol. 438, col. 187, 25 January 1983.

43 See Beck, *The Falkland Islands as an International Problem*, op. cit., pp. 49–55.

44 *The Disputed Islands*, op. cit., p. 29.

45 FCO, 10 November 1982, *HCFAC 1982–83*, p. 1; *HCFAC 1982–83*, 17 January 1983, p. 168; Sir Ian Sinclair, FCO legal adviser, in Charlton, *The Little Platoon*, op. cit., pp. 3–6.

46 Julius Goebel, *The Struggle for the Falkland Islands: a study in Legal and*

Diplomatic History, New Haven, Yale University Press, 1927; Beck, *The Falkland Islands as an International Problem*, op. cit., p. 52.

47 Beck, *The Falkland Islands as an International Problem*, op. cit., p. 52.

48 The question is covered in C078/175/6 files, Public Record Office, Kew, London. Note Wilfred Down, 'The Occupation of the Falkland Islands', unpublished Ph.D. thesis, Cambridge University, 1927.

49 The 1982 war, though prompting some releases, appears also to have caused a tightening up on sovereignty-related files, such as to prevent access to British documents through dominion archives. See Peter J. Beck, 'Research Problems in Studying Britain's Latin American Past: the Case of the Falklands Dispute 1920–1950', *Bulletin of Latin American Research*, vol. 2, no. 3, 1983, pp. 5–13.

50 Interview with Professor Christopher Platt, Director of the Latin American Centre, University of Oxford, October 1982.

51 Caputo, 16 November 1987, Argentine government press release.

52 Menem, United Nations General Assembly Records (UNGA) A44/PV5, 25 September 1989, p. 33.

53 Argentine government to Britain, 2 January 1888, quoted in Beck, *The Falkland Islands as an International Problem*, op. cit., p. 70.

54 J. Ruda, 9 September 1964, in Perl, *The Falkland Islands Dispute*, op. cit., p. 363.

55 UNGA A40/PV92, 26 November 1985, p. 3.

56 De Rozas to UN, 6 May 1976, in Perl, *The Falkland Islands Dispute*, op. cit., p. 401.

57 J. Ruda, 9 September 1964, in Perl, *The Falkland Islands Dispute*, op. cit., p. 368.

58 J. Ruda, 9 September 1964, in Perl, *The Falkland Islands Dispute*, op. cit., pp. 364–5; Argentine government to US State Dept., 29 April 1982, ibid., p. 475.

59 Argentine government to US State Dept., 29 April 1982, in ibid., pp. 478–9; Akehurst, *A Modern Introduction to International Law*, op. cit., p. 295.

60 Jack Child, *Geopolitics and Conflict in South America: Quarrels among Neighbours*, New York, Praeger, 1985, pp. 41–3; Virginia Gamba-Stonehouse, *Strategy in the Southern Oceans: A South American View*, London, Pinter, 1989, pp. 71–133; Jack Child, 'Latin Lebensraum: the Geopolitics of Ibero-American Antarctica', *Applied Geography*, vol. 10, no.4, 1990, pp. 291–3.

61 Carlos Escudé, 'Argentine Territorial Nationalism', *Journal of Latin American Studies*, vol. 20, 1988, pp. 156–60; Carlos Escudé, 'The Malvinas Conflict – 1', *Buenos Aires Herald*, 18 November 1985.

62 Press release, Argentine Ministry of External Relations, 10 June 1990.

63 Peter J. Beck, 'Argentina's Philatelic Annexation of the Falkland Islands', *History Today*, vol. 33, no. 2, 1993, pp. 39–44.

64 SOCMERC opinion poll, March 1990, South Atlantic Council Press Release, 26 March 1990; *Clarin*, 26 March 1990; Felipe Noguera and Peter Willetts, 'Public Attitudes and the Future of the Islands', The Falklands Conflict Conference, University of Keele, September 1990. The Keele conference papers appear in A. Danchev (ed.) *International Perspectives on the Falklands Conflict: A Matter of Life and Death*, London, Macmillan, 1992.

65 *Manual Estrada 4° Grado* (3rd edn), Buenos Aires, Angel Estrada, 1988, pp. 106–7; Susana Molfino, *La Argentina: La Tierra, El Hombre, Sus Recursos* (2nd edn), Buenos Aires, Kapelusz, 1985, p. 167. See also Peter J. Beck, 'Whose Island Story?', *History Today,* vol. 39, no. 2, 1989, pp. 8–11.

66 For example, see Jorge M. Ramallo, *Historia 3*, Buenos Aires, Ediciones Braga, 1988, pp. 11–13; Ernesto Palacios, *Historia de la Argentina 1515–1983* (15th edn), Buenos Aires, Abelado-Perrot, 1988, pp. 316–17.

67 Escudé, 'The Malvinas Conflict – 1', op. cit.

68 Carlos Escudé, 'The Malvinas Conflict – III', *Buenos Aires Herald*, 25 November 1985.

69 Carlos Escudé, 'The Malvinas Conflict – IV', *Buenos Aires Herald*, 27 November 1985; Escudé, The Malvinas Conflict – 1, op. cit.

70 Quoted, in Charlton, *The Little Platoon*, op. cit., p. 102.

71 Destefani, *The Malvinas*, op. cit., p. 5.

72 *La Nacion*, 2 April 1991; *Ambito Financiero*, 3 April 1991.

73 *Buenos Aires Herald*, 3 April 1991.

74 Ibid.

75 *La Nacion*, 11 June 1991; *La Prensa*, 11 June 1991.

76 There was a critical editorial in the English language *Buenos Aires Herald*, 4 April 1991.

77 Joseph S. Tulchin, *Argentina and the United States: A Conflicted Relationship*, Boston, Twayne Publishers, 1990, pp. 17–18.

78 Ibid., p. 155.

79 Beck, *The Falkland Islands as an International Problem*, op. cit., p. 130.

80 Conservative Central Office, Press Release, 3 July 1982.

81 Raphael Samuel (ed.) *Patriotism: the Making and Unmaking of British National Identity*, London, Routledge, 1989, vol. 1, pp. x–xi; see also Anthony Barnett, *Iron Britannia*, London, Allison & Busby, 1982.

82 Letter by S. Miller to the author, 21 September 1987.

83 Beck, *The Falkland Islands as an International Problem*, op. cit., pp. 169–92.

84 Peter J. Beck, 'Fisheries Conservation as a Basis for a Special Anglo-Argentine Relationship', *The World Today*, vol. 47, no. 6, 1991, pp. 102–3.

85 Associated Press Dispatch, Buenos Aires, 10 July 1989.

86 BBC Radio World Service broadcast, 22 December 1989, London, Prime Minister's Department, 1989.

87 For example, see *La Nacion*, 23 November 1990; *La Prensa*, 23 November 1990; *Clarin*, 23 November 1990; *Buenos Aires Herald*, 23 November 1990. Compare Nicanor Costa Mendez, 'South Atlantic Stand-off', *Buenos Aires Herald*, 15 May 1985.

88 Beck, 'Fisheries Conservation', op. cit., pp. 103–6.

89 John Major, 'Christmas message to the Falkland Islanders', 12 December, London, Prime Minister's Department, 1990.

90 Marplan Ltd, 2 April 1986 poll on 'what kind of sovereignty do you want for the Falkland Islands?': 94.5 per cent for British sovereignty, 0.3 per cent for Argentine sovereignty.

91 Clifton, UN Committee of Twenty Four, Press Release, 13 August 1990. See William Luxton, *Legco*, 19 and 28 May 1990, pp. 79–80.

92 Geoffrey Howe, 'Sovereignty and Interdependence: Britain's Place in the World', *International Affairs*, vol. 66, 1990, pp. 676, 691.

93 Ferro, *The Use and Abuse of History*, op. cit., p. vii.
94 HCFAC 1982–83, *Report*, p. xxiii.
95 Sir Anthony Parsons, 'Comment', The Falklands Conflict Conference, University of Keele, September 1990, p. 2.
96 *The Independent*, 16 July 1990; Norman Stone, 'What Mrs Thatcher Really Thinks', *The Times*, 16 July 1990.

10 Buddy, can you spare a paradigm?

American academics and the debate on foreign direct investment in the USA

Michael Hodges

[America's] growing dependence on foreign capital ... is too
reminiscent of America's former dependence on foreign oil, and just
as we shook ourselves loose from the OPEC cabal, we must reduce
our craving for foreign money.

Professor Susan Tolchin[2]

In America the frontiers between the groves of academe and the
corridors of power have experienced considerable cross-traffic. No less
than three presidents (James Garfield, Woodrow Wilson and Bill
Clinton) held academic positions before entering politics. Henry Kissinger left Harvard to become Secretary of State (1973–77), while
George Kennan went from being head of the State Department's Policy
Planning Staff (1947–53) to the position of resident scholar at the
Institute for Advanced Studies at Princeton, where he remained for over
forty years. During this century there has also been a tradition of
departing presidents creating libraries as depositories for their papers,
often directly connected to American universities, or close to university
locations. The very large number of political appointments in any
American administration – about three thousand in all – also gives
opportunities for academics to enter the policy-making establishment,
while the practice of American universities in employing adjunct
professors as part-time teachers has permitted many government and
other public officials to teach on a part-time basis.

It is not therefore surprising that American academics have long
played a prominent role in the debate on public policy in the United
States, with special emphasis on foreign policy. American universities
welcome the additional recognition they gain from having their faculty

take a prominent part in public policy debates; testifying before a Congressional committee is not in itself sufficient to gain tenure, but it certainly conforms to the conception of public service which plays an important role in the tenure and promotion process in American universities. In the academic world, as in commerce, the rewards go to those who succeed in producing a differentiated product for which there is a ready market. For many social scientists, especially those who do not necessarily have a ready outlet in business consulting, debates on public policy provide an opportunity to gain a wider stage for themselves and greater prominence for their views.

Although considerable attention, and not a little criticism, has been directed towards lobbyists – both lawyers and others operating interest groups (within the Beltway surrounding Washington, DC) aimed at influencing public policy and legislation – relatively little attention has been paid to the role of academics. While certain think-tanks, such as the Brookings Institution (Democrats) or the Heritage Foundation (Republicans) have some reputation for housing both the has-beens and wannabees of former and future administrations, the majority of their staff are either full-time researchers or academics on secondment – and it is these think-tanks, together with individual academics operating from their home base, which play a prominent (if not always influential) role in the debates on public policy. The apparent need to provide a 'balanced ticket' of witnesses at Congressional hearings, the frequency of election campaigns (with the need of candidates to gain access to expert knowledge on the issues), the attempts by interest groups to invest their views with the credibility of independent academic expertise, and the imperative of foundations to differentiate their philanthropy by promulgating agendas of significant issues, all encourage the participation of academics in the public policy debate – awaiting the call from Washington like longshoremen clustering around the union hall at the start of the morning shift.

As with life on the waterfront, some players are more equal than others. Academics from the most prestigious institutions will find it easier than those from less ivy-covered halls to plug into the network, and junior academics will often lack the necessary *gravitas* to break through to the major leagues. The criteria for tenure and promotion stress research output, with emphasis on articles published in refereed journals and monographs published by a university press – outlets which are slow in bringing research to market and consequently handicap those academics wishing to address contemporary policy issues. Foresight or sheer dumb luck are therefore required if an academic is to catch the tide of debate with the product of his or her research; think-tanks are somewhat better equipped to produce timely contributions, but usually award fellowships to those who already have an established expertise in a particular issue-area and have sufficient seniority at their home institution to negotiate a leave of absence.

On foreign investment questions, one of the most important points of intersection between a modern state and its external environment, research has of necessity to be empirically based, and data collection is expensive; consequently academics have had to depend on foundations or government research funding agencies to finance data collection (not plentiful before the late 1980s, because inward foreign investment was not considered to be a problem meriting priority in the US) or else use data collected by public authorities – federal, state and local – which was often so aggregated that analysis of issues such as foreign control of a given sector, or the comparative economic performance of foreign-owned and domestic firms, was difficult or impossible. Academic contributions to the debate on foreign investment in the US have therefore been reactive rather than proactive, and have until quite recently been confined to methodological critiques of government data collection rather than the advancement of new paradigms for the assessment of the costs and benefits of foreign investment.

FOREIGN DIRECT INVESTMENT IN THE USA AS AN ISSUE

It might be expected that American academics would have paid considerable attention to foreign direct investment (FDI) flowing into the United States after the Second World War, particularly in the late 1970s and 1980s when it increased considerably in volume and significance. In fact, apart from a handful of books dealing with subjects such as Japanese investment in Hawaii or the operations of foreign banks in New York, until the late 1980s American academics published little on foreign investment in the United States – preferring instead to concentrate on the operations of American corporations abroad, or macroperspectives on the position of the US in the international economic system. The linkage between foreign investment and national security (in terms of the structure of foreign control over strategic industries or technologies in the US) is an issue which might be expected to exercise scholars in political science and international relations; yet the literature on declining US hegemony touches on it briefly or not at all. Joseph Nye mentions it in passing; Henry Nau and Paul Kennedy omit it; and even one of the leading European international political economists, Susan Strange, deals with foreign investment only in the context of North–South relations.[3] Even by the 1990s, very little had been contributed to the debate by political scientists: Theodore Moran, in a pamphlet published in 1993, argued that the policy choice lies between 'sophisticated neomercantilism' and 'transnational integration', but offered no prescription or criteria for choice beyond a warning that 'nationally self-interested measures may be used as substitutes for the fundamental changes in American behavior needed to reverse the country's decline'.[4]

In part this neglect of the FDI issue was because inward foreign investment has for quite a long time been uncontroversial in the United States. Both Democratic and Republican administrations have pursued a policy of 'neutrality with encouragement' with regard to inward investment. As President Reagan said on the 9 September 1983: 'The United States welcomes foreign direct investment that flows according to market forces . . . We believe there are only winners, no losers, and all participants gain from it.' The dominance of the liberal economic paradigm in American economic thinking, and the higher status given to abstract theoretical economics, meant that much of the research on foreign direct investment was carried out not by academics (although there were notable exceptions, such as Raymond Vernon and Charles Kindelberger) but by economists in governmental organisations such as the Commerce Department's Bureau of Economic Analysis or the Federal Reserve Bank of New York. Academe seems to have trailed behind in the debate on foreign investment, with government setting the agenda: an agenda which, until the early 1990s, was skewed in favour of minimal restriction on inward investment. Where analysis of inward foreign investment was carried out, this emerged almost exclusively from departments of economics and business, in which political economy was a distant historical memory and the liberal economic paradigm prevailed.

Academics from political science and international relations were certainly interested in America's relative power in the international system, and the role of US-owned multinational corporations in the projection of American power overseas, but the inward flow of foreign investment into the US was not high on their list of concerns. FDI might be useful as one indicator of complex interdependence and transnationalism, but even among economic historians there was little interest in the role of foreign capital in constructing the American economy: the first comprehensive historical study of foreign investment in America (by Mira Wilkins, an economist and former associate of Raymond Vernon's research programme on multinational enterprises at Harvard) did not appear until 1989, documenting the crucial part played by foreign capital and technology in developing American industry and infrastructure – notably the railroads:

> The more than \$7 billion from abroad invested in the American economy at the eve of outbreak of war in Europe represented a sum equal to almost 20 per cent of the U.S. gross national product in 1914. The benefits derived by the U.S. economy from this sizable foreign investment far surpassed the costs.[5]

It was not until America became a debtor nation once more (in 1985) that foreign investment in the US became a focus of attention. According to UNCTAD statistics, the annual rate of growth in foreign direct investment into the US was, at 42 per cent in the 1984–88 period (and only slightly lower growth in the early 1980s), almost twice that of inflows into the EC and other developed countries (about 22 per cent), while in the case of Japan there was a net disinvestment by foreigners in several of those years.[6] The phenomenon attracting most attention was the rapid increase in Japanese direct investment in the United States – which by March 1988 had made the United States the destination for 38 per cent of total Japanese foreign direct investment, and over half of all Japanese direct investments made during the 1988 financial year.[7]

This rapid increase played into America's preoccupation with its perceived decline in power as a result of 'imperial overstretch', a phrase used by Professor Paul Kennedy of Yale in his book *The Rise and Fall of the Great Powers*, which spent several months on the *New York Times* best-seller list in 1987. Aside from books about America's decline, one of the few growth industries in the United States in the late 1980s was writing books about the Japanese threat to American economic well-being. This burgeoning literature – to which American academics contributed quite significantly – tended to obscure the fact that although Japanese manufacturing investment in the United States grew quite rapidly in the latter part of the 1980s, in fact Japan lags well behind the UK and is only just ahead of the Netherlands as an investor. By 1989 – the peak year for foreign investment in the United States – the total amount of foreign direct investment in the US represented some 8 per cent of US gross national product – compared to over 20 per cent in 1914.[8] The foreign-controlled share of US industry as a whole is below 10 per cent in terms of assets, sales and employment – compared to approximately twice that level in the UK, France and Germany.

Given that less than a fifth of the total stock of foreign direct investment in asset terms comes from Japan (compared to about a third from the UK and a sixth from the Netherlands), this obsession with Japan is a little at variance with the facts. Few people worried that such icons of American culture as Burger King (owned by Grand Metropolitan of the UK) or the Watergate building in Washington (owned by the British Coal pension fund) were in foreign hands, but much public concern was raised by the Japanese acquisition of Rockefeller Center in New York and Columbia Studios in Hollywood.

THE COMMITTEE ON FOREIGN INVESTMENT IN THE US

The hysteria about Japanese investment has some echoes from a decade earlier, after the energy crisis of 1973–74, when there were fears of petrodollars pouring into the USA to buy up ranches in Montana, office blocks in Los Angeles, and apartment buildings in New York, and over seventy bills were introduced into Congress from 1972–76 aiming to restrict foreign investment. None were passed, largely because the Ford Administration bowed to pressure from free trade advocates and undertook a far-reaching benchmark survey of foreign investment in the United States, finding it to be at a very low level in comparison with the other OECD countries, and also set up an inter-agency committee – The Committee on Foreign Investment in the United States – to review foreign acquisitions where defence or national security considerations were involved. This committee was chaired by the Treasury, which is more concerned about the American balance of payments and about possible restrictions on capital inflows than it is about preventing foreign investment in the United States; and from the time of its formation in 1975 until 1988 it met on average only twice a year.

It is worth noting that only the US and Germany among the OECD countries have never had a comprehensive formal review process for inward investment. Indeed, FDI matters have largely been the responsibility of the US Trade Representative since 1979 (perhaps as a result of a tendency to see FDI as import substituting in effect). However, some sectors of the American economy have long been effectively closed to direct control by foreign investors – civil aviation, production and utilisation of nuclear energy, and most domestic maritime transport, as well as broadcasting (unless the Federal Communications Commission grants an exception). With the exception of some Canadian and British firms which have a long record as reliable suppliers to the Department of Defense, there has also been an unwritten convention of major firms engaged in large-scale defence contracting having to be American owned, or at the very least insulated from direct control by the parent company by a trust controlled by US nationals. With these exceptions, the US government has traditionally pursued a policy of 'neutrality with encouragement' toward inward foreign direct investment – undoubtedly a reflection of the relatively small-scale foreign investment in the United States until the late 1980s and the pragmatic view that American investors overseas might suffer retaliation if FDI in the US were restricted.

The rapid growth, if not the relative size, of foreign direct investment in the latter part of the 1980s did oblige the Reagan Administration to accede to some nominal restrictions on inward investment in order to allay public concern. A Gallup poll conducted in October 1989 found 51 per cent of respondents asserting that foreign investment was bad for the US economy and 60 per cent thinking that US firms should avoid foreign investors.[9] The Exon–Florio Amendment to the 1988 Trade Act gave the President power to block foreign takeovers on national security grounds – although not on the grounds that they would affect 'essential commerce', as the sponsors of the Amendment had originally wanted.

The Committee on Foreign Investment in the US (CFIUS) was designated the review body under the Exon–Florio Amendment. The Committee represents nine agencies and offices (including Treasury and Defense), but has only a very small staff – six part-time staff in 1990 – and is obliged to complete its review of foreign acquisitions within ninety days of referral: it has thirty days to decide whether to investigate the case, then forty-five days to complete the investigation, and a final fifteen days for the President to act on the Committee's recommendations. Companies are not obliged to notify CFIUS if they intend to take over US corporations, but if they do not do so and the Committee considers that national security is being undermined or violated in consequence, there is no time limit on CFIUS ability to open investigation of a takeover or annul it. The time-scale for reviews and investigation by CFIUS – and the need to safeguard confidentiality – means that academics can make no input into its work and that they acquire little information about the reasoning underlying CFIUS decisions.

The CFIUS reviews a number of factors including: (1) the domestic production needed for projected national defence requirements; (2) the capability and capacity of domestic industries to meet these requirements, including availability of human resources, technology and materials; (3) the control of domestic industries and commercial activity by foreign citizens as it affects US ability to meet the requirements of national security, and (4) the past record of the participants in fulfilling export control regulations. By 1992 the CFIUS had received over 700 notifications by companies intending to take over US firms: of these less than a dozen proceeded to formal investigation, with only two being formally blocked – the acquisition of Mamco (a supplier of metal aircraft components to Boeing and other companies) by the China National Aero-Technology Import and Export Company (CATIC) in 1990; and the attempt in 1992 by Thompson CSF, a French government-controlled electronics firm, to buy the missile division of LTV Corporation.

The CFIUS has been careful not to be seen as a 'Japan-basher' – the companies investigated have come from Germany, Japan, Sweden/ Switzerland, India, France and China. Of the cases investigated only a minority have involved Japanese companies – the 1989 attempt by Tokuyama Soda to bid for General Ceramics, a producer of components for nuclear weapons (where the deal was finally approved after Tokuyama Soda agreed to spin off the nuclear weapons component division); and Nippon Sanso's $23 million acquisition in 1990 of Semi-Gas Systems Incorporated, the world's leading producer of 'gas cabinets' for semiconductor production. Despite heavy lobbying from Sematech, a research consortium of leading US semiconductor producers, CFIUS decided in July 1990 that the sale of Semi-Gas to Nippon Sanso should not be blocked, on the grounds that the acquisition would not undermine national security and that there were other sources of the technology.[10] A third Japanese deal, the takeover by Fanuc of Moore Special Tools Incorporated in early 1991, a machine tool manufacturer supplying to the Energy Department for the nuclear weapons programme, was approved after modification.[11] Early in 1993 there was some controversy when CFIUS approved the acquisition by a Japanese company of the only American manufacturer of some computer components used in the Patriot and Trident missiles – the Applied Magnetics Corporation.

For the most part the academic community has not paid much attention to, nor had much impact on, the procedures or criteria employed by CFIUS. To some extent this has been due to the speed and confidentiality of the CFIUS review and investigation process, but these characteristics have not prevented lawyers with experience of acting for companies affected by the Exon–Florio Amendment from commenting on its activities, nor has it inhibited various interest groups from either praising or criticising CFIUS.

One such interest group, the Association for International Investment (a lobby group funded by various, mainly European, firms and a number of US state governments), was of the opinion that Exon–Florio had worked well, but that there was a danger of 'economic security' becoming linked with the CFIUS remit of defending 'national security', of the CFIUS process being used as a delaying tactic by target firms in hostile takeovers, and CFIUS becoming a target for political pressures emanating from Congress and elsewhere (Larschan testimony, 26 February 1991, p. 63). Christopher Wall, an attorney who had represented several clients in CFIUS transactions, and one of the few CFIUS investigations, testified before a Congressional Committee that the Exon–Florio Amendment 'embodies the right policy, and the law has worked well . . . Vague phrases like "economic destiny" cannot substitute for a close examination of the facts of each case.'[12] Linda Spencer of the Economic Strategy Institute (a think-tank headed by Clyde Prestowitz, a former Commerce Department Counsellor for Japan Affairs and one of the leading revisionists on Japan and its closed markets) argued that CFIUS's 'ineffectiveness . . . stems largely from a lack of political will'.[13] The only academic to testify at the hearings quoted above, Professor Theodore H. Moran, made an extremely ingenious suggestion that CFIUS, in its reviews of foreign acquisitions, should develop measures of international concentration of foreign suppliers because such dependence poses danger to US interests only when 'substitutes are few, the lead-time to develop alternatives is long, and stockpiling is not feasible'. He suggested a rule that national security threats could be measured objectively according to 'whether or not four countries or four companies control more . . .than 50 per cent of the market', and that performance requirements should be imposed if that test was met.[14] The Subcommittee did not pursue his suggestion, but adjourned for lunch; one CFIUS member later criticised it as overly mechanical and simplistic.

Professors Graham and Krugman, writing in 1989 (two years earlier) had argued that there are 'no simple criteria that can be used to prescribe performance criteria that are actually in the public interest. As a result, efforts to impose performance requirements will inevitably become more of a political than an economic exercise.' They also raised similar objections to the use of seemingly objective criteria to screening of investment: 'The fact is no such criteria exist. In their absence, any US government screening process would become either highly politicized or turn into a largely irrelevant rubber stamp.'[15]

Professor Susan Tolchin (in a book co-authored with her husband, Martin Tolchin of the *New York Times*'s Washington Bureau) criticised CFIUS as a 'paper tiger', on the ground that since 1988 it had vetoed only one (two by 1993) foreign takeover on national security grounds, clearly showing that 'it is futile to give the president more power than he intends to use' and noting that firms faced with a choice of bankruptcy or foreign takeover had no real option unless the US government was prepared to provide more funds for the maintenance of indigenous technological capabilities.[16] Professors Woodward and Glickman observed that the Reagan Administration's international policy was incoherent and lacked direction and focus; their book was published in the early months of the Bush Administration, before some of the more controversial CFIUS decisions (and its first veto, of Boeing subcontractor MAMCO Manufacturing's acquisition by CATIC – owned by the Chinese government – in January 1990). They did, however, detect an obsessive hostility in the Reagan era toward acquisitions by state-owned foreign companies.[17]

Academic opinion was therefore divided on the utility of the CFIUS process, though all agreed that its original remit was fairly narrowly defined and that it did not pose a significant barrier to foreign investment in the US. Graham and Krugman probably spoke for most academic experts when they argued that certain actions of foreign firms should be regulated, but that equal restrictions should be placed on domestic firms, on the grounds that 'there exists a strong general economic case against monopolization'.[18]

If there is a change to be seen in the relatively permissive enforcement of domestic US anti-trust regulation in the post-Reagan/Bush years, however, it is more likely to stem from a reaction to the excesses of liberalisation in the 1980s than from arguments by academics about the economic case for competition, which support rather than influence the tide of public opinion. Certainly the Labor Secretary Robert Reich, formerly a Harvard academic, has argued forcefully that foreign ownership is irrelevant as a criterion for evaluating the activities of a firm in the US, given that production is now irreversibly global and national economies are ceasing to have meaning as almost every factor of production becomes more mobile. His answer to the fundamental question 'who is us?' (as opposed to 'them') is that only labour is relatively immobile, and that the US (and other countries) can only prosper by policies designed to 'increase the potential value of what its citizens can add to the global economy, by enhancing their skills and capacities and by improving their means of linking those skills and capacities to the world market'.[19]

This view may not necessarily extend to a willingness on the part of the Clinton Administration to stand aside from the flow of non-human resources across national frontiers: the Chair of President Clinton's Council of Economic Advisers, Professor Laura D'Andrea Tyson, argued in a book published shortly before her appointment that 'cautious activism' in both opening foreign markets for US exports and intervening domestically to ensure technological competitiveness (as the Europeans have done with Airbus) is justifiable.[20] Vigorous debates – an area of comparative advantage for academics – may be expected in the White House.

COLLECTION OF DATA ON FOREIGN DIRECT INVESTMENT

If academics are united on any point, it is that governments should provide more information – preferably in machine-readable form so that it can be scanned, collated, and correlated to provide the substance for their publications. American (and other) academics are singularly fortunate that the US government is arguably more liberal than any other in providing information about its activities and about the transactions carried out within and across its borders. This liberality probably has more to do with the democratic, pluralist political culture of the US than with fulfilling the needs of academics, but academics have had some influence in reinforcing a culture of free flows of information from the government to the governed. In this issue-area, academics can invest their opinions with great credibility: data sets are their business, and lack of data the all-purpose alibi for failures to analyse the pressing issues of the age.

In terms of the data available for analysis, analysts of foreign investment flows in and out of the US have been better served by the US government than by most other countries. American official statistics on foreign investment – both inward and outward – have long been the most reliable and comprehensive of any of the industrialised countries; academics have rarely criticised the US government's efforts to collect and present data on FDI and have never found it guilty of politically inspired manipulation. Even so, as academics increasingly complained in the late 1980s, the official data do not permit the analysis of a number of important questions concerning the impact (positive and negative) of foreign direct investment in the US.

The full extent of foreign ownership of specific sectors, the employment effects of foreign investment, the degree of value-added in specific foreign-owned plants, and many other topics, cannot be analysed rigorously because data series are often not compatible, differ in the definition of key variables (such as the definition of full-time employee), and are frequently aggregated to protect the confidentiality of the companies supplying the information.

While over two dozen Federal agencies collect data on some aspect of foreign direct investment in the US, the prime responsibility for collecting and reporting information on foreign investment lies with the Departments of Commerce (for foreign direct investment, involving direct managerial control over the assets involved) and Treasury (for portfolio investment, owned for a financial return, but where the assets are not managed by the owner). The US, along with other OECD countries, defines foreign direct investment as investment resulting in the foreign ownership or control of 10 per cent or more of the equity in a US business.

The collection of FDI data is the special responsibility of a division of the Commerce Department, the Bureau of Economic Analysis (BEA), which under the terms of the International Investment Survey Act of 1976 collects data on the ownership of foreign direct investment, its cost and the sectoral distribution of sales of the foreign-owned affiliate in order to classify the foreign investment by industry. Data on transactions between US affiliates and their foreign parent companies are collected quarterly in order to prepare balance of payments accounts; financial and operating data (such as balance sheets, information on employment, exports and imports) are collected annually. In addition, every five years a benchmark census is undertaken by BEA so as to cover a wider range of information; the last such census took place in 1993, and the results of the 1987 census were still being published in revised form in 1992. The information is published in aggregate form classified by foreign country, by industry affiliate and – where appropriate – by state within the United States, except where this would identify individual companies. Information for individual firms cannot be released outside the statistical agencies designated by the President to perform functions under the International Investment and Trade in Services Survey Act, whose intent is to supply the government and other users with the aggregate information needed to assess the impact of foreign direct investment in the US. Full and accurate reporting by the firms involved in the survey is encouraged by the provision that the data cannot be used as a basis for actions against these firms (for example, on anti-trust matters by the Justice Department or on taxation by the Internal Revenue Service) or which would provide information about their operations to potential competitors. Failure to file any of the required forms is punishable by a civil penalty not exceeding $10,000, and wilful failure to file is punishable by a fine not exceeding $10,000 and imprisonment for not more than one year, or both.[21]

Another branch of the Commerce Department, the International Trade Administration, collects and publishes annual reports on individual transactions based on a monitoring of publicly available sources, including company filings with the Securities and Exchange Commission, press reports and direct contacts. Unlike the BEA statistics, these data specify the company name of both the US affiliate and the foreign parent firm. The ITA publishes transaction reports annually which contain information about each investment in terms of its sector, its location, its type and value as well as the country of the foreign parent company. Unfortunately these cannot be compared directly with the aggregated BEA statistics, and are not comprehensive because of the lack of mandatory reporting requirements.

The data collection procedures try to balance the need of policy-makers to know more about inward direct investment into the United States (especially important given its explosive growth during the 1980s) with the equally important goal of maintaining confidentiality of sensitive business information, safeguarding the integrity of the data collection system and controlling the costs associated with maintaining the database. One of the criticisms made by academics of the existing data on FDI are the inconsistencies between the classification of the data collected by the BEA, which maintains data at the business enterprise level – and thus classifies all business activity of that enterprise in accordance with its primary business activity, regardless of other secondary business activities in which the firm is engaged – and the actual activities of foreign-owned firms. This leads to some significant distortions in the data: for example, a firm whose primary business is the importation and distribution of cars, but which also assembles cars in the US as a secondary business activity, will have all its operations classified under wholesale trade. Thus Honda, Toyota and Nissan – all of which have assembly plants in the US – are classified as wholesalers rather than car manufacturers in the BEA data.[22]

The BEA collects three distinct classes of information about inward direct investment: on the balance of payments; on financial and reporting data on foreign-earned subsidiaries in the US; and acquisition and establishment of new enterprises. Each type of information is designed to provide a different perspective on the role of inward investment in the US economy. The balance of payments data reveal cross-border flows of capital and investment income flows between a foreign-owned subsidiary in the US and its parent company abroad, to measure the direct investment position of foreign investors in the US in terms of the book value of their equity (including retained earnings) and loans to foreign-owned subsidiaries in the US. It is designed to measure flows relating to the US balance of payments: capital flows between a foreign parent company and its American affiliate, in terms of equity, inter-company debt and reinvested earnings; income flows such as retained and distributed profits for the foreign parent, payments for royalties and licence fees and other services between the parent and its subsidiary in the US. All this data is used to measure the book value of inward direct investment.

The second set of data – financial and operating data – of foreign-owned firms in the US is designed to give information about the overall operations of that subsidiary including transactions with its foreign parent. This consists of standard balance sheet items such as assets, liabilities, net worth, sales and capital expenditures (including R&D spending), net income, US and state taxes paid, interest and dividend payments and remitted profits. In addition, information on employment and total compensation paid to employees is provided as well as information on imports and exports. This information is then aggregated by industry and nationality of the parent company to provide a broad view of the economic performance of foreign-owned firms operating in the US economy. The information is collected through an annual survey and a larger benchmark survey conducted every five years – the most recent survey having been carried out early in 1993 for the 1992 tax year. The results of the 1987 survey were published in preliminary form in 1989 and in revised form in 1990 and 1992. The 1987 benchmark survey was based on reports from over 8,000 companies representing almost 22,000 individual business operations. The BEA estimates that the information it receives from its annual survey represents fully 95 per cent of the value of operations of all foreign-owned firms in the US.[23]

A third category of information collected by BEA is on acquisitions of existing US businesses by a foreign company or by the subsidiaries of foreign companies and the establishment of new business enterprises by foreign investors. Reporting is required if the new business or acquisition has total assets in excess of one million dollars or owns at least 200 acres of land.

The BEA data is widely used by US government agencies, international organisations, state and local governments, and academic and other researchers. A Royal Institute of International Affairs study noted in 1989 that the US government 'already publishes more complete information on the domestic operations of FOF's (foreign-owned firms) than any other country'.[24]

In terms of the information available about foreign direct investment to American policy-makers, the BEA collects data on all the major categories that they might be expected to need: the magnitude and trends in FDI; international capital and income flows; international trade; competition and market structure; corporate finance; industrial relations and labour policy; public finance and fiscal matters; and national security in terms of the control by foreign investors are sources of supply of vital raw materials, technology or products essential to national security. The data on R&D spending, ownership of patents by foreign-owned firms and payments for licences, royalties and other forms of technology transfer also provide information on US competitiveness.

The main issue is the level of detail at which this information is available – although the BEA does not collect information on, for example, the degree of unionisation or the demographic characteristics of the labour force, which would be useful for human resource policy. The BEA data is classified in terms of industry group and does not go down to the level of class of products produced – at that level of detail the main source of information to the US government is that collected by the Bureau of the Census, the government's principal data collection agency, which is prohibited by law from sharing information at the enterprise or plant level with the BEA. In terms of geographic detail, important for assessing the employment effects of foreign investment, the BEA provides regional and state breakdowns annually for employment, property holdings and land owned but not for most of the other categories. Since the mid-1980s there have been several attempts to introduce legislation in Congress to improve the level of detail of foreign investment statistics reported by the BEA, notably several measures considered in 1990 to require the Bureau of the Census to provide data to the BEA to enable it to undertake more refined industries and geographic analyses of the operations of US affiliates of foreign parents. Some of these measures were vigorously opposed by organisations such as The Association for International Investment (a lobby group headed by Elliot L. Richardson and financed by a number of foreign-owned companies and state governments) which argued that some of the measures – notably the Bryant Bill – would require foreign companies to disclose more information than was the case for US companies, and would deter foreign investors. Eventually a compromise measure was passed which has resulted in more detailed classification of the sectoral distribution of foreign investment in the US: this resulted in the publication in 1992 of a more informative breakdown of the 1987 benchmark statistics.

These newly detailed statistics revealed that foreign investment accounts for only 1.1 per cent of all firms and employs 3.7 per cent of the workforce (but 6.9 per cent of manufacturing employment) – 66,678 firms employing 3.23 million workers. In some sectors the foreign share of employment was much higher: 55 per cent in zinc and lead mining, 43 per cent in liquor distilling, 40 per cent in consumer audio and video manufacturing – but only 5.4 per cent in automobile production, the source of so much *angst* about the Japanese invasion.[25]

Professor Susan Tolchin, co-author with her husband Martin of a best-selling book on foreign investment in the US, *Buying Into America*, asserted in 1988 that 'most experts believe that at least 50 per cent of all foreign investment [in the US] goes unreported, but gave no evidence to support this'.[26] Graham and Krugman concluded that there is 'no reason to believe that any significant degree of misreporting takes place'. They were also unable to find any discrepancies within the US data and concluded that criticisms of such discrepancies have been caused by misinterpretation rather than faults in the data collection process itself.[27] Some of these discrepancies, such as the differences between Canadian data on Canadian investment in the United States and US data on Canadian investment are caused by differences in definitions and standards applied – thus the Canadian government classifies as outward direct investment some transactions which the United States classifies as portfolio investment.

Even the BEA admits that it cannot track every direct investment and that therefore the data it collects understate the total amount of direct investment in the United States. None the less, it is clear that the BEA data covers most FDI transactions and that the discrepancies are largely caused by the dividing line between portfolio investment (i.e. foreign entities controlling less than 10 per cent of a given enterprise) and direct investment. The BEA data, however, is not problem-free: it is often difficult to track down the ultimate beneficial owner of an enterprise – thus Fairchild Semiconductor, which was owned by Schlumberger, an oil field services electronics firm, was considered to be based in the Netherlands Antilles, even though its ultimate owner was a French family.

The requirement not to disclose information about individual companies also presents problems for analysts: thus the amount of chemical employment in Delaware is not published in the data because most of it is accounted for by Dupont. This is in order to prevent the government from disclosing confidential information about the individual operations of firms. Moreover, the practice of gathering information on a fully consolidated basis means that the firm's overall industry classification is based on its primary activity and does not include its secondary activities, which may in fact be quite important. It is thus very difficult to measure with any accuracy the extent of foreign ownership in detailed industrial categories. The many different data series on employment produce different percentages for the amount accounted for by foreign-owned firms, depending on which employment series is used.

Similarly, measurement of the overall extent of foreign direct investment will vary according to whether one measures the foreign direct
investment position, in terms of the book value of the parent company's
equity in a loans to their subsidiaries in the US, or whether one uses
the total financial structure and operations of foreign-owned affiliates
in the US, which would produce a much larger figure.

Even if one accepts that the data gathered by the BEA and other
government agencies is reasonably accurate and representative, there
are significant limitations on the possible uses of existing data. There
is at present no means of determining the sources of growth in the assets
of foreign firms or of assessing whether foreign-owned firms achieve
higher labour productivity than domestically owned enterprises. While
accepting the need for confidentiality, Graham and Krugman suggest
that reporting firms should be able to decide for themselves whether
their submissions should be open to the public – as is the case in Japan.
This would avoid collection of data having a chilling effect on foreign
direct investment and continue to provide a strong measure of confidentiality: data could be made available to researchers on an aggregated basis that does not divulge confidential information.[28] In this
respect it is possible to discern some influence from academics: the
Graham and Krugman recommendations were broadly followed in the
provisions of the Foreign Direct Investment and International Financial
Data Improvements Act of 1990 and permitted data linkage between
the BEA, the Bureau of the Census and the Bureau of Labor Statistics
of the US Labor Department. One of the bills on which the Act was
based, the Sharp Bill, included in its letter of introduction direct
references to the Graham and Krugman recommendations.[29] The
changes made to BEA publication of statistics from 1990 go some way
to meeting the criticism of academics outlined above, although it seems
likely that the greater precision and detail offered was seen more as an
antidote to ill-informed public hysteria (or mail-bag-induced xeno-
phobia on Capitol Hill) than to satisfy the needs of academia. In
general, academics may have helped to refine the FDI statistics at the
margin, but they have otherwise been reduced to the position of half-
interested, ineffectual spectators.

IT AIN'T WHAT YOU DO, IT'S THE WAY THAT YOU DO IT

Why did American academics play such a marginal role in the debate
on foreign direct investment, one of the most salient political issues in
the United States' redefinition of its relations with the outside world?
Certainly it was not because the political establishment in the US

suppressed debate on FDI – indeed, most of the debates on FDI were initiated by legislators impelled by post-bag politics and the importunings of special interest groups (such as those in the automobile and semiconductor industries) faced with intensified foreign competition on their home turf. Although the Reagan and Bush Administrations were unworried (even complacent) about inward FDI, they certainly did nothing to suppress debate on the subject (beyond failing to inspire researchers by providing government funding in this area) and continued to supply the high-quality data on which academic research depended, even improving that data in response to pressure from academe and Capitol Hill.

In part, the silence of the academic dog in the night can be explained by the fact that the FDI issue straddles established disciplinary boundaries, and that it has never reached the level of penetration in the US economy where present (as distinct from future) national security has been threatened: consequently FDI has primarily been analysed from an economic standpoint, through the prism of the liberal economic paradigm. Even economists who have flirted with strategic trade policy and some government intervention in the market, such as Krugman and Tyson, have argued that the overall impact of inward foreign investment on the US economy has been beneficial, except where it stifles competition or induces excessive dependence on foreign suppliers.

Political scientists and international relations specialists, however, have had little interest in – and consequently negligible impact on – the policy debate. In part this was because their preoccupations have been – in the case of political scientists – with the decay of the US internally, and foreign investment has made a small but positive impact in promoting the development of some of the less affluent states, such as those in the south. For international relations specialists, preoccupied by the position of the US in the world at large in the post-hegemonic era, the low level of foreign investment in the US in comparison with all other industrialised countries (except, notably, Japan) and the symmetrical character of inward and outward direct investment (with total stocks of FDI by the US overseas and foreign investment in the US more or less in balance by the early 1990s) provided no evidence that the ability of the US to project its power abroad was significantly affected by the foreign industrial presence in America. The linkages between the economic and political aspects of foreign policy, and between domestic and international trends, seem to have been neglected in this case, despite the pointers to such problems provided by the theorists of international political economy and foreign policy analysis over the last twenty years. The fall in inward investment flows from

1990 then acted as a further disincentive to investigate the problem, since the FDI debate in Congress and elsewhere vanished like a summer storm and attention became focused on America's decaying infrastructure, health care and deficit reduction. Before most academics had even woken up to the possibilities the party had moved on, and the players were packing up their instruments for the next gig.

NOTES

1 *Business Week*, 27 October 1986, p. 84.
2 Testimony before the US Senate, Committee on Commerce, Science and Transportation *Hearing on Federal Collection of Information on Foreign Investment in the US*, S. Hrg. 100–650, 24 March 1988, p. 75.
3 Nye notes that 'It would be ironic if fears of American decline led to policies of . . . resistance to foreign investment.' Joseph Nye, *Bound to Lead: The Changing Nature of American Power*, New York, Basic Books, 1990, p. 228; Henry Nau, *The Myth of America's Decline: Leading the World Economy into the 1990s*, New York/Oxford, Oxford University Press, 1990; Paul Kennedy, *The Rise and Fall of the Great Powers*, New York, Random House, 1987; Susan Strange, *States and Markets: An Introduction to International Political Economy*, London, Pinter Publishers, 1988, p. 214.
4 Theodore H. Moran, *American Economic Policy and National Security*, New York, Council on Foreign Relations, 1993, p. 81.
5 Mira Wilkins, *The History of Foreign Investment in the United States to 1914*, Cambridge, Mass., Harvard University Press, 1989, p. 625.
6 *Financial Times*, 21 July 1993, quoting from UNCTAD, *World Investment Report 1993: Transnational Corporations and Integrated International Production*, 1993.
7 Michael Hodges, 'The Japanese Industrial Presence in America: Same Bed, Different Dreams', in Kathleen Newland (ed.) *The International Relations of Japan*, London, Macmillan, 1990, pp. 50–1.
8 Figures from Edward Graham and Paul Krugman, *Foreign Direct Investment in the United States*, Washington, DC, Institute for International Economics, 1989, p. 30; and Mira Wilkins, *The History of Foreign Investment*, op. cit., p. 625.
9 *The Polling Report*, Washington, DC, 4 December 1989, vol. 5, no. 5, p. 1.
10 James K. Jackson, *Foreign Investment: The Exon–Florio National Security Test*, Library of Congress, Congressional Research Service, 26 September 1990, pp. 7–9.
11 US Congress, House of Representatives Committee on Energy and Commerce, Subcommittee on Commerce, Consumer protection, and Competitiveness, *National Security Takeovers and Technology Preservation*, 26 Feb. 1991, 102nd Congress, Serial no. 102–23; testimony of Bradley R. Larschan, pp. 59–60.
12 Hearing of the Subcommittee on Commerce, Consumer Protection, and Competitiveness of the Committee on Energy and Commerce, House of Representatives (102nd Congress) *National Security Takeovers and Technology Preservation*, Washington, USGPO, 12 June 1991, p. 165.

13 Ibid., p. 154.

14 Ibid., pp. 178–80; see also Theodore H. Moran, 'The Globalization of America's Defense Industries: Managing the Threat of Foreign Dependence', *International Security*, vol. 15, no. 1, Summer 1990, pp. 57–100.

15 Graham and Krugman, *Foreign Direct Investment in the United States*, op. cit., pp. 119, 116.

16 Martin and Susan Tolchin, *Selling Our Security*, New York, Knopf, 1992, p. 45.

17 Norman Glickman and Douglas Woodward, *The New Competitors: How Foreign Investors are Changing the U.S. Economy*, New York, Basic Books, 1989, p. 265.

18 Graham and Krugman, *Foreign Direct Investment in the United States*, op. cit., p. 121.

19 Robert Reich, *The Wealth of Nations: Preparing Ourselves for 21st. Century Capitalism*, New York, Knopf, 1991, p. 8.

20 Laura D'Andrea Tyson, *Who's Bashing Whom? Trade Conflicts in High-Technology Industries*, Washington, Institute for International Economics, 1992, esp. pp. 42–5.

21 US General Accounting Office, *Foreign Investment: Federal Data Collection on Foreign Investment in the United States*, Washington, GAO/NSIAD–90–25BR, October 1989.

22 See Graham and Krugman, *Foreign Direct Investment in the United States*, op. cit., pp. 140–1.

23 See the testimony of Elliot L. Richardson, Chairman of the Association for International Investment in Subcommittee on Commerce, Consumer Protection, and Competitiveness, Committee on Energy and Commerce, House of Representatives (101st Congress, 2nd session), *Foreign Investment in the United States* (Serial no. 101–194), 13 June 1990, pp. 92–127.

24 Deanne Julius and Stephen Thomsen 'Foreign-Owned Firms, Trade and Economic Integration' *The Tokyo Club Papers*, no. 2, London, RIIA, 1989, p. 202.

25 Associated Press Financial News, 24 June 1992.

26 Martin and Susan Tolchin, *Buying Into America: How Foreign Money is Changing the Face of Our Nation*, New York, Times Books, 1988, p. 264.

27 Graham and Krugman, *Foreign Direct Investment in the United States*, op. cit., p. 139.

28 Ibid., p. 142.

29 See Edward Graham and Paul Krugman, *Foreign Direct Investment in the United States* (2nd edn), Washington, DC, Institute for International Economics, 1991, pp. 174–5.

Part V
Conclusion

11 The two worlds

Natural partnership or necessary distance?

Christopher Hill and Pamela Beshoff

In this book we have been attempting to throw some light upon the complex relationship between the respective inhabitants of the two worlds of international relations of our title – the scholars and practitioners of world politics. By scholars is meant primarily, but not exclusively, university academics who teach as well as research, while practitioners are taken to be all those – public or private, political or administrative, diplomats or home-based – who have a role in making events. To do this, the answers to three questions in particular have been sought: the 'history question', concerning the degree to which academic International Relations necessarily shares the same contemporary focus as that of the practitioner; the 'ideological question', or the role of normative concerns in the origins and conduct of research; and, thirdly, the 'professional question', which highlights the pressures on the academic which may accrue from greater involvement with policy-makers.

In so far as common themes have emerged out of the nine separate cases examined by our contributors, they will be summarised below. But the analysis does not only concern the solipsistic world of academe. Chapter 1 also raises questions about how practitioners can best use academic work, and in what ways their choices are shaped, knowingly or otherwise, by what intellectuals (admittedly, a category not coterminous with that of academics) produce. A degree of generalisation is also possible about these issues. Underlying both sets of problems, however, is a single broad dilemma on which all of us take positions. In general terms, this final chapter will try to determine whether academics and practitioners are natural partners who ought to work closely together, or whether – in the field of international relations at least – a certain mutual detachment would be in the interests of both sides.

THE 'HISTORY QUESTION'

With the heightened role of the communications industry in the transmission of instant news, amply demonstrated during the 1990s in commentary on the Gulf War and the civil war in the former Yugoslavia, international relations have gripped the imagination of people across the world more than ever before. Clearly, in such periods as 1912–20, 1936–45 and 1957–63 any half-informed person in any country would have looked outwards for the major events of the day. But only in recent times has there emerged a general awareness of the notion of an international community, with its own patterns and dynamics, let alone the sense of an academic subject specialising in the comprehension of such a community. Now, especially after the fractured world of the Cold War has come to an end, the concept as well as the consequences of international relations is all too familiar to the millions who tune in to daily news bulletins or scan the front pages of their newspapers. Correspondingly, the academic subject of International Relations is finally achieving a sound footing in the universities (although continental Europe still lags behind the Anglo-Saxon world), not least because students think it important, and more student interest means more money.

This new salience has given academics the opportunity to influence public opinion, and thereby to influence policy-makers indirectly as well as through such direct channels as exist. The obverse of such an opportunity is the burden of explanation. Increased information has meant that open season has been declared on international relations by every barbershop and tap-room pundit, without any real understanding of the complexity of the issues involved.[1] Yet academics are not necessarily best equipped to explain their understanding of complexity to a mass audience, and to the extent that they do seek to emulate A.J.P. Taylor in that regard,[2] they risk sinking under a much heavier general workload than thirty years ago.

Through judicious contributions to the media, and inviting journalists to the right conferences, academics can at times certainly raise the level of the public debate of foreign policy. Perhaps this is already the principal motive for many in the profession. For others, and for the subject as a whole, this is only one objective, and a secondary one at that, among several in the study of international relations. The academic contributors to this book naturally disagree amongst themselves as to the degree of attention which they should give to current issues: Christopher Hill sees scholarship as being at risk from too enthusiastic a commitment to the policy debate, while William Wallace is strongly of the view that the subject only takes its life and energy from its contemporary relevance. Pamela Beshoff, (perhaps as the result of having worked at one time as a practitioner) is concerned as much with the risk of poor communication between the two sides as with the dangers of mutual involvement. In general the academic contributors show in their work a persistent concern for the ever-changing contemporary world without wishing to depart far from their basic specialisms or from their distinctively academic rules of engagement. Beck, for example, criticises policy-makers' neglect of historical data in the Falklands dispute, but he does so from the position of expert knowledge acquired over years of study. Without that knowledge he and other colleagues would have had no *locus standi* in the debate over sovereign rights which suddenly raged after 2 April 1982. Conversely, special knowledge of that kind will only occasionally bring the academics concerned into the glare of political attention. For most of the time, even if working on a policy-relevant issue, a specialist will rely on influencing his or her respective opposite numbers in government or in pressure-group through scholarly books and journals, and direct contact through conferences or consultancies.

In more general terms, the evolution of an academic subject like International Relations will be powerfully affected by events or, more precisely, by how those who pursue it respond to events. On human rights, for example, as pointed out by John Vincent, 'sufferings about the world of experience are what incites concern in the first place'. The wide dissemination of facts about what may be happening in Somalia, Bosnia, East Timor or elsewhere, to 'outrage the conscience' at least of Western electorates, has important implications for the development of theory, at the levels of both human rights theory itself, and wider theories of international society. In April 1991, United Nations Security Council Resolution 688, which saw a rare coalescence of condemnation of the treatment of the Kurdish population of Iraq, contributed significantly towards the erosion of international orthodoxy on the question of intervention.[3] Intervention, or rather non-intervention – that is, the prohibition, enshrined in this century in the UN Charter, of interference in the affairs of sovereign states by outside bodies, whether other states or international institutions – is historically and philosophically a matter of excruciating delicacy.[4] The ghost of interventions past has stood behind the negotiators' chair during considerations of how to respond to the Bosnian crisis, and indeed not only to Bosnia but to the fate of all minorities in what was Yugoslavia. The horror of events on the ground has impacted on the development of theory: massacres in Bosnia call in question the validity of non-interventionist doctrines and legitimise theorising about the expanding role of the United Nations. This can lead, in a transitional phase before the congruence of theory and practice is re-established, to confusion in the citadels of policy-making, with practitioners casting around for new conceptual certainties and, until they settle down again, making policy 'on the hoof'. Here the scholarly debate on the possibility of a 'paradigm shift' becomes of interest even to the practitioner harried by the dictates of in-trays and out-trays.[5]

On the academic side, far from academic interest in contemporary events leading to turf disputes and distractions from scholarship, it might actually be an essential stimulus to the advance of theoretical work – so long as the tail does not wag the dog and scholarship remains a central value. The paradox here is that theory and practice need to be congruent, but in order to inform practice theory needs to be autonomous and ahead of the practical game, rather than chasing behind it – as Hodges (Chapter 10) shows they were in the US debate over foreign investment.

But is there evidence from practitioners that they find academic International Relations useful, or that they see the relationship as a natural partnership? Historically, there has been nothing systematic in Britain about the ties between the academic subject and the Whitehall machine, certainly by comparison to what occurs in Washington. Among our contributing practitioners Berman has shown clearly that the Foreign and Commonwealth Office's lawyers feel themselves to be a part of a professional community with international lawyers outside their own employ. They, foreign governments, and international tribunals often rely on the practical wisdom and the conceptual independence of legal scholars. International law, of course, is not international relations proper, but it is an intimately related subject and books on such subjects as sovereignty and intervention genuinely straddle the divide and draw practitioners attention. If recent talk about contracting-out to academics some of the work currently done in the FCO's Research Department ever comes to fruition, there is a precedent at hand in the surprisingly interpenetrated world of government and academic international lawyers.

Our two other practitioners are a former diplomat who is also a well-known scholar, and a campaigning member of Parliament. In Chapter 6 the former gives revealing insights into the deeply ambivalent relationship between academics and practitioners in the 1960s. The FCO Planning Staff were beginning to argue that academics in their field should not be ignored, but despite making certain efforts to understand the new approaches to international relations then proliferating, their efforts to talk to theorists and the profession as a whole generally foundered (notably in what seems to have been a scene worthy of Tom Sharpe at the Foreign Secretary's lunch for 20 professors), leaving contacts with the 'geographers' (i.e. regional specialists), the think-tanks (Chatham House and IISS) and distinguished and/ or forceful individuals (John Erickson and Patrick Honey) as the main points of contact. As Sir James Cable's career illustrates, there will also be the occasional scholar-diplomat inside the Foreign Office, who can encourage their colleagues to look out more often towards the universities (this is, however, much less true than of the legal advisers, who themselves form a significant part of the international law community in Britain, as in other countries). Cable's analysis starts from the criticisms made elsewhere by William Wallace, one of our academic contributors, and he accepts that the area of planning is an obvious place for an academic contribution to be made. But he also outlines the difficulties involved in bringing academics into an organisation where the 'operators' were already suspicious of anything abstract and unfamiliar. For its part the world of the campus, concludes Cable, is just as stand-offish, with the result that IR remains stuck in an 'ivory tower as an elegant piece of show-business for planners'.

This depressing conclusion is not shared by Tam Dalyell (Chapter 7), from his position as gadfly critic of the foreign policy establishment, suffering as all such figures do from the lack of resources with which to challenge a powerful, secretive, governmental machine. His contacts in academia have been invaluable in providing him with ammunition to use in guerrilla campaigns against ministers in the House of Commons. These contacts have varied from friends who have shared his own passions, whether an Argentinian Ph.D. student or members of the Bradford Department of Peace Studies, to august members of the Royal Society and the Smithsonian Institution who joined him over a particular issue. As Dalyell says, 'Any campaigning politician, if he is to take on Her Majesty's ministers, must have sources of information as expert as those available to HMG'. Dalyell also stresses the importance of the first-class scholarly training enjoyed by many of the Clerks of the House of Commons and in the International Affairs Division of the Commons Library. He takes equal heed of the views of 'intellectual heavyweights' on the other side of the argument from himself. On the other hand, for him academics are only one source of expertise among many – journalists, fellow-campaigners and local people on the ground being just as important – while the divisions between International Relations and other subjects which so exercise researchers are to him of little consequence. Moreover, on issues like the bombing of Libya from UK bases in 1986, no amount of outside learning would suffice either to change the action or to find out whether it really had been Libya, as Washington alleged, behind the La Belle Discotheque bombing in Berlin that occasioned the raid.

Thus the practitioners are well able to see, from their various perspectives, that academics are an important resource to draw on in foreign policy-making, but that the process is necessarily haphazard and individualistic. As a corollary, academics' value consists in sticking to their last, so that when on occasions their concerns do intersect with those of policy, they have something distinctive to add. Such a proposition seems uncontentious when considered in the context of Tam Dalyell's expert on the properties of coral limestone, and his relevance to the Aldabra Atoll dispute. But in international relations, the lure of generalisation and of the present is ever-present, and the number of arcane specialisms far less than in the natural sciences – or in history, where experts like Peter Beck (Chapter 9) are surprised ever to get their chance of fifteen minutes of fame.

Ironically, some historians are more active in the media than their IR colleagues, seemingly enjoying liberation from the claustrophobia of their normal archival constraints. There is also a political and popular tendency to assume that historians have special access to 'lessons of the past' which enable them to advise on the present.[6] Historians have been employed by the Foreign Office either permanently, or as consultants, on an *ad hoc* basis from the same era (the 1920s) as that in which International Relations was being introduced as an academic subject in British universities. On the other hand, the historian's role in influencing policy formation, as Zara Steiner's examination of the British foreign office (Chapter 3) demonstrates, has not been as dominant as might have been supposed, and for good reasons. There is little evidence, for example, to suppose that there can ever be general agreement on what the lessons of history are, or whether they will be well taken even when evident to the specialists. Other, political and cognitive elements tend to intrude when the time comes to operationalise such lessons, a point borne out in Beck's discussion of the exploitation (or lack of it) of the historian's expertise in the run-up to the war in the South Atlantic in 1982.

THE 'IDEOLOGY QUESTION'

The item on which historians tend to choke more than on any other in the menu of International Relations tends to be that of theory, with all the conceptual baggage of paradigms and norms that theory brings with it. Like most practitioners, they tend to discount such questions on the assumption that what needs to be done is the measurement of the gap between actions and interests, rather than a philosophical discussion of the nature of interests, duties, communities and values. This may or may not reflect the long-standing *de facto* dominance of the 'realist' school in Western foreign offices, which, by virtue of their own methodology, historians of diplomacy study but rarely question at the level of first principles. Take the state – a concept fundamental to all academic theorising in International Relations. Such theorising rarely concerns the practical man or woman. It can, none the less, be shown to have significant implications for international relations practice. Those scholars who are currently developing the arguments of international political economy stress the inability of the state to function in face of the ineluctably changing rules of the game from one played primarily by states to one governed by the demands of the international economy. As Roger Tooze puts it (Chapter 4), 'national policy-makers consistently tend to overestimate the role and power of states in the global political economy'.

The implications for national (or federal) foreign policy of such a disjunction are profound. Even the language of journalistic and of parliamentary debate, particularly over the vexed question of European union, has by no means taken on board the implications of the fact that 'the state' is changing significantly but is not yet dying. The notion of 'interdependence', for example, may have been part of the vocabulary of statesmen and women since the 1970s, but public discussion of it rarely rises above the banal. The extensive IR debate has not percolated through into the public realm, despite the best efforts of Susan Strange, William Wallace, and others.[7]

In all the major theoretical developments in international relations, whether over interdependence, IPE, or human rights, there is a continuing two-way dynamic in the relationship between events and the evolution of theory. The emergence of new 'paradigms', a question which has occasioned much burning of the midnight oil in the studies of academic theorists of International Relations, is in the end always a matter also for practitioners. If, for example, we are to make the quantum leap from the 'mercantilist' state, in Paul Kennedy's phrase,[8] to that of a liberal global economy, or from realism via liberal institutionalism to some post-modern condition, then practitioners had better be aware of what is going on at the level of ideas as well as events. The questions then become: how best to interpret change, how to translate ideas into policy, and how to provide leadership in a mass society impatient of abstractions? Such matters are difficult in the extreme, and their interpretation challenges academics and politicians alike.

We now need to build on this in order to improve our understanding of how best the transmission of knowledge, or, to put it another way, the implementation of theory, might be worked out. There are not only the well-known dangers, memorably articulated by Keynes, of carrying out the theories of long-dead economists, or, in Wallace's reformulation, of long-dead geo-politicians. There is also the danger of theoretical overload, or imbalance, in the policy-maker's intellectual make-up. Asked whether a politician is any better for having studied politics and economics, a former Commonwealth prime minister gave a revealing response. While acknowledging that the study of political theory and history had its uses, Michael Manley, former prime minister of Jamaica, stressed its weaknesses:

> [I]f you succumb to an over-theoretical view of political process that is not sufficiently rooted in an understanding of your own culture I think you can make tremendous mistakes. I think I made tremendous mistakes in the 1970s. And, when I look back at them, a lot of them were the product of a theoretical concept, and although I had been a trade unionist I had not enough appreciation of the dynamic of the culture around me.[9]

There remains the large question of normative concerns within the field of international relations. Although the academics writing in this book have often had something to say in this regard, the practitioners have been more reticent. Officials tend to regard values as a matter for politicians, while the latter are taken up with issues and rarely have time to focus on the possible trade-offs between sectional, national and global concerns. Tooze has put this in the context of a wider metaphysical consideration, concluding, in effect, that practitioners too often assume that they are making 'value-free' judgements, when the opposite is invariably the rule. What happens all too often is that practitioners pick up those voices they wish to hear from the academic world, and by legitimising them inevitably affect the balance of research in the universities. Thus Tooze argues that policy-makers and classical economists have been locked into something of a slow waltz since 1945, marginalising the very different – and in his opinion far more truthful – view being developed in approaches within the field of political economy. The latter, however, may have the last laugh.

Perhaps academics could do with a little less of the disciplinary introspection which irritated Cable,[10] while practitioners should probe more into their own 'unspoken assumptions'.[11] It might well be, for example, that Western decision-makers have in fact slowly been losing, or transforming, their infamous realism, and over a longer period than that of the few years since the Berlin Wall fell. Such a possibility would repay analysis by scholars just as it should lead decision-makers to reflect on the fundamental nature of the criteria they should be using in the conduct of foreign policy.

Vincent provides powerful support for this view when he points to the nature of human rights as an 'energising, global ideology', and quotes Walzer's argument to the effect that human rights provide the 'key to unlock the whole question of the legitimacy of international ethics'. The Universal Declaration on Human Rights was adopted in 1948, but it was not until 1976 that these rights were embodied in treaty form in the two conventions on Civil and Political Rights and Economic, Social and Cultural Rights. Even then, codification is one thing, adhesion another. Yet the most hard-headed diplomat must now acknowledge that many governments' definitions of national interests are partly conditioned by domestic support for the values embodied in these conventions. Scholars of International Relations have, on the whole, been chary of moralising because of their awareness of the diversity of beliefs in the terrain which their subject covers. But they have not been slow to understand the importance of ethical considerations in foreign policy, even in the years of reaction against 'idealism'. This means that they are well-placed to explain the changing value-systems which determine international politics. There can be no doubt that the question of human rights is one which has both universal appeal and ethical foundations. It is an area in which the intellectual challenge for the two worlds, the one of ideas and the other of implementation, is at its most compelling. Each has its distinctive contribution to make.

THE 'PROFESSIONAL QUESTION'

The problem for the international relations academic of undue pressures by policy-makers has also been one of the concerns of this book. In a world where competition for funding between various academic institutions is intense, this is more than over-sensitivity on the part of academics. It is not, however, a problem encountered by them alone. Berman's elucidation of the way in which the international lawyer works is instructive, particularly in its description of how the delicate balance is struck between working within the confines of a known policy and satisfying the duty, the overriding duty, of the international lawyer to the law, which means 'to expound the law as it is, without trimming his views to suit the preconceptions of the client – or indeed the client's interests'. Tooze raised in Chapter 4 the question of knowledge as a 'social product'. It is an argument which, reformulated, has exercised the mind of the international lawyer, *vide* the quotation from Sir Gerald Fitzmaurice: 'how can anyone actually working in a department of government and dependent on it for his salary, give it really dispassionate advice? Will he not tend to tell it what he thinks it wants to hear, rather than what he knows it ought to be told?' Fitzmaurice's answer, that governments do not seek 'impartial', but rather 'accurate and judicious' advice, as any client would, is expanded by Berman when he points out also that the independence of the international lawyer is the 'more easily guaranteed when the exclusive, or predominant, function of the departmental lawyer is advice than when he carries also a responsibility for formulating or executing *policy*' – as is the case under the French and German models. In this relationship there are, none the less, clear strains, potential or actual, whatever form it takes.

Outside the walls of government, Wallace's reflections on think-tanks suggest the conclusion that the balance of academic concern should be to get a hearing, rather than being unduly worried about the dangers of being (intellectually) suborned. Tooze tends to agree with him, at least for Britain, where we are a long way from the American model of the virtual interchangeability of academic and practitioner. But Tooze stresses the importance of combining the surrender of 'value-free' academic knowledge, as the basis of intellectual independence, with a long historical perspective and a critical approach to the conventional wisdoms of governments and their favourite academics. His argument is critical of orthodox realism and its tendency to mirror the conventional wisdoms of diplomatic practice. Henry Kissinger made his reputation as a balance of power theorist, riding the crest of the wave made by his study of Metternich, but this not only did not help him to understand Third World demands in the 1970s for a New International Economic Order (the theoretical background of which lay more probably in the work of Latin American and African dependency theorists) but positively diverted him from them. In consequence Kissinger neglected the Third World and political economy, and by his own account had to undertake crash courses in economics, history and culture when turning his attention to such problems as China, OPEC and Rhodesia.[12]

The Kissingers of this world are, however, exceptional figures. The problem of academic freedom is at once more banal and more insidious for most in the profession. The international comparisons in Wallace's chapter show that where the academic base of International Relations is weak or politically compromised, it is difficult to achieve the 'open market for ideas', and the pressure on policy-makers to think, and to think critically, which is essential in a healthy democracy (long-term thinking is also important, but as the Japanese case shows, it can sometimes be espoused as a way of *avoiding* any rocking of the official boat). Wallace shows that even think-tanks – always under attack from both academics and practitioners – can maintain an independent role if they have an internal culture which stresses research values, and if they exist in a national political culture which is genuinely competitive. But they need the support of a healthy and relatively detached tradition of university scholarship. However good the state-funded Stiftung fur Wissenschaft und Politik at Ebenhausen, it is no substitute for the lack of a proper International Relations community in German universities.

From their different perspective, that of historians with one foot in the International Relations camp, both Beck and Steiner also suggest that we do not need to be too pessimistic about 'the professional problem'. Historians have a longer tradition of being consulted by governments, given that International Relations is a relatively young subject. And their profession has not been overly compromised as a result. However, all the evidence suggests that this is at least in part because they have not often been listened to very seriously, even when heard. Much, again, depends on the political culture. It has been very difficult for Argentinian historians to write about the '*Las Islas Malvinas*' except in the context of '*nuestro derecho*', while post-war Japanese governments have influenced school history textbooks to gloss over Japan's pre-war role in China and Korea. In Britain as well, the lack of truly vigorous public debate on foreign policy has made life difficult for those researchers dependent on official assistance. Beck reports the case of the 1927 Ph.D. student too cowed to look at 'closed' files inadvertently given to him (the times were not yet ripe for Peter Hennessy), while Steiner reminds us of the struggles between the Foreign Office and the 'tender consciences' of official historians since the 1920s, and points out that it is too early to form a judgement on the worth of the many officially sponsored publications of the post-war years.

The difficulty of getting the ear of policy-makers tends to strike historians in different ways. Beck, for example, wants them to be listened to more, along the lines of Mrs Thatcher's famous Chequers meeting in 1990 with experts on Germany, and is ironical about the fact that Latin American diplomats have been far more likely to seek out the views of British Latin Americanists than have their FCO counterparts (it should be noted that one consequence of their so doing might have been the reinforcing of Argentina's tendency to underestimate British reactions to an attack on the Falklands). He also points out the importance of communication between the two worlds: 'The detailed academic monograph or article has little attraction to a diplomat working to a deadline and seeking a clear, concise summary of relevant points'. This is where the think-tanks come in. An established, independent and high-quality institution will be able to transmit ideas and research in digestible form to busy practitioners. Good conferences can have the same effect, although a surfeit can have the opposite effect to that desired. Otherwise, academics should be content to let their ideas slowly percolate through society, and exert their influence on policy indirectly. This requires patience, but who is to say that it is any the less effective? As Steiner concludes, if academics stay largely outside the policy machine, their voice will be clearer and more distinctive, if more distant.

CONCLUSIONS

The line dividing outsiders from the world of practice is becoming more difficult to draw. Wallace showed how even in the 1920s educated individuals moved easily back and forth between a number of professional milieux. In the post-war period, with the expansion of the universities and the professionalisation of social science, a sense of two separate (and possibly competing) communities evolved, but now, with the growing academic respectability of International Relations, and the removal of a rationale for the 'security state' through an end to the Cold War, we are once again becoming more relaxed about interchange, human and intellectual, between the 'pure' and the 'applied' aspects of work to improve human society.

On the other hand the working environment of the late twentieth century is profoundly different from that of the cultured and leisured classes who debated Keynes's criticisms of Versailles in the early 1920s. If not more issues to discuss, there are very many more points of potential contact in government machines, while the growth of democratic values and of international organisations has opened up foreign societies to the curious researcher. Within the academic world, the requirements of teaching and administration have increased immeasurably. Like most other professions, university teaching and research is now very often hard graft, with little energy left over for what might be loosely called civic responsibilities.

Conversely, where a dialogue with the world of policy is achieved, there are likely to be opportunity costs in terms of the time available for basic research. The downside of increased access and respectability for academic International Relations is that these costs might make it less likely in the long term that academics have anything distinctive to say. This is not to mention the problems of agenda-setting which occur through the need to seek grants from government-sponsored bodies, or from charitable foundations eager to be seen doing something about this year's crisis or next year's intellectual trend. Academics are almost always conscious of the need to protect their independence, but beneath the surface, as Edward Said has recently pointed out, 'if your eye is on your patron, you cannot think as an intellectual, but only as a disciple or acolyte. In the back of your mind there is the thought that you must please, not displease.'[13]

It is worth re-emphasising that to the extent that academics are likely to be distracted from their main business it is not only governments, their bureaucracies and the various foundations which orbit around them which do the distracting. At a deeper level it is the world of events which is irresistible, with our twentieth-century addiction to change and to 'news' making it seem as if as the world has turned upside down every second week. To react in such a way is a wholly human response for someone alert to their environment and living in the 1990s. Whether it is 'modern' or 'post-modern' matters little more than whether one was a Futurist or a Vorticist during the Great War. To live with a sense of overwhelming change is our paradigm, our fate.

Yet this may be all the more reason to build on traditions of thought which are at one remove from events, and to work in that much-derided ivory tower which provides the freedom to be eccentric. For *some* of yesterday's eccentricities will turn out to be today's conventional wisdoms. A senior British practitioner, the diplomat Brian Crowe (a descendant of the famous Sir Eyre Crowe), argued in an academic journal recently that 'in our new global village and with the spread of intermestic issues . . . domestic opinion on domestic matters in individual countries is becoming more and more a matter of concern to others'.[14] It was less than twenty years ago that 'buzzwords' like Marshall McLuhan's 'global village' or Bayless Manning's 'intermestic' were being greeted with derision by those in positions of practical responsibility, and the general analysis in Crowe's article was certainly prefigured in some of the theories which Sir James Cable was disappointed with when he read the digest commissioned from Joseph Frankel in the early 1970s.[15]

Even if we discount the importance of scholarship for its own sake – and in the long-run the social and cultural arguments against discounting it seem to us immensely strong – the above example makes it clear that in the end practitioners, and perhaps even more the barely empowered millions who bear their decisions, actually *need* academics to be independent, eccentric, critical and apparently irrelevant, even if they think they need them to be amenable, sensible, practical and relevant. As Martin Wight pointed out thirty years ago, International Relations has a sound pedigree in terms of charting the evolution of the international system. As a subject of study it had been around for a long time before the First World War, and did not spring 'from the head of Andrew Carnegie when he set up his Endowment for International Peace (1910), or from that of President Wilson when he thought up the League of Nations, or of David Davies and the Cassel Trustees when they founded chairs in Aberystwyth (1919) and London (1923)'.[16] The world of academic International Relations has the evidence on which to make a robust defence of its record in reaching and disseminating a sophisticated understanding of how foreigners cope with each other (its essential subject-matter) and it should not be too fastidious in so doing. If the core of academic work is basic research, both theoretical and empirical, by which we mean research which takes a longer and wider perspective than that enjoyed by decision-makers, then we shall actually be in a stronger position to contribute to policy when the occasion (that is, society, our conscience, or the logic of the research) demands.

NOTES

1 Some barbers have now given up, witness the following notice on the mirror of a Taunton shop in April, 1993: 'Politics, business and the international situation are now so complicated that not even hairdressers can solve them' (*Guardian*, 13 April, 1993).

2 A.J.P. Taylor was the first and most brilliant populariser of modern history, whether through Workers Educational Association lecture tours, columns in the Beaverbrook press or unscripted lectures on television. In his day he was vilified by fellow academics for being too political and too popular. See Taylor's autobiography, *A Personal History*, London, Hamish Hamilton, 1983. Nowadays there are fewer such restraints.

3 See Paul Taylor and A.J.R. Groom, *The United Nations and the Gulf War 1990–91: Back to the Future?*, RIIA Discussion paper no. 38, London Royal Institute of International Affairs, 1992. But see also James Mayall, 'Nonintervention, self-determination and the "new world order"', *International Affairs*, vol. 67, no. 3, July 1991.

4 See R.J. Vincent, *Non-Intervention and International Order*, Princeton N.J., Princeton University Press, 1974.

5 See Chapter 1, note 4, for a reference to the idea of competing paradigms. Many academics think their subject (and the world) is long overdue a shift

away from what they see as the dominance of the realist paradigm. For a recent discussion see John C. Garnett, 'States, State-Centric Perspectives, and Interdependence Theory' in John Baylis and N.J. Renger (eds) *Dilemmas of World Politics: International Issues in a Changing World*, Oxford, Clarendon Press, 1992, pp. 64–84.

6 See Richard Neustadt and Ernest May, *Thinking in Time: The Uses of History for Decision Makers*, New York, the Free Press, 1986, a book whose importance has been referred to by more than one of the contributors to this volume.

7 See Susan Strange, *Casino Capitalism*, Oxford, Blackwell, 1986, her most popular work; also the series of articles written in *International Affairs* since the 1970s by William Wallace in a sustained attempt to raise the level of British debate about foreign policy.

8 Paul Kennedy, *Preparing for the 21st Century*, London, HarperCollins, 1993, Ch. 7.

9 Interview with Michael Manley, in Geoffrey Stern, *Leaders and Leadership*, London, BBC World Service and London School of Economics, 1993, pp. 91–9.

10 And see G.M. Dillon's scathing reference about the tendency of International Relations to fall back on 'the inbred retelling of its story' in his review of a recent survey of the subject, *International Affairs* vol. 68, no. 4, October 1992, p. 707.

11 The phrase is James Joll's, in his inaugural lecture '1914: the Unspoken Assumptions', London School of Economics, 1968.

12 See, for example, Henry Kissinger, *White House Years*, London, Weidenfeld & Nicolson, 1979, p. 704.

13 Edward Said, 'Gods that always fail', BBC Reith Lecture of 28 July 1993, printed in *The Independent*, 29 July 1993.

14 Brian L. Crowe, 'Foreign Policy-Making: Reflections of a Practitioner', *Government and Opposition* 28(2), Spring 1993, p. 183.

15 See Chapter 6, p. 105. Frankel's book was *Contemporary International Theory and the Behaviour of States*, London, Oxford University Press, 1973. Marshall McLuhan's work is best approached through *Understanding Media: the Extensions of Man*, London, Routledge & Kegan Paul, 1964, and the much less conventional *War and Peace in the Global Village* (with Quentin Fiore), New York, McGraw-Hill, 1968. For 'intermestic' see Bayless Manning, *The Conduct of US Foreign Policy in the Third Century*, Claremont, Calif., Claremont University Press, 1975, cited in Lincoln Bloomfield, *The Foreign Policy Process: A Modern Primer*, Englewood Cliffs, N.J., Prentice-Hall, 1982, p. 27.

16 Martin Wight, 'Introduction', in Martin Wight, *International Theory: The Three Traditions*, edited by Gabriele Wight and Brian Porter, Leicester, Leicester University Press for the Royal Institute of International Affairs, 1991, p. 5.

Index